Shakespeare in Practice

Series Editors
Bridget Escolme
London, UK

Stuart Hampton-Reeves
Preston, UK

The books in this series chart new directions for a performance approach to Shakespeare, representing the diverse and exciting work being undertaken by a new generation of Shakespeareans and combining insights from both scholarship and theatrical practice.

More information about this series at
http://www.palgrave.com/gp/series/14484

Bridget Escolme

Shakespeare and Costume in Practice

palgrave
macmillan

Bridget Escolme
London, UK

Shakespeare in Practice
ISBN 978-3-030-57148-1   ISBN 978-3-030-57149-8   (eBook)
https://doi.org/10.1007/978-3-030-57149-8

Cover illustration: Tom Piper: 'Botswain as Ceres', design for '*The Tempest*', designed by Tom Piper, directed by Michael Boyd, Royal Shakespeare Company 2002.

This Palgrave Macmillan imprint is published by the registered company Springer Nature Switzerland AG.
The registered company address is: Gewerbestrasse 11, 6330 Cham, Switzerland

To my mother, Hilary Escolme, and dear friend Frances Babbage, with whom talking about clothes is always such a joy.

ACKNOWLEDGEMENTS

Shakespeare and Costume in Practice is part of the *Shakespeare in Practice* series, which I co-edit with Stuart Hampton-Reeves. My first thanks go to him, for his vision in creating the series, and for his invaluable insights and indefatigable patience working on this volume. It has also been a great pleasure to work with Eileen Srebernik and Jack Heeney at Palgrave Macmillan, whose enthusiasm and creativity have recently reinvigorated the series. Many thanks indeed to designer Tom Piper for the beautiful cover image of his costume design for *The Tempest*, generously donated from his own notebooks.

A large part of research for this book happened during sabbatical leave granted to me by Queen Mary University of London (QMUL). Thanks to all of my Queen Mary colleagues for their inspiration and support. I am particularly indebted to Jen Harvie and Aoife Monks as Directors of Research in the Department of Drama, for their encouragement and kindness as I completed this book, and to Aoife for her inspiring contribution to theatre costume design as a field of study. These colleagues, and the School of English and Drama at QMUL, led by Markman Ellis, Warren Boutcher and our beloved and much missed Catherine Silverstone over the period of this book's creation, and the Department of Drama, led by Caoimhe McAvinchey, then Dominic Johnson, brilliantly support research at every stage: practically, intellectually and emotionally. I must also thank Bev Stuart without whose help and patience my sabbatical application might never have been completed.

This book is about the work of theatre and costume designers, all of whose work I am indebted to and many of whom have given of their time, and insights into their creative brilliance, in conversations with me. I would like to thank Susan Mayes, Richard Hudson, Chloe Lamford and Tom Piper for showing me private archival material, and to these designers as well as theatre directors Phelim McDermott and Jatinder Verma, and live artist Dickie Beau, for their generous insights into their work and profession when I spoke to them.

I have benefited enormously from the dedicated work and expertise of librarian and archivists, who care for and curate costumes, designs, images and all of the production documentation that allow performance scholars to begin to reconstruct productions that they have not seen and to recall those they have. Many thanks to Liverpool John Moores University Library (Everyman Archive); the Brotherton Library, University of Leeds; the Library of Birmingham (Birmingham Rep Archive); the National Theatre Archive; Shakespeare's Globe Library and Archive; the Shakespeare's Birthplace Trust (Royal Shakespeare Company Archive), with special thanks to Alistair McArthur, Head of Costume at the RSC, for permission to view costume bibles; the V&A Theatre Collections.

Profound thanks also to Farah Karim Cooper, Head of Higher Education and Research at Shakespeare's Globe, and her research team at the Globe, especially Will Tosh, for the inspiring conferences and events that have informed my thinking, particularly the Shakespeare and Race symposium of 2018 and the London Shakespeare Centre and Shakespeare's Globe Second Graduate Conference, 2020: 'Negotiating Boundaries: Early Modern Texts and Cultures', for which thanks also to Gordon McMullan and Kings College London, where parts of this work were received so generously. Thanks to the Quorum seminar team at Queen Mary, the Society for Theatre Research, to Kiki Lindell and the organisers of the *Much Ado About Nothing* in Performance workshop at the University of Lund, Sweden, and to Gabriella Reuss and the Hungarian Society for the Study of Drama in English, all of whom hosted papers in which this work was developed. Thanks and gratitude to Michael Dobson at the Shakespeare Institute, University of Birmingham, for his inspiring work on *Much Ado about Nothing* and for providing invaluable feedback on my chapter on the same, and to Tony Howard for his insights into Jonathan Miller's *Tempest* productions. Many thanks to Ella Hawkins and Amy Borsuk for permission to cite their superb theses before publication. Many thanks, too, to Queen Mary graduate students—now Doctors—Alessandro Simari and Amy Borsuk, whose work on Shakespeare sites and performances has inspired me throughout the research process. Yet more thanks go to Amy Borsuk for her invaluable proofing help.

Finally, thanks, as ever, to my husband Gary Willis, for his endless patience, encouragement, support and proofreading.

CONTENTS

Abbreviations

BBC	British Broadcasting Company
des.	Designer
dir.	Director
HUSSDE	Hungarian Society for the Study of Drama in English
NT	National Theatre
NTCP	Non-traditional Casting Project
RSC	Royal Shakespeare Company
V&A	Victoria and Albert Museum

CHAPTER 1

Introduction

Costume design can be a site of experimentation, playfulness and transgression in the theatre; it can also follow convention and reiterate cliché. Theatrical costume can trap the body in weary historical conventions of racialised or gendered display; it can also undo cultural binaries and demand that an audience think again about what power, race and gender are supposed to look like. Costume can suggest that an audience wants its money's worth, that we will need to see plenty of conspicuous consumption on stage; or it can put visual conventions of class and power into theatrical quotation marks, asking an audience to examine those conventions rather than assume they are stable or true for all time. *Shakespeare and Costume in Practice* examines how costume creates meaning on stage in Shakespeare production. In this book, I demonstrate how a culture's relationship with the past is reflected and interrogated through clothing on stage. I reflect on what costume means in practice, and what it allows Shakespeare to mean. I begin with a performance meditation on *Hamlet*, which demonstrates the power of costume to perform both the expected and the unexpected.

At the Almeida Theatre, London, in 2016, lip-synch artist Dickie Beau performed his one-man show *Re-Member Me*, late at night, on the set of the theatre's production of *Hamlet* (an exceptionally well-received modern-dress production with Andrew Scott in the lead). Dickie Beau's performance began as a gossipy mash-up of actors talking about their experiences of playing Hamlet. Hilariously, empathetically and always with

© The Author(s), under exclusive license to Springer Nature Switzerland AG 2020
B. Escolme, *Shakespeare and Costume in Practice*, Shakespeare in Practice, https://doi.org/10.1007/978-3-030-57149-8_1

uncanny precision, dressed in *Fame*-style work-out or running gear, perhaps to remind us, as one critic put it, that performing Hamlet is 'something of a competitive sport' (Gardner 2017), Dickie lip-synced the
recorded words of celebrated Hamlets past—Jon Gielgud, Peter O'Toole,
Ian McKellen, Jonathan Pryce. *Re-Member Me* featured five shop window
dummies clothed in items from the National Theatre's costume store
(Beau 2017). 'It is…always surprising to see a costume's theatrical life
frozen on display, missing the intimacy of the body', says Barbara Hodgdon
of her visit to the RSC's costume archive (Hodgdon 2007, 72), and at first
these costumes seemed, too, to miss that intimacy as they hung limply on
their dummies or on the backs of chairs, lined up across the stage. Their
lifeless presence foregrounded the actor's voice as real and human by contrast: voice became the external expression of Hamlet's 'that within which
passeth show' (1.1.85), whilst costume was staged as the empty show
itself. The ghostly embodying of actors' words achieved by the precision
of the lip-synch artist drew attention to the minute, individuating detail of
each voice, whilst the male dress-maker's dummies in their slightly shabby
costumes seemed to represent any (male) bodies and none. Taken apart
and reassembled, dressed and undressed throughout the piece (the arms
of one dummy were used in hilarious extension of Dickie's own arms as he
lip-synched an interview with a theatre dresser) the body in costume was
made to seem comically theatrical, the voice full of emotional depth and
meaning.

Dickie Beau describes how he went to the National Theatre's costume
store in something of a rush to hire 'anything that looked like a costume'
for *Re-member Me* (Beau 2017). For the version of the piece that I saw, he
had picked out items such as a romantic, loose white shirt; a doublet and
hose; a tuxedo with a flashy gold collar; a red women's blouse. The white
shirt looked like the ones so many Hamlets have worn and been as 'pale
as', revealed beneath the Prince of Denmark's standard black doublet as it
becomes 'all unbrac'd' (2.1.75), to fit Ophelia's description. The sandy
brown doublet and hose could have been worn by just about any male
character in an Elizabethan-styled production, other than the mourning
Hamlet. The tailcoat recalled Claudius in a modern dress production such
as the Royal Shakespeare Company's (RSC) of 2008, in which the state is
represented by the pompous archaisms of 'modern' ceremonial and evening dress. The red blouse could have been part of a 'modern dress' costume for Gertrude. The mere placing of costumes on shop window
dummies, in the context of *Hamlet*, seemed to recall a set of precise

references to *Hamlets* past; at the same time, the clothes looked like any or all costumes from countless productions of the play. As Dickie said, if it looks like a costume, it looks like a *Hamlet* costume (Beau 2017).

The costume that took on a particularly precise life—and indeed an intimate life, *pace* Hodgdon—in *Re-Member Me* was a pair of striped pyjamas, which at first I took to be a nod to Mark Rylance's first Hamlet for the RSC in 1989. In fact, they referenced the actor Ian Charleson, who took over from Daniel Day-Lewis in the role when Day-Lewis left Richard Eyre's National Theatre production in the middle of a performance. Charleson's story became the eventual narrative focus *for Re-Member Me*; the actor played Hamlet whilst suffering from the AIDS-related illnesses from which he eventually died, and his pyjamas were used tenderly to dress a re-assembled dummy, which lay prone between two chairs to stand for Charleson on his death bed. One of the lip-synched figures in the piece is the dresser who had to help Daniel Day-Lewis's understudy, Jeremy Northam, into his Hamlet costume on the night Day-Lewis collapsed off stage and said he could not continue. The dresser had hurriedly to remove parts of Day-Lewis's costume to get them ready for the understudy, taking one Hamlet apart to assemble a new one in the middle of Day-Lewis's crisis. The voice of theatre critic John Peter was also lip-synched in the piece: he was the only mainstream British critic to review Ian Charleson's Hamlet when Charleson replaced Day-Lewis. David Benedict opened his obituary piece for Charleson in the *Independent* by commenting that 'When Daniel Day-Lewis walked out halfway through the run of Hamlet at the National, everyone talked. When Ian Charleson took over the role a few weeks later, nobody noticed' (Benedict 1995). Although Benedict goes on to relate how John Peter's review remedied this situation somewhat, the tale of Day-Lewis's departure from the production gained the status of theatrical myth/popular ghost story (see Trueman 2012) whereas the intense poignancy of Charleson's performance, undertaken whilst already ill, may well have been news to some of Dickie Beau's audiences.

Re-Member Me is partly a performance about playing Hamlet and the inevitable critical attention an actor in the role gets (unless, it seems, he is a gay actor who replaces a well-known straight one). To an audience used to the knowing archness of Queer lip-synching performance, or the explicit body of performance art, the costumes might have read as something of a joke about theatrical costume cliché. But as dummy parts were reassembled and dressed in the striped pyjamas, Ian Charleson's dying body was tenderly evoked in ways that reminded me of theatre costume's simultaneous particularity and iconicity. The pyjamas recalled: Mark Rylance's 1989 Hamlet; Hamlet's madness as recalled by imagery from some generic, pseudo-historical psychiatric ward; and the last days of the sick Charleson. As Aoife Monks has argued, theatre costume is kaleido-scopic in nature, 'with the same ingredients creating new effects and out-comes depending on how it is viewed' (Monks 2010, 11). *Re-Member Me* reminded me that different effects and outcomes of actors in costume are produced all at once in certain theatrical moments. Here, costume was placed in theatrical quotation marks so as to draw focus to the issues of memory and repetition that are both a problem for performers of this best-known of all Shakespeare plays, and are at the heart of its meaning.

I have opened *Shakespeare and Costume in Practice* with *Re-Member Me* because the performance both seemed to laugh at how generic and clichéd theatre costumes can look, and reminded me of how powerfully detailed and multivalent they can be. Some of the costumes in the Shakespeare productions analysed here do what is conventionally expected of them; others stage the self-consciously new and innovative. Some stage costumes are inextricably linked to character or period; they are designed to be looked *through*, as film scholar Stella Bruzzi puts it, rather than at (Bruzzi 1997, 36), and to a degree, this is the norm for the modern film or theatre audience who is, in Monks' words, 'trained to repress the visibility of cos-tume' (Monks 2010, 11). Other costumes draw deliberate attention to themselves: to the ways they display actors' bodies, to their gendered or racialised meanings; to their place in the construction or disruption of power; to their relationship with history. In this book, I want to consider moments when costume is consciously staged as a maker of meaning for the audience, but also to think about costume as something that is always making meaning, whether directors or designers want us to pay particular attention to it or not. In one sense, *Re-Member Me* could not have been less 'about' costume. It drew attention to costume's potential for tired theatrical reiterations, tropes and conventions and it privileged the voice as the site of lively, individuated, actorly subjectivity. However, in the moment when the pyjamas were placed on the prone dummy's body, the garments managed all at once to recall: the material reality of how fabric feels (com-forting or irritating on the body of a sick man); histories of Hamlets past and histories of 'madness'; histories of HIV and the gay community; and the very particular story of a gay actor's erasure from the history of British theatre. I hope that this book will sensitise the reader to the multiple meanings made by costume in Shakespeare production in moments like this, when costume is the centre of theatrical attention, but also in moments where productions seem to be asking that we see it only as a sign for period or an aspect of character.

COSTUME IN THEORY: CULTURAL MATERIALISM AND MATERIAL CULTURE

Theatre costume has emerged this century as a significant field for scholars of theatre and theatre history. In the introduction to Patricia Lennox and Bella Mirabella's important essay collection *Shakespeare and Costume*, the editors remark that twenty years after Jean MacIntyre's *Costumes and Scripts in the Elizabethan Theatres* first paid sustained attention to the relationship between the language of clothing in early modern plays and costumes on the early modern stage, 'a rich discussion and exploration of many aspects of costume in Shakespeare performance' has begun (Lennox and Mirabella 2015, 3). An important inspiration for this discussion has been Ann Rosalind Jones and Peter Stallybrass's *Renaissance Clothing and the Materials of Memory*, the core project of which is neatly summed up by Lennox and Mirabella's introduction: Jones and Stallybrass's book 'argues that the construction of and exchange of clothing is central to the very construction of Renaissance culture' (Lennox and Mirabella 2015, 3). *Renaissance Clothing* is not only a book that deals with 'material culture'—historical clothing itself—but is part of a cultural materialist project that began to dominate early modern studies during the 1980s, which reminds us that all culture is produced within and by power structures that access, restrict and govern it. *Shakespeare and Costume in Practice* is a work of cultural materialism, in that it, too, regards quotidian clothing and stage costume as both produced by and constitutive of visual regimes of power, of class, of gender and of race. The phrase 'cultural materialism' suggests that this critical approach is always to do with material production; but cultural materialism as it has been applied to the analysis of drama has become a semiotic project, an intellectual endeavour that privileges *reading* culture as though it were a text whose parts make sense like a language does. Just as the scholar has to be literate in the language of Elizabethan emblems to fully understand what Queen Elizabeth I's clothing means in her portraits, so the cultural materialist scholar has to be literate in the discourses of Elizabethan gender, race and power. Indeed, cultural materialism privileges discourses of power and its subversion as the means through which the 'material' of 'culture' is read. This book is a cultural materialist project in that it draws upon discourses around gender, race and power to develop readings of what costume does in practice.

There are moments in *Shakespeare and Costume in Practice*, on the other hand, when the focus is 'material culture' rather than 'cultural materialism', moments when the stuff of clothing and costume is privileged over its place in a wider visual 'text'. 'Material culture is just what it says it is', remarks Jules David Prown in his opening essay to the collection *American Artifacts: Essays in Material Culture*:

> namely the manifestation of culture through material productions. And the study of material culture is the study of material to understand culture, to discover the beliefs—the values, ideas, attitudes, and assumptions—of a particular community or society at a given time. (Prown, in Prown and Haltman 2000, 11)

In his essay, Prown describes art and literature as belonging to different orders of objects from quotidian artefacts, because art and literature self-consciously express the values and beliefs of a culture—they are its 'most obvious expressions of belief' (Prown, in Prown and Haltman 2000, 15), whereas artefacts are primarily functional. They may express cultural meanings that are taken for granted and so are difficult to uncover centuries later, or even cultural meanings that a society needs to repress. The introduction to the collection of which Prown's essay is a part elucidates his own method of analysis and interpretation of artefacts from the past, from choosing an object to consider, through describing and sketching it, to deducing evidence from it, entertaining informed hypotheses and composing a polished interpretive analysis (Prown and Haltman 2000, 2–7). Starting from historical objects as a means of understanding a historical culture is what a social scientist might call an inductive, 'bottom up' process rather than a deductive, 'top down' process (see O'Reilly 2009, 104) and the study of material culture invariably works in this way: from a direct, often tactile relationship with an object, to a theory about its meaning in a historical culture. But whilst Prown suggests that this is how a culture's unspoken, hidden or repressed meanings might best be uncovered, and implies that art and literature are not necessarily the best places to find these meanings, cultural materialist scholars often have remarkably similar scholarly aims when they examine art and literature to the scholar of material culture examining an object. Far from assuming that the meanings inherent in art and literature are open to the consumer of the cultural product and self-consciously displayed, cultural materialist scholarship often suggests that repressed cultural anxieties, or subversions of dominant power structures, are to be found beneath the surface of, for example, a comedy that ostensibly and simply celebrates cultural norms (see, for example, Catherine Belsey's analysis of 'Meaning and Gender in the Comedies' in the foundational essay collection of cultural materialist early modern studies, *Alternative Shakespeares* (Belsey 2002, 166–90). Thus, cultural materialism and material culture can do the same scholarly work in different directions: the study of material culture induces cultural meaning from artefacts; cultural materialist literary criticism starts from an understanding of how power and production works in a culture and looks at art and literature through that lens.

Historical clothing and stage costume offer a particularly interesting set of cultural objects for both scholars of material culture and cultural materialists. Certain kinds of clothing can seem just as functional as the eighteenth-century teapot through which Prown explains the study of material culture: it might take exactly the kind of material analysis and deduction described by Prown to excavate the cultural meanings of labour, class and gender inherent in a working woman's dress from 1600, and one might learn more about class, culture and power by doing that analysis. Another dress from the same period might obviously have been produced to display wealth rather than simply to cover and protect, but a detailed and accurate knowledge of, say, the lace trim at its neckline, might contribute to a more nuanced understanding about the wearer, her social class, and her culture's attitudes to conspicuous consumption. I am suggesting here that attention to material culture can make for better cultural materialism: examining costumes and clothing carefully and inductively, from the 'bottom up' can enrich the kind of understanding of how power is at work in a culture that a cultural materialist invariably seeks.

I use the example of lace here, because it is the artefact with which Catherine Richardson opens her brilliant exploration of the relationship between material culture and the politics of sex and power on the cross-dressed early modern stage. In her chapter on 'Dressing and Cross Dressing' in *Shakespeare and Material Culture,* Richardson teases out the ways in which early modern dress *replaces* the body in the visual regimes of the theatre, and in early modern culture more broadly. I draw upon her work in the chapter on *Hamlet* below. Citing Marjorie Garber, whose monograph title *Vested Interests: Cross-dressing and Cultural Anxiety* is underpinned by some of the key principles of cultural materialism, Richardson argues for the 'primacy of the material construction of cross-dressed identity' on stage. If one does not understand the explicit roles of clothing in early modern life, she and Garber argue, 'the...eye glides absentmindedly past lists of incomprehensible garments in search of moral or emotional (or even sexual or political) context' (Richardson 2011, 82; Garber 1992, 35). *In Shakespeare and Costume in Practice,* I assume that the study of 'material culture' and scholarship based on the theoretical premises of 'cultural materialism' are co-dependent, and there are moments when I start, like Richardson, with the physical stuff and manufactured objects of clothing to suggest that they both reflect and produce meanings, hierarchies, norms and behaviours in cultural life.

This book is also underpinned by the cultural materialist theories of 'subjectivity' that emerged in the academy from the 1980s in Britain and via the New Historicism in the USA. These theories are useful to a study of theatre costume because they deliberately set out to challenge the idea that the 'subjects' of drama—the characters in a play, the figures on stage, the different 'selves' that abound on stage and page—represent some kind of stable human nature that is true for all time and in every place. Instead, works published in the 1980s such as such as Catherine Belsey's *The Subject of Tragedy* (1985), Francis Barker's *The Tremulous Private Body* (1984) and Stephen Greenblatt's *Renaissance Self Fashioning* (1980) suggested that the very notion of self-hood is bound up in historically specific social and economic structures of power. The idea that we are all the same under our clothes is one that viewers of film and television 'costume dramas' are used to; many of these dramas suggest that the emotional lives of people who lived in the English country houses of the past are very similar to our own. These characters might have more formal manners (from the restrictions of which they are generally longing to burst) but they ultimately speak, move, emote just like people of today, only in lovelier clothes. *Shakespeare and Costume in Practice* posits that costume is an important area of study because human beings are not all the same under their clothes—they are rather partially constructed *by* their clothes. As Stephen Orgel reminds us in his study of *Spectacular Performances,* 'the permanence and impenetrability of the self beneath the costume, and therefore the essential superficiality of the costume, has not always been taken for granted' (Orgel 2011, 36).

The Elizabethan government was highly aware of the power of clothing to construct the social subject and repeatedly attempted to reinforce sumptuary legislation via royal proclamations (see Hunt 1996, 311–321). As

Catherine Richardson argues, 'status outside the theatre was most commonly communicated through the cloth, cut and ornament added to dress' (Richardson 2011, 72) and as Ninya Mikhaila and Jane Malcolm-Davies note in their work on reconstructing sixteenth-century dress, *The Tudor Tailor*:

> To know who you are in Tudor society was less about understanding yourself and more about knowing your place. Clothes did not broadcast the wearer's individuality but rather where s/he fitted into society. (Mikhaila and Malcolm-Davies 2006, 11)

'Plato, the Bible, Erasmus and Shakespeare all agree that clothes demonstrated a person's inner self through exterior display' and that 'inner self' had more obviously to do with 'financial and spiritual worth' and social status than people with access to fashion like to imagine their choices of clothing have today (Mikhaila and Malcolm-Davies 2006, 10). Mikhaila and Malcolm-Davies also remind us that clothes of this period 'moulded the body rather than the other way around' (2006, 10). No-one in Shakespeare's London would have talked about clothing expressing their personality, or even suiting their body shape, as clothing in this period *produced* the body's shape. Gender and class were both expressed and moulded by clothing in more strictly defined ways than they are for Western consumers now.

On the other hand, the early modern period was one of mercantile expansion and new consumer choice: as new dyes, threads and fabrics were made available to those with disposable incomes, clothing became part of what Stephen Greenblatt named as *Renaissance Self-Fashioning*, a self-conscious and fluid construction of the self in the social world. Whilst the range of styles available to even the very richest Elizabethan or Jacobean might seem limited to anyone interested in fashion today, the notion of making choices of clothing to fashion a social self emerges as a source of interest and anxiety in the writings of Shakespeare and his contemporaries. To readers who have multiple choices of self-realisation, the early modern period is one in which a person's sense of self might seem much more rigidly socially constructed; but it was also a period in which choices of social behaviour—including choices of clothing—produced a great deal of social play and social anxiety. Can costume engage a modern audience with dominant, residual and emerging forms of self-hood, to use Raymond Williams's (1977, 121–7) terms, as they were staged in the early seventeenth century, or does the modern actor in costume inevitably reflect our own subjectivity back at us? *Shakespeare and Costume in Practice* explores how costume might heighten rather than erase the simultaneous sense of recognition and strangeness potentially encoded for us in a 400-year-old play.

Costume: An Invisible Problem

Although this book considers what clothes meant on Shakespeare's own stage—I begin Chaps. 1 and 3 with considerations of what the first Hamlet and the first Caliban might have looked like—I am predominantly concerned with costume in recent production. In considering the theatre production of the more recent past, I inevitably turn to reviews of theatre productions for one set of evidence about reception. Reviews are problematic as evidence because journalistic criticism (especially given its limited word count) tends towards reading costume as reflective of meaning already decided by a director, at the expense of discussion of the ways in which clothes—and the ways in which actors wear them—*produce* meaning. Even in the most 'conventional' British Shakespeare production today, set designs are frequently relatively abstract, while costume is richer in the recognisable historical or contemporary detail that produces period setting. When a critic declares that a production is 'set' in 1950s' Cuba or 1640s' England, it is often costume that gives the visual clue. Less obviously, when critics discuss what they might broadly term acting or character interpretation, they are often reading clothes. Reviews, then, are useful pieces of evidence when considering theatre production, but one often has to read through them, or alongside visual documentation, to recover the effects of costume from a past production one has not seen, or saw long ago. An example: in the Royal Shakespeare Company's most recent *Romeo and Juliet* at the time of writing (designed by Tom Piper, directed by Erica Whyman) a number of critics comment on the cross-gender casting of some of the characters, particularly Mercutio played by Charlotte Josephine, and assume rather than make explicit the work costume is doing to produce gender. Michael Billington in the *Guardian* remarks

> Josephine, who has written and performed a play called Bitch Boxer about a 21-year-old pugilist, plausibly plays Mercutio as a tough, crop-haired female bruiser always ready for a scrap. (Billington 2018)

Here, 'crop-haired' and 'female bruiser' become a short-hand for the kind of woman Billington wants the reader to imagine; but the image of Josephine that accompanies the review online allows for a more detailed analysis of clothes that mix archetypes of masculinity. She wears a leather jacket, with its connotations of a particular kind of 'hard' masculinity; gym wear to signify fitness; plain black trousers and belt that signal a 'neutral', masculine unfussiness; and a tight-fitting net top that 'feminises' her sporty crop-top. Billington goes on to suggest that if *Romeo and Juliet* contains a critique of violent masculinity, then for him, 'casting one of the key knife-wielders as a woman' is a problem for the production However, Josephine's costume read to me as though designer, actor and director were at some level aware of the contradictions staged by casting the play with an eye to twenty-first-century gender fluidity when the text itself contains such rigid gender binaries (indeed, the title of Billington's review is 'RSC's gender-fluid tragedy of youth'). Costume here is not just 'everyone in contemporary clobber', as Dominic Cavendish has it in the *Daily Telegraph* (Cavendish 2018). The production uses 'modern dress' in ways that deliberately seem to heighten and productively alienate aspects of the play's gender politics. A central aim of *Shakespeare and Costume in Practice* is to make costume visible in the documentations of its reception: to suggest where the audiences of the recent past might have been reading costume, even where they were not conscious of doing so.

Costume: A Spectacular Problem

As Monks has pointed out in her introduction to *The Actor in Costume*, a number of factors have led to a disinclination to take costume seriously in theatre scholarship: a long history of privileging the textual over the visual in Western theatre; a tendency to consider clothes as a superficial, a bourgeois, or an implicitly feminine concern; and a critical habit of conflating actor's costume and actor's body in reading the theatre event (Monks 2010, 10). One might add to Monks' suspicion that costume has been considered 'not worthy of serious masculine analysis' (2010, 10) a contention that it has not been considered worthy of serious critical analysis in the field of Performance Studies because costume is a key element of theatrical spectacle. Since Guy Debord wrote *The Society of the Spectacle* in 1967, the notion of spectacle has been associated in radical humanities scholarship with obfuscating consumerist illusion that conspires to divorce human beings from material truths about their conditions of existence.

Recent citations of Debord from the field of Performance Studies have included Jen Harvie's critique of superficial spectacles of social participation in performance (Harvie 2013, 42); Theron Schmidt's analysis of Yvonne Rainer's task-based performance as 'a way of circumventing the 'pretence of theatre, and its mimetic distance from 'real' experience' (Schmidt 2019, 159-62, 159); Martin Puchner's examination of Debord's work, in which Puchner suggests that the 'strategies of the neo-avant-garde cannot be easily transferred to a traditional theatrical form' (Puchner 2004, 4). Perhaps costume has largely not featured as an object of study in the field of Performance Studies because it is implicitly regarded as intrinsic to superficial, mimetic, traditional forms of theatre that the field eschews as part of the obfuscating spectacle of late capitalism. Further, the twentieth-century focus on the body in performance art and the key works of scholarship that have followed it has made the body the site of the radical and the subversive rather than what covers it. Even within the study of Shakespeare in contemporary performance, costume becomes a suspicious political operator: Peter Holland compares an exciting late twentieth-century research focus on the early modern body (he lists Gail Kern Paster (1992) on the Foucaudian discipline of shame and early modern body; Jonathan Goldberg (1992) on 'the sodomised body'; Peter Stallybrass (1986) 'on the enclosed body'; Jonathan Sawday (1995) on the dissected body; Laura Levine (1994) on the gendered body, amongst others) with theatre voice coach Patsy Rodenberg's 'banal account of how the early modern body differs' from the modern. In his examination of Rodenberg's historical fantasy of an alert, upright, centred early modern body (Rodenburg 2002 16 in Holland 2005, 42) Holland describes Rodenberg's vision as one of 'the body dependent on costume-drama, the body in costume'. In Holland's critique, then, 'costume-drama' becomes the ultimate form of commodified silliness to be held up against the astute cultural politics of the scholar's interest in a body without clothes. Holland goes on to hold up Shakespeares's Globe's interest in early modern dress research as the logical result of a fetishisation of costume. Rodenberg's 'vision of the body dependent on costume-drama' contains, he argues,

> the kind of assumption that has led productions at Shakespeare's Globe in London to trumpet their recreation of Elizabethan through the use of the right dyes, including urine, and their use of early modern underwear, which the actors reported as transforming their bodies into the right walk for Shakespeare but which we could see as an invisible fetishization of the newly

marketable commodity of the early modern authentic as a liberation for their bodies. (Holland 2005, 42)

Holland's critique of Rodenberg's particular fetishisation of the perfect body to deliver Shakespeare is an astute and important one, and it is interesting that his markers for the political lie of commodification are costumes. The dye made from urine and historically researched underwear—costume elements so close to the body—feature as the ultimate in costume-led consumerist obfuscation here.

If actors wearing historical costumes have been part of a spectacular problem for Performance Studies, perhaps it is safe to assume that costume is more significant to the 'Shakespearean' scholar, because it is essential to the material culture of early modern stage and society. Costumes were, after all, the most expensive items owned by early modern theatre companies; as Jonathan Gil Harris remarks, 'Much has been made of the fact that companies who paid £6 commissions for new works could also pay in excess of £20 for a new single costume' (Gil Harris 2002, 48; see also Bruster 2002, 72; Richardson 2011, 65-6). But perhaps 'much has been made' of this fact because it is surprising to scholars that early modern cultural objects which are now so intellectually and artistically valuable—early modern plays, particularly those by Shakespeare—were once less economically valuable than costumes. Although, as we have seen, there has been important work done by Jones and Stallybrass in their cultural materialist analysis of Renaissance material culture, what performers looked like in the clothes that they wore on the public stage, and what this might have meant to early modern audiences, has been given little exclusive analytical attention outside of: Jean McIntyre's *Costumes and Scripts* and Robert I. Lublin's *Costuming the Shakespearean Stage*; moments from Peter Hylands's work on *Disguise on the Early Modern Stage*; Jenny Tiramani's conclusions about early modern stage and costume design from her 'original practices' work at Shakespeare's Globe (see Tiramani 2008); one essay collection, Lennox and Mirabella's *Shakespeare and Costume* (2015); Stephen Orgel's chapter 'Seeing through Costume' in *Spectacular Performances: Essays on Theatre* (2011); and Richardson's chapter in *Shakespeare and Material Culture* (2011). In addition, at the time of writing, Ella Hawkins has recently completed a doctoral project on the meanings of 'Jacobethan' costume on the English stage; this focuses on twenty-first-century performance but includes a particularly significant study of the likely absence of the ruff from early modern stage costume practices (see below page 49). A wider literature survey might be done of moments of costume analysis in works on early modern masque performance (and see, e.g. Ravelhofer 2006 and Mickel 2003 for extensive work on these costumes), no doubt because we have Inigo Jones's designs extant to analyse. But if, as Catherine Richardson suggests in the abstract to the collection *Clothing Culture 1350–1650* (2004), early modern clothing has 'been discussed in relation to various disciplines' but 'has not in many cases found a place as a central topic of analysis in its own right', this has been even more the case for that clothing as it appeared on the early modern public stage.

What *Shakespeare and Costume in Practice* aims to do is not simply to continue the work of placing costume at the centre of the scholarly stage but to bring it into dialogue with a range of theoretical positions that are not often associated with the pragmatics of theatre making. The book is structured around three play-based case studies—of *Hamlet, Much Ado About Nothing* and *The Tempest*—each of which frames an analysis of costume in theatrical practice with a theoretical approach. 'Inky Cloaks and Solemn Black. *Hamlet*, Mourning and the Disappearing Costume' draws upon cultural materialist studies of dramatic 'subjectivity', which in their turn, particularly in the case of Catherine Belsey's work, have used *Hamlet* as a founding text. The critical frame within which I examine costume designs for *Much Ado*, in 'Tires and Rebatoes, Corsets and Lace. *Much Ado About Nothing*, Restorative Nostalgia and the Costume Drama' is framed by Sveltana Boym's cultural history of nostalgia. 'The Post-colonial *Tempest*: Costume and Race' connects the post-colonial turn in *Tempest* criticism, and more recent scholarly critiques of whiteness, with British stage production. In each chapter, a theoretical position helps me to think about how costume practice makes meaning from a 400-year-old text: how costume suggests Hamlet is a 'modern' psychological subject; how costume frames the very way we think about the past—in critically reflective or nostalgically restorative terms—in *Much Ado*; how costume realises debates about colonialism, race and identity visually in *The Tempest*. Each of the studies focuses on the spectacular in the literal sense of 'that which is to be looked at'. The *Hamlet* chapter works against the privileging of psychological interiority in the play and aims to restore the visual as a primary constituent of its political meanings. The chapter on *Much Ado* puts productions of the play into conversation with the notion of the 'costume drama', with all its connotations of mere or trivial spectacle, and suggests that a productive politics of clothing can emerge from costumes that are consciously flagged as beautiful. The *Tempest* chapter draws on the work of critical race theorists to suggest that it is neither possible nor productive to be blind to colour as we stage this play, even where casting makes attempts at 'colour-blindness', a shifting and contentious term the usefulness or otherwise of which is discussed in the chapter.

COSTUME AND CLOTHING HISTORIES: PERFORMING THE PAST

Shakespeare and Costume in Practice does not give an overview of the history of costuming Shakespeare, although Chap. 1 does offer a history of British (mainly London) Hamlet costumes as it explores costume's role in the development of dramatic subjectivity. Attempts to mark broad movements in costume history can be helpful: Russell Jackson's 'General Overview' in the Lennox and Mirabella collection takes the reader deftly from early modern eclecticism, through Victorian 'pictorialism', then into the 'freer, happier [twentieth century] world of choosing your period for interpretive reasons—though with an understanding of the theatre culture of Shakespeare's own time' (Jackson in Lennox and Mirabella 2015, 9). Particularly suggestively, Jackson points to the eclecticism of early twentieth-century costume design that might look strictly 'period' to the casual viewer of photographs today. Even William Poel, in his 'Elizabethan' stagings of Shakespeare, designed costumes that 'could be eclectic, mixing periods and styles' (Jackson 2015, 16).

    Shakespeare and Costume in Practice pays particular attention to how costume allows for, indeed heightens, the multiple senses of familiarity and strangeness, comfortable recognition and alienation, that watching a Shakespeare play can entail for audiences 400 years after his time. Jackson is right to suggest that costume which does this eclectic work has a long history, punctured by relatively short periods of pictorial consistency, stage naturalism and devotion to 'historical authenticity'. Jonathan Bate, too, as part of his discourse on the Peacham drawing, or Longleat Manuscript, of a scene from *Titus Andronicus*, suggests that modern eclecticism is a return to something essentially Shakespearean:

> The Peacham drawing provides us with the valuable evidence about costumes: as the play addresses issues in contemporary history via a Roman setting, so the costumes mingle ages. Titus wears a toga but his soldiers are Elizabethan men-at-arms with halberds, while Tamora's dress is vaguely medieval. There could be no better precedent for modern productions

which are determinedly eclectic in their dress, combining ancient and modern. (Bate 1995, 43)

I am happy to agree with Bate that the much-cited Peacham drawing may be an example of early modern theatre's costuming eclecticism (see Levin 2002 for a summary of a range of arguments around the document)—indeed, the notion of this eclecticism underpins my analysis of a putative first *Hamlet*. However, costume in Shakespeare's period participates in other visual regimes of cultural meaning—pageants, jousts, court display, masque, the presentation of the self in everyday life in a culture that legislated on class and dress—so that the theatre is not singular in its kaleidoscopic costuming effects (see Monks 2010, above 4). Martin Holmes suggests that Titus's sons, in their mix of Roman armour and Elizabethan dress, look like the audience's ideas of St George in a pageant, or recollections of Essex in the tilt yard, or Ralegh coming home from an expedition abroad. It is less important that they should look like real Romans than that they be immediately recognisable as national heroes, thus they would be wearing such modern or near-modern armour as was available (Holmes 1972, 153, see also Escolme 2012, 131).

Holmes is not suggesting here that Shakespeare's company made conscious aesthetic decisions about how 'issues in contemporary history' might be recalled 'via a Roman setting' (Bate 1995, 43), as a modern costume designer might, but rather draws our attention to how early modern London performs politics through a range of sartorial display and shows how spectacles of heroism inevitably get re-staged in a play where nobles return triumphant from a war.

Theatre costume, in Shakespeare's period and our own, may be 'eclectic' but the clothing culture which Elizabethan and Jacobean stage practice shared was very different from today's. Fashion seems to offer the twenty-first-century Londoner an infinite variety of 'looks', changing each 'season' and ranging from startlingly cheap clothes made in the world's sweatshops, to recycled garments for sale in vintage and second-hand stores, to 'status brand' bags, shoes and watches with prices comparable to a deposit on a house. But whilst a designer or clothing company's wares might signify a particular income bracket or social group, clothing in modern Western culture is also regarded as a significant means of self-expression, a concept which would not have meant much to an early modern London theatre-goer, as we will see in Chap. 1. Most early modern Londoners, even the richest, would have owned far fewer clothes than many people living in that city on even relatively modest incomes today. They would have been part of a much slower-changing, socially and legally restricted system of fashion that read in terms of social status in more obvious and codified ways than high fashion does now. Shakespeare's audiences, I want to suggest, went to the theatre to look at clothing, rather than through it, to use Stella Bruzzi's binary again (1997, above 4), not only because the clothes on stage were so lavish and expensive but because these audiences were used to looking at clothes and reading their overt social meanings and performative functions. In addressing questions of how costume makes meaning in Shakespeare's theatre and our own, *Shakespeare and Costume in Practice* aims to cast something of an early modern eye over the stage: to restore ways of looking at clothes on stage as though they are always doing particular cultural work, rather than assuming that they are the primarily means of individual self-expression for modern psychological subjects.

Of course, to restore the early modern eye and mindset accurately and entirely is impossible. But 400-year-old plays draw attention to clothing in a range of fascinating ways, and paying the attention they demand will, I hope, lead to new ways of bringing past and present into dialogue. Rather than assuming that period costume offers a transparent window onto the past, or that modern dress connects Shakespeare's world directly with our own, this book attends to how costume produces the past and the present and explores the kinds of past and present that theatre productions seem to assume, desire or believe in. If the Peacham drawing is truly a depiction of a production, then clothing on Shakespeare's stage colluded with the plays to reflect on both past and present; *Shakespeare and Costume in Practice* contends that it is not only eclectic costume design that does this work but all stage clothing.

INKY CLOAKS AND SOLEMN BLACK. *HAMLET*, MOURNING AND THE DISAPPEARING COSTUME

Shakespeare and Costume in Practice is divided into three play-based case-studies and two practitioner interviews. The first study begins by asking what Hamlet might have looked like in the black mourning cloak that his mother wants him to 'cast...off' (1.2.67) in the second scene of the play. It considers how the public theatre heightened and played with the assumptions its audiences might have made when they saw clothes on actors' bodies in the theatre. It offers a history of *Hamlet* costumes on the London stage, landing on the reception of Henry Irving in the leading role in 1874, then moves to recent productions of the play. The chapter explores how costume for this play seems to 'disappear' at certain periods in theatre history, particularly in the unremarkable black shirts and trousers of modern Hamlets who, at a time when black never seems to go out of fashion, barely registers as being in mourning at all. At the end of this chapter, having looked at some of Hamlet's recent neutral, casual blacks and greys, I consider a Hamlet costume that re-stages the Prince as rebellious artist in a riot of colour. This is the RSC's most recent *Hamlet* at the time of writing and its first with a black actor in the lead; it is set in an imagined African country, which gives rise to some problems around cultural specificity and appropriation. But it fascinatingly and literally re-paints the play and portrays Hamlet as a young artist, struggling to find his own way between Claudius's opportunistic new world order and the 'much older cosmos', to site Catherine Belsey (1985, 42), represented by his father. I use it as an example of the dialogue between past and present that this play can create when recent stage conventions of the 'disappearing costume' are rejected for a theatrically conscious foregrounding of fabric and colour.

TIRES AND REBATOES, CORSETS AND LACE. *MUCH ADO ABOUT NOTHING*, RESTORATIVE NOSTALGIA AND THE COSTUME DRAMA

This chapter focuses on *Much Ado About Nothing* as a 'Costume Drama', with all that label's connotations of nostalgic prettiness. It draws on Svetlana Boym's definitions of two kinds of cultural nostalgia: the first she names restorative nostalgia, which looks back at an idealised set of tropes and traditions and imagines them as ultimate truths; the second is reflective nostalgia, which owns its own longings and contradictions more reflectively and critically. The chapter uses these definitions as starting points for a consideration of *Much Ado* at the Royal Shakespeare Company and its relationship to film and television 'costume dramas', or 'heritage films'.

In the case-study pairs of *Much Ado* productions I examine in the chapter—two productions set in India; two sets of Carolinian costume designs; two productions set in the 1950s; and two productions with very specific historical settings designed with an almost televisual realism—I suggest that the examples of costume designs that demand one looks *at* clothes make this comedy a more productively awkward, unsettling experience for modern audiences than some of the beautiful designs that ask that one looks *through* clothes. Stella Bruzzi's film studies binary (1997, see above 4 and 17) thus becomes a useful one for a consideration of this play in the theatre. I also look at some 'period' set and costume designs that mimic the luxurious period detail tropes of the film and television industries, which generally ask us to look *through* clothes; some of the avowedly beautiful costumes for these productions serve to erase the social and gender troubles of this play in a haze of lovely period detail. Chapter 2 draws on my experiences of looking at the Royal Shakespeare Company's 'costume bibles' alongside photographs and video recordings held in the company's archive. It references the pleasure of looking at and touching fabric in order to reconstruct a production one has either not seen, or saw years previously. I close the chapter with some questions about reflective nostalgia and the study of material culture.

THE POST-COLONIAL *TEMPEST*: COSTUME AND RACE

Chapter 3 explores how costume might interrogate or critique racial and colonial stereotypes and where it might be in danger of reiterating them. Drawing on Edward Said's critique of orientalism, scholars of 'whiteness' as a racial/cultural trope have demonstrated that whiteness tends to reproduce itself as a norm in various cultural contexts, producing 'blackness' as the exotic, violent, sexualised other. The chapter looks at how black and white bodies are clothed, exposed and staged in *The Tempest*. I begin with some speculation as to what an early modern Caliban might have looked like at the King's Men's Blackfriars theatre—'a man or a fish?', as Stephano asks himself. I trace the implications for power relations in the play that are contained in more monstrous and more human possible early 'costume designs' for Caliban and asks how 'other' to Prospero and Miranda the first Caliban might have appeared. I then consider the costumes worn by black Ariels and Calibans commanded by white Prosperos, in the productions directed by Jonathan Miller in 1970 and 1988, and demonstrate how the RSC drew again upon a colonial reading and colour-conscious casting in 2002. I consider how black and white actors are costumed in productions where the master/slave relationship between Prospero and the Islanders is not figured in obviously colonial terms but where a post-colonial sensibility might still be said to underpin casting: productions in which characters other than Ariel and Caliban, particularly Prospero, are cast with people of colour.

A modern audience potentially experiences an early modern drama dually, as both familiar and historically alien at different points in a performance; costume design can be part of what produces this experience, rather than a means of erasing historical difference. In this chapter, I argue similarly about race and casting. Ayanna Thompson writes that the 'practice of colorblind casting cannot resolve the larger societal tensions in which [theatre productions] are enmeshed' (Thompson 2006, 8). I am not suggesting that casting which has centred *The Tempest* on a black Prospero solve or erase these tensions. I rather contend that costume can draw attention to these tensions one moment, erase them the next, just as production foregrounds and erases the 'past-ness' of a play.

DESIGNING SHAKESPEARE NOW: CHLOE LAMBARD AND TOM PIPER

The final section of this book comprises interviews with two theatre designers about the work of costuming Shakespeare. As in the case of most British theatre design today, Chloe Lambard and Tom Piper design both sets and costume for their theatre productions. Piper was one of the RSC's most prolific designers under the artistic directorship of Michael Boyd and was Associate Designer there between 2004 and 2014. His work on the RSC's 2002 *Tempest* features in Chap. 3 and, I would argue, represents some of the RSC's most significant recent work in its playful approach to 'period' shapes and fabrics. Here, I discuss with Piper his methods for designing costume as part of an overall scenographic vision, his work with actors and directors and how meaning is made collectively in large-scale production, and how he works with historically inflected designs for a company which insists on the continuing contemporary significance of Shakespeare.

Lambard is more obviously a designer of contemporary theatre. Her work on the Donmar Warehouse's all-women 'Shakespeare Trilogy' *Tempest* features in Chap. 4 here, but she is better known for her installation work and design for new writing. I ask her how working with insistently contemporary themes inflected her work on *The Tempest* and on *Ophelias Zimmer*, an installation work directed by Katie Mitchell which staged Ophelia's time off stage in *Hamlet*. Both productions use modern clothes which appear, superficially, to typify the self-effacing neutrality of 'modern dress' but which, I suggest to Lambard, build a dramaturgy of dress through both productions, crucial to their meanings and effects. The purpose of this section of the book is to give voice to two costume designers and to demonstrate the ways in which the practical and aesthetic vocabularies of design might infiltrate academic discourse about theatre in future scholarship. The work of the costume designer, particularly where they design both costume and set, is remarkably broad in practical, aesthetic and intellectual scope. The designer must be able to communicate with actors, directors and audiences their understanding of plays and their historical and aesthetic contexts; of dramatic 'characters' and their place in a play's and a production's dramaturgy; of actors' bodies wearing clothes and how they signify on stage. The vocabulary of the theatre designer, then, holds a rich potential for developing and extending academic discourse about the theatre, involved as it is in both theatre's material culture and its semiotics. I hope that these interviews, and this book as a whole, will create new dialogues between theatre practice and scholarship, and allow the languages of design to inflect and infect the theatre academy in new ways.

PRODUCTIONS DISCUSSED

Beau, Dickie, and Jan Willem van den Bosch. 2016. *Re-member Me*. London: Almeida Theatre.

HAMLET

National Theatre (1989), Richard Eyre, (director), Liz Da Costa (costume designer), John Gunter (set designer), Olivier Theatre, National Theatre, London.
Almeida Theatre (2016), Robert Icke (director) and Hildegard Bechtler (designer) (2016), Almeida Theatre, London.
Royal Shakespeare Company (1989), Ron Daniels (director) and Antony MacDonald (designer), Royal Shakespeare Theatre, Stratford upon Avon.
——— (2008), Greg Doran (director) and Robert Jones (Designer), Royal Shakespeare Theatre, Stratford upon Avon.

ROMEO AND JULIET

Whyman, Erica (director) and Tom Piper (Designer) (2018), Royal Shakespeare Company, Stratford upon Avon.

WORKS CITED

All references to plays by Shakespeare are from the *RSC Shakespeare: Complete Works* (2007) ed. Jonathan Bate, Houndsmills, Basingstoke: Palgrave Macmillan
Barker, Francis. 1984. *The Tremulous Private Body: Essays on Subjection.* Ann Arbor: University of Michigan Press.
Bate, Jonathan. 1995. *Introduction to William Shakespeare Titus Andronicus, The Arden Shakespeare Third Series.* London: Routledge.
Belsey, Catherine. 1985. *The Subject of Tragedy Identity and Difference in Renaissance Drama.* London: Methuen.
———. 2002. Disrupting Sexual Difference: Meaning and Gender in the Comedies. In *Alternative Shakespeares,* ed. John Drakakis, 169–193. London: Routledge.
Benedict, David (1995) 'Theatre: Goodnight Sweet Prince' *The Times,* 6 January 1995, http://www.independent.co.uk/arts-entertainment/theatre-good-night-sweet-prince-1566786.html
Bleeker, Maaike, Adrian Kear, Joe Kelleher, and Heike Roms, eds. *Thinking Through Theatre and Performance.* London: Bloomsbury, Methuen Theatre.
Boym, Svetlana. 2001. *The Future of Nostalgia.* New York: Basic Books.
Bruster, Douglas. 2002. The Dramatic Life of Objects. In *Staged Properties in Early Modern English Drama,* ed. Jonathan Gil Harris and Natasha Korda, 67–96. Cambridge: Cambridge University Press.
Bruzzi, Stella. 1997. *Undressing cinema: Clothing and Identity in the Movies.* London: Routledge.
Cavendish, Dominic. 2018. *Romeo and Juliet* at RSC, review - a fresh, fleet, blade-sharp revival. *The Telegraph,* May 2. https://www.telegraph.co.uk/theatre/what-to-see/romeo-juliet-rsc-review/
Debord, Guy. 2009. *Society of the Spectacle.* Eastbourne: Soul Bay Press.
Dickie Beau, Interview with Bridget Escolme (2017), London.
Drakakis, John. 2002. *Alternative Shakespeares.* 2nd ed. London: Routledge.
Escolme, Bridget. 2012. Costume. In *Shakespeare and the Making of Theatre,* ed. Stuart Hampton-Reeves and Bridget Escolme, 128–145. Basingstoke: Palgrave.
Ferguson, Margaret, et al., eds. *Rewriting the Renaissance.* Chicago: University of Chicago Press.
Garber, Marjorie B. 1992. *Vested Interests: Cross-dressing and Cultural Anxiety.* London: Routledge.

Gardner, Lynn (2017) '"Re-member Me" Review: A Seance of Hamlets from O'Toole to Day-Lewis', *Guardian*, 20 March https://www.theguardian.com/stage/2017/mar/20/re-member-me-review-a-seance-of-hamlets-from-otoole-to-day-lewis.

Gil Harris, Jonathan, and Natasha Korda, eds. 2002. *Staged Properties in Early Modern English Drama*. Cambridge: Cambridge University Press.

Goldberg, Jonthan. 1992. *Sodometries: Renaissance Texts, Modern Sexualities*. Stanford, CA: Stanford University Press.

Greenblatt, Stephen. 1980. *Renaissance Self-fashioning: From More to Shakespeare*. Chicago: University of Chicago Press.

Harvie, Jen. 2013. *Fair Play – Art, Performance and Neoliberalism*. Houndsmills, Basingstoke: Palgrave Macmillan.

Hawkins, Ella Kirsty (2020) 'The Significance of Jacobethanism in Twenty-First-Century Costume Design for Shakespeare', University of Birmingham, PhD thesis.

Hodgdon, Barbara. 2007. Briding the Shrew: Costumes that Matter. *Shakespeare Survey* 60: 72–83.

Hodgdon, Barbara, and W.B. Worthern, eds. 2005. *A Companion to Shakespeare and Performance*. Oxford: Blackwells.

Holland, Peter. 2005. Shakesepeare's Two Bodies. In *A Companion to Shakespeare and Performance*, ed. Barbara Hodgdon and W.B. Worthern, 36–56. Oxford: Blackwells.

Holmes, Martin. 1972. *Shakespeare and His Players*. London: J. Murray.

Hunt, Alan. 1996. *Governance of the Consuming Passions: A History of Sumptuary Law*. Basingstoke: Macmillan Press.

Hyland, Peter. 2011. *Disguise on the Early Modern Stage*. Farnham: Ashgate.

Jackson, Russell. 2015. Brief Overview: A Stage History of Shakespeare and Costume. In *Shakespeare and Costume*, ed. Patricia Lennox and Bella Mirabella, 9–21. London: Bloomsbury.

Jones, Ann Rosalind, and Peter Stallybrass. 2000. *Renaissance Clothing and the Materials of Memory*. Cambridge: Cambridge University Press.

Lennox, Patricia, and M. Bella, eds. 2015. *Shakespeare and Costume*. London: Bloomsbury.

Levin, Richard. 2002. The Longleat Manuscript and *Titus Andronicus*. *Shakespeare Quarterly* 53 (3): 53–40.

Levine, Laura. 1994. *Men in Women's Clothing*. Cambridge: Cambridge University Press.

Lublin, Robert I. 2011. *Costuming the Shakespearean Stage: Visual Codes of Representation in Early Modern Theatre and Culture*. Farnham: Ashgate.

MacIntyre, Jean. 1992. *Costumes and Scripts in the Elizabethan Theatres*. Edmonton: University of Alberta Press.

Mickel, Lesley. 2003. Glorious Spangs and Rich Embroidery: Costume in the Masque of Blackness and Hymenaei. *Studies in the Literary Imagination* 36 (2): 41–59.

Mikhaila, Ninya, and Jane Malcolm-Davies. 2006. *The Tudor Tailor: Reconstructing 16th-Century Dress*. Hollywood, Calif: Costume and Fashion Press.

Monks, Aoife. 2010. *The Actor in Costume*. Basingstoke: Palgrave Macmillan.

Orgel, Stephen. 2011. *Spectacular Performances: Essays on Theatre, Imagery, Books, and Selves in Early Modern England*. Manchester: Manchester University Press.

O'Reilly, Karen. 2009. *Key concepts in Ethnography*. London: SAGE.

Paster, Gail Kern. 1992. *The Body Embarrassed*. Ithaca, NY: Cornell University Press.

Peter, John (1989) 'A Hamlet who would be King at Elsinore' *The Sunday Times*, 12 November.

Prown, Jules David, and Kenneth Haltman. 2000. *American Artifacts: Essays in Material Culture*. East Lansing: Michigan State University Press.

Puchner, Martin. 2004. Society of the Counter-Spectacle: Debord and the Theatre of the Situationists. *Theatre Research International* 29 (1): 4–15.

Ravelhofer, Barbara. 2006. *The Early Stuart Masque: Dance Costume and Music*. Oxford: Oxford University Press.

Richardson, Catherine. 2011. *Shakespeare and Material Culture*. Oxford: Oxford University Press.

———. 2004. *Clothing Culture 1350 – 1650*, 2004. Farnham: Ashgate.

Rodenburg, Patsy. 2002. *Speaking Shakespeare*. New York: Palgrave Macmillan.

Said, Edward W. 2003. *Orientalism*. London: Penguin.

Sawday, Jonathan. 1995. *The Body Emblazoned*. London: Routledge.

Schmidt, Theron. 2019. How Does Theatre Think through Work? In *Thinking Through Theatre and Performance*, ed. M. Bleeker, A. Kear, J. Kelleher, and H. Roms, 158–170. London: Bloomsbury, Methuen Theatre.

Stallybrass, Peter. 1986. Patriarchal Territories: The Body Enclosed. In *Rewriting the Renaissance*, ed. Margaret Ferguson et al. Chicago: University of Chicago Press.

Tiramani, Jenny. 2008. Exploring Early Modern Stage and Costume Design. In *Shakespeare's Globe: a Theatrical Experiment*, ed. Christie Carlson and Farah Karim Cooper. Cambridge: Cambridge University Press.

Thompson, Ayanna, ed. 2006. *Colorblind Shakespeare: New Perspectives on Race and Performance*. London, New York: Routledge.

Trueman, Matt. 2012. 'Did Daniel Day-Lewis See his Father's Ghost as Hamlet? That is the Question' *Guardian*, 29 May, https://www.theguardian.com/stage/2012/oct/29/daniel-day-lewis-hamlet-ghost.

Williams, Raymond. 1977. *Marxism and Literature*. Oxford: Oxford University Press.

CHAPTER 2

Hamlet, Mourning and the Disappearing Costume: Inky Cloaks and Solemn Black

*And then you have some again that keeps one suit Of jests, as a man is
known by one suit of Apparel, and gentlemen quote his jests down In
their tables before they come to the play, as thus: 'Cannot you stay till I
eat my porridge?' and 'You owe me A quarter's wages', and 'My coat
wants a cullison', And 'Your beer is sour'.*
Hamlet Quarto 1, scene 9.

The speech above is from Hamlet's advice to the Players as it appears in
the First Quarto edition of *Hamlet*.[1] Here, the prince warns the players
against clowning which is so clichéd that wealthy young wags in the

---

[1] As Zachary Lesser summarises, the first printed edition of *Hamlet* has been rehabilitated
as a lively, theatrical version of the play in both the nineteenth and twentieth centuries: 'A
nod towards the "theatricality" of Q1 seems by now almost obligatory in editorial introduc-
tions and essays on Q1…' (Lesser 2015, 216; see for example David E. Jones 1988, 104–10;
Orgel 2006, 13–54, 22; Holderness and Loughrey 2014, 14–6; Irace 1998, 20; see Marcus
1996, 150–2 for a somewhat sceptical account of Q1's possible performance origins; see
Dillon for a detailed critique of the assumption that Q1 is a performance text). See Lesser for
a detailed history of editorial responses to Q1. Lesser suggestively points out that theatrically
inflected rehabilitations of this edition, notoriously named a 'bad' Quarto by Duthie in
1941, are part of a long scholarly project of deflecting questions about the historical origins
of this text (217). However, the passage quoted here, exclusive to this edition of the play, and
the reference to the Ghost's night-gown (on which Lesser bases a chapter) certainly offer
insights into theatrical practice that the 'authoritative' texts do not.

© The Author(s), under exclusive license to Springer Nature
Switzerland AG 2020
B. Escolme, *Shakespeare and Costume in Practice*, Shakespeare in
Practice, https://doi.org/10.1007/978-3-030-57149-8_2

audience are able to write the clown's jests down 'before they come to the play', perhaps so that they can shout them out during the performance and spoil the jokes that everyone knows are coming. Bad clowns are known by their repertoire of jokes 'as a man is known by one suit of apparel', and this disparaging remark of Hamlet's provokes questions about what it means to be known by one's clothes. Is Hamlet suggesting that whilst most people are known by just one suit of clothes, theatrical jesting should be more varied and unpredictable? Or is he conjuring 'a man' who is visually marked as odd, or poor, by owning only one suit? Certainly, even the richest citizens of early modern London would have owned fewer items of clothing than those on average incomes living there today, so to be known by one suit of apparel might not have been as eccentric in 1600 as it might be now. On the other hand, being marked by the singularity of one's dress is something the audience have been introduced to earlier in the play, when Hamlet is asked by his mother to 'cast [his] nightly colour off' (1.2.67): Hamlet persists in wearing mourning for his father when everyone else at court has changed out of it, to celebrate Claudius and Gertrude's marriage. Further, having warned the Players about clowns who interrupt the plot, our hero proceeds to behave similarly himself during The Murder of Gonzago. Perhaps this irony plays out in the Q1 advice to the Players, too, as Hamlet, the sole figure on stage dressed in funereal black, uses the example of the man with one suit to lecture the Players about theatrical cliché.

This chapter examines some key moments in the history of dressing British productions of *Hamlet* and argues that Hamlet's mourning dress plays a significant role in constructing the cultural and political meaning of the self, or subject, in the play. In 1600, theatre costume was a bricolage of stock clothing and newly bought and made garments. These garments were all clothes, not costumes especially adapted for stage use as 'period' costume often is today. But I want to suggest that quotidian clothing accrued significance on stage differently from how it read in everyday life, not only because ordinary theatre goers were offered the pleasure of getting close to the clothing of the aristocracy when a King or Queen entered, but also because of the slippery relationship between individual and type, and between moral, social and psychological meaning in the early modern theatre. In 1600, Hamlet's inky cloak and suits of solemn black were a personal choice, a visual symbol, and a political statement. *Hamlet*, I will suggest, foregrounds clothing politically in ways that become culturally and aesthetically unfashionable centuries later, when theatre and society need the play to be a play about a single, tortured mind.

Hamlet first walked onto the stage at the 1600 Globe Theatre as a startling figure in a big black cloak. This may already have been a familiar image for some audience members given the existence of a lost *Hamlet* play before Shakespeare's (Knutson et al. 2018), though we have no way of knowing whether Shakespeare's intriguingly twisted staging of this revenge or malcontent figure at a wedding celebration was original. Since then, Hamlet has morphed into a stylish but sartorially nondescript young man in modern dark shirts, sweaters and trousers. Here, I am going to consider: the impact of actor Richard Burbage's funeral wear for the first production of *Hamlet*; the moment when a medieval tunic becomes the standard costume for Hamlet during the second half of the nineteenth century, which I mark as the beginning of costume's 'disappearance' in the play; a 1980s and a 2000s Hamlet in which the Ghost disappears into a costume; and a recent Hamlet at the RSC in which costume is reinscribed as central to the play's meaning. As we will see, there are phases in the stage history of *Hamlet* when costuming for the Prince becomes standardised, to the point where he is indeed a 'man...known by one suit of apparel', and moments when costuming tradition seems to shift sharply and significantly, to reflect or produce new possible meanings for the play.

HAMLET: THE GLOBE, THE CHAMBERLAIN'S MEN, C.1600

In this section, I speculate as to how clothing might have signified in the first performances of *Hamlet*. Jean MacIntyre has suggested that the dominant semiotics of clothes in the play's first staging would have signified social decorum rather than the moral journeys of the earlier morality and religious traditions; the play

> uses and changes costume mainly if not exclusively according to decorum. It uses the familiar codes of public symbolism for mourning and rejoicing and of theatre symbolism for journeying and madness, but not to show changes of fortune or moral condition. (MacIntyre 1992, 182)

Whereas in plays of the mystery and miracle traditions, 'everyman' figures wore clothes that denoted their place on a journey towards heaven or hell (see Richardson 2011, 76, on how Mankind's 'progressively short-ened coat' reflected his 'diminishing virtue'), by the time of the first per-formance of *Hamlet*, actors were wearing clothes that befitted the social occasions depicted on stage: court celebration, funeral, journey. MacIntyre suggests that decorum and the proper behaviour of people in their social roles—'maid, wife, widow, brother, nephew, son, father, husband, king, scholar, and, most of all, avenger'—are a central concern of *Hamlet* (MacIntyre 1992, 181). These are important observations but I would suggest that on the early modern stage, decorum and moral condition are not easily separated: the first is a sign of the second. Hamlet believes that his Mother and Uncle's swift shift to marriage—and out of the mourning indicated by black clothes—is both morally degenerate and a grotesque failure to uphold proper decorum. What early modern spectators saw on stage when they attended a production of *Hamlet* were individual bodies, social types and moral conditions, all dressed in and expressed through clothing; the strictly hierarchical tropes and systems of late Elizabethan dress, and the social and moral condition of each figure in the play, col-luded to make meaning.

This social and theatrical collusion was strengthened by economic real-ity: the extraordinary expense of dressing actors in aristocratic roles and the fact that early modern stage clothes were not especially designed stage costumes, created for comfort, ease of movement and quick changes, but early modern garments complete with pins, ties and lacing (see Tiramani 2009), meant that many actors would have likely worn the same basic costume throughout the performance of a play. Costume changes, in line with MacIntyre's comment on decorum, may have indicated social occa-sion and role but not, I would suggest, the passing of time, as in a modern realist drama. Even occasion-based costume changes are likely to have been simple—cloaks and hats to indicate, say, mourning or a journey, if only because getting dressed and undressed in the early modern period is such a time-consuming business. Brett Gamboa's study of doubling in Shakespeare's repertoire supports this conclusion when he equates the early modern theatrical trope of disguise with the costuming practices of doubling:

Costume changes…were typically simple, the actors likewise comfortable with the fact that the outward changes necessary to convince fellow charac-ters need not seem convincing to the spectators. On the contrary, convinc-ing the spectators might diminish their experience of the play, once enhanced by watching onstage audiences be taken in by impersonations and disguises that echo those transacted by every actor onstage before the offstage audience. (Gamboa 2018, 66)

Thus, Gamboa suggests, part of the pleasure of watching an early modern play is imagining that a simple change of garment can indicate a complete change of character. Clothing on the early modern stage, then, has both a functional and a social iconicity: to indicate a court occasion a King might wear a crown, to indicate a journey he might don a cloak and a hat rather than continue to wear a crown to indicate his kingly status. I contend that complete costume changes for such narratives are unlikely for economic and practical reasons and might indeed have been kept to a minimum because, as Gamboa demonstrates, they also indicate doubling.

A basic costume worn by an actor through a play, with minimal practical and socially decorous changes, was thus also representative of a broad social and—sometimes, still—moral type. Take Horatio, who Richardson (2011, 72–3) and Lublin (2014, 641) agree would have worn a dark, scholar's gown in *Hamlet*. In production today, even one with an Elizabethan-inflected costume design, the actor playing Horatio might don outdoor wear for the watch scenes, then a variety of different, student-appropriate costumes to indicate the passing of time, including something passably smart for the court occasion of the play within the play. In 1600, one dark scholarly gown over a suit from company stock or the actor's own clothes would have made him Horatio the Scholar, and thus made him reasonably cheap to costume. This meant that his presence as the social type 'student' would have permeated the play, reminding the audience that Hamlet has been refused permission to return to the life of scholarly contemplation from which his friend is only visiting, and positioning Horatio as one who stands outside of the corruption at the core of the state of Denmark—like Hamlet himself, who is also wearing dark clothing, of course. Hamlet admires his friend as a stoic, unaffected by emotional turmoil; for early modern audiences, his scholarly, philosophical distance from the turmoil of the play would have been indicated in his costume. Whilst a 'real' wealthy young scholar just returned from a famed place of learning might have changed into more courtly attire for the wedding celebrations and formal court pronouncements of a royal family, Horatio may rather have made the visual statement 'scholar' throughout *Hamlet*. Practicality and iconography converge to make meaning on the early modern stage.

INKY CLOAKS: HAMLET AND FUNERAL DRESS

My interest in Hamlet's own dark clothes—his mourning dress—was first piqued by a collection of illustrations of Elizabethan funeral processions kept by the British Library. Drawn by an unknown artist (possibly by historian and herald William Camden) not long after the death of Elizabeth I and culminating in a depiction of the Queen's own funeral, these images are remarkable for the time and care that has been taken to draw and ink in figure upon figure over many pages, all of whom are wearing mourning cloaks or gowns (with the exception of ceremonial tabards for those with particular heraldic office) and a large number of whom therefore look very much alike. The only face that has been drawn as clearly demonstrating any kind of emotion in the whole of this collection is Helena, Marchioness of Northampton, Elizabeth I's chief mourner, who is pictured looking down and carrying a handkerchief. No-one else needs to look sad in the illustrations, and the way in which some figures are painted as if turned towards each other reads rather oddly to the modern viewer, as though funeral-goers are using the occasion to have a pleasant gossip. To the early modern eye, it was presumably enough that their clothing performs their mourning. Accustomed as I have been to seeing Elizabethan-inflected *Hamlet* productions dressing the lead in elegant black doublet and relatively slender breeches, of which more later, these images of funeral wear challenge the modern playgoer's notion of what Hamlet's 'inky cloak' might have looked like.

Hamlet's mourning obstructs Claudius's public presentation of smooth-running statecraft just as women's mourning more literally obstructs Richard III when the female relatives of his murder victims forestall the march to his coronation (Escolme 2014, 194–7; Goodland 2006, 152–3). In early modern culture, aristocratic funeral ceremonies engaged mourners in visual statements of both remembrance and allegiance. Principal and important mourners attended the funeral of a powerful personage dressed in mourning clothes provided by his or her family, in order to honour the dead and to express a political relationship with those that remained. In his work on performances of mourning in Shakespeare's theatre and early modern culture, Tobias Doring writes of mourning as:

> A political performance at the interface between commemorative and imperative behaviour, …[which] draws on available forms of expression in

religious and material culture while trying to bridge the gap between bereavement and belonging. (Doring 2006, 25)

At the aristocratic or royal funeral, everyone performed both sorrow for loss and allegiance to the ongoing regime. By aggressively insisting on wearing mourning months after his father's death, Hamlet himself chooses bereavement *over* belonging, by refusing to relinquish his inky cloak and suits of solemn black and integrate visually into Claudius's court. He keeps re-performing his father's death, with the 'vailed lids' and downward gaze (1.2.69–71) of Queen Elizabeth's chief mourner.

In Robert Lublin's article "Apparel oft proclaims the man": Visualizing *Hamlet* on the Early Modern Stage, Lublin and Adam West have produced a conjectural drawing of how Hamlet might have first appeared in the play (Lublin 2014, 631); but it is not clear from this how his inky cloak and customary suits might have looked different from the clothing of any fashionable young man wearing black in 1600. In her essay 'The Diversity of Black', written for an exhibition catalogue to accompany the National Gallery of Victoria, Australia's exhibition 'Black in Fashion— from Mourning to Night', Laura Jocic (2008) comments on the painting of the Somerset House Conference between England and Spain, painted only three or four years after the first performances of *Hamlet*, in which all of the representatives of the two great powers are wearing black, as are four out of five figures in the portrait of Robert Carey and Elizabeth Trevannion, 1st Earl and Countess of Monmouth and their family, also held in the UK's National Portrait Gallery; there are countless examples in late Elizabethan and Jacobean portraiture of black as fashion as opposed to black as mourning. The Puritan pamphlet writer Philip Stubbes, writing satirically on English fashions in 1583 writes of black as a colour worn by ordinary men of his father's generation (Stubbes 2002, 143), but also lists black velvet shoes (147) and black cloaks (150) amongst the decadent items of apparel worn by the wealthy (Stubbes 2002; see also Evans 1998, 131). Production of black dye, relates Jocic, was still a lengthy and therefore expensive process, even after 'Spanish colonization of the New World led to the discovery of the logwood tree in Central America [and t]he heart of this tree produced a good black dye when combined copper or iron mordant' (Jocic 2008, 17). It was a fashionable colour not only worn for mourning, so in order to read it as mourning dress on the stage of the first *Hamlet*, it is a fair assumption that the rest of the Danish court was dressed in conspicuously brighter colours, especially if one assumes, as Catherine

Richardson does, that Claudius and Gertrude have literally just come from their wedding in 1.2. Richardson points out that 'mourning clothes were... a strong statement intended to abjure status distinctions in favour of the advertisement of loss' and although 'in practice...the distinctions between costly and cheap black cloths were considerable' they were less 'instantly visually appreciable' than distinctions between clothes for courtly display. This is certainly borne out by the illustrations of Elizabeth I's funeral procession. Thus for Richardson, Hamlet not only reads as 'incongruous in relation to the celebration [and] to the court setting' but also 'to his own status there' in relation to the monarch (Richardson 2011, 74). If, as I want to argue, Hamlet is wearing the clothing that was actually provided for his father's funeral, rather than just fashionable (albeit for Claudius and Gertrude overly gloomy) black, then as Richardson suggests, he cannot be read as part of the court hierarchy that Claudius is trying to secure.

This is to contradict Jean MacIntyre, who writes of Hamlet's mourning in passing, whilst discussing the '*all in black*' stage direction of the first scene of *All's Well That Ends Well*: 'The black costumes are plain mourning like Hamlet's, not the special cloaks and gowns worn used in aristocratic funerals' (MacIntyre 1992, 197). MacIntyre presumably assumes this because she thinks it would be particularly odd to wear funeral gear at a celebratory court occasion. I contend that this is just what Hamlet might have done, and that this could doubly have disconcerted Claudius, because in 1600 it was still customary for those paying for an aristocratic funeral to dress the key mourners at their own expense. An early modern audience might have assumed that the funder in the case of Old King Hamlet's funeral was his brother, as the incoming monarch: Hamlet's uncle might have provided the cloth for the inky cloak that Hamlet persists in wearing, much to that new King's embarrassment. David Cressy cites a range of references to mourning gear paid for by Elizabethan aristocrats and gentry in advance of their deaths (Cressy 1997, 440–2); but Hamlet's father went to his own death 'unhouseled, disappointed, unaneled' (1.5.82) and thus possibly unprepared for his funeral in terms of these kinds of sartorial funds and instructions.

It is worth noting that a long cloak as a sign of mourning is remarked upon as a feature of the unusual figure cut by one Sir Kenelm Digby when, to avoid the 'envy and scandall' that John Aubrey suggests followed the sudden death of his wife, he is described as retiring to Gresham College London, where '[h]e wore a long mourning cloake, a high crowned hatt, his head unshorne, Look't like a Hermite, as signes of sorrowe for his beloved wife' (Aubrey 1962, 188; see also Taylor 1983, 100). If the first Hamlet wore full funeral regalia, the long cloak and high-crowned hat of Digby's isolated, hermit-like mourning, for a court occasion in which the present and future are being celebrated, this would have been a truly aggressive visual statement. Claudius insists on celebration; Hamlet looks as though he is literally at a funeral. This is something of a different 'look' from the variety of 'Elizabethan' Hamlets theatre audiences have been offered since a theatricalised version of doublet and hose was introduced to the stage in the late eighteenth century; different, even, from the painstakingly researched but distinctively stylish black velvet clothes and long black boots that Mark Rylance wore at the Globe in 2000 (dir. Giles Block, des. Jenny Tiramani), in a production that the company discussed as 'modern dress circa 1600' (Bessel 2001, 7); and certainly different from the generalised doublet and not-too-historically-alienating narrow hose of a number of twentieth- and twenty-first-century Hamlets. These versions of Elizabethan dress are more dashingly attractive to the modern eye than historical funeral wear and even they have been frequently replaced on the London stage by the modern psychological subject in casual black, as we will see. A voluminous black mourning cloak obviously makes no sense in a modern costume scheme, and even in an Elizabethan one makes a young male lead look 'like a hermit'; it has been, perhaps unconsciously, rejected for its lack of sex appeal as well as for its emphasis on the social role of the funeral over mourning as private and intimate. Interestingly, the only recent British Hamlet to be dressed in a long, dark and relatively shapeless gown for large parts of the play has been Simon Russell Beale at the National Theatre in 2000 (dir. John Caird, des. Tim Hatley), who was nearly 40 when he played the role and whose atypical body type for romantic heroes was occasionally commented on by reviewers.[2] A stout, less-than-young Hamlet does not recall recent Hamlets past—a fact that Russell Beale played to his advantage, as it left him reliant on his own precise vocal performance and many reviewers were struck by the clarity and newness he gave the familiar speeches.

For most of the rest of the play, I suggest that Burbage's Hamlet would have continued to wear black. The kind of voluminous mourning cloak depicted in the funeral drawings would have been impractical for the whole of the action of *Hamlet*, and a hardy traveling cloak was a likely

[2] The most notorious instance, purportedly from a local paper, was a review title "Tubby or not tubby, fat is the question" (Croall 160).

change for the return from England: Hamlet himself mentions his 'sea-gown scarfed about me' (5.2.14), which could be quickly removed so that Laertes and Hamlet confront one another over Ophelia's grave in similarly sombre dress. Hamlet does, of course, agree to obey his mother 'in all [his] best' (1.2.120) during their first encounter in the play, which might suggest that he takes off his mourning at her request. But he makes this reply not to her plea that he change clothes but to her later one, that he stay in Denmark rather than return to university in Wittenberg; his answer to Gertrude's comment on his 'nightly colour' is, famously, that taking off black clothes, the 'trappings and suits of woe', will not change his mournful inner state (1.2.67, 86). I concur with Tobias Doring when he argues that for Hamlet, the outward signification of mourning 'is only dismissed in order to revalue it, that is in order to reinvest the old 'suits' with new signifying power' (Doring 2006, 12); I suggest that obeying his mother in the best way he possibly involves staying in her presence rather than relinquishing the authentic performance of his inner self produced by his black clothing.

MOURNING AND MADNESS: OPHELIA

A consideration of Hamlet's mourning dress raises the question of who else might have worn mourning in the Chamberlain's Men's *Hamlet*. The ambivalent nature of Ophelia's death and the 'hugger mugger' interment of Polonius possibly justify a lack of costume change to black for Claudius and Gertrude and attendants, so that when the court parade enters for Ophelia's funeral, a powerful visual replay of the entrance at 1.2 could have taken place, with Laertes as the only figure in the royal procession wearing black rather than Hamlet. As Hamlet watches the family enter behind Ophelia's body, he is still wrapped in his sea-gown: thus Laertes takes Hamlet's place here as the dark figure from 2.1, and whereas Laertes is keen to be off to Wittenberg in the early scene, Hamlet is the traveller here (see also MacIntyre 1992, 187). Pleasing though the idea of this mirroring might be, however, not to wear black funeral cloaks to Ophelia's burial would have seemed extraordinarily indecorous, even for Ophelia's doubtful interment, and all of the characters in 5.1 must be assumed to own them: the audience will have heard Hamlet's barbed remarks about how recent his own father's funeral was in relation to his mother's later marriage. The more likely symbolism of this scene works around the funereal black that Claudius and Gertrude want banished from their court in 1.2.

In *Hamlet* productions after Shakespeare, mourning black has not been the norm for Ophelia in her 'mad' scenes, even though the Q1 stage direction indicating that her hair is down when she enters in that edition's equivalent of 4.5 (*Hamlet* Q1 13.14 *sd*) suggests not just madness but extreme grief, as Alan Dessen has noted (Dessen 1984, 36). Queen Elizabeth in *Richard III* is similarly directed but is, as Roger Apfelbaum remarks, 'completely sane, only temporarily in an extreme state of grief through loss' (Apfelbaum 2004, 82). Further, in her exposition of the place of the lute in the Q1 stage direction, Deanne Williams relates the state of Ophelia (or Ofelia in Q1)'s hair to her maidenhood rather than her 'distracted' state:

[the lute] also allows her performance of madness to play off dramatically against an image, and an implied history, of skillful, educated girlhood. While *haire down singing* is usually understood in the context of other stage directions for hair that convey madness, such as 'loose,' 'disheveled,' or 'about her ears,', young unmarried women are also typically represented with their 'haire down', signaling their maidenhood. A classic example of this is the famous Coronation Portrait of Elizabeth I, roughly contemporaneous with *Hamlet*. (Williams 2012, 119–20)

Presented with this image of 'skillful educated girlhood' in a state of distraction, this young woman who has, perhaps gathered herbs with meanings particular to her distress (Newman 1980; Laroche 2011), an early modern audience might have accepted a degree of decorousness from such a figure: Ophelia could have donned some individual items of mourning black for her father whilst becoming increasingly 'distracted'. This would not have amounted to a wholesale and expensive costume change but would have indicated her loss and—as with Hamlet, her inner state—visually. If it is anachronistic to imagine early modern audiences thinking about such off-stage action, it might be more productive to suggest that Ophelia represents not so much a 'real' young woman in a state of severe mental stress but a more fragmented icon of decorous and grief-distracted womanhood, with her rosemary for remembrance, missing violets (4.4.180, 185), maidenly/mad hair and a black funeral cloak.

Nevertheless, white garb had become conventional for Ophelia by the nineteenth century: it represented feminine innocence and perhaps glanced at the night shift of the asylum patient. In 1896, when Ellen Terry discussed her costume for the role with Henry Irving's advisor Walter Lacy, he told her in no uncertain terms that 'there must be only one black figure in this play, and that's Hamlet!' (Terry 1908, 157) There followed some notable exceptions: a year later, Mrs Patrick Campbell donned a black veil to wear across her white dress at the Lyceum, as did Nell de Silva at the same theatre in 1905. Gertrude Elliot wore a black dress as Ophelia in the Lyric performance of 1902 (Mander and Mitchenson 1952, 114) but in the silent film based on her Drury Lane performance of 1913 she wears floating white, as if a medium so dependent on the visual could not but revert to recent type. Interestingly, Poel's one-off 'Elizabethan' stage revival, with its all-male cast, dressed Master Barrington's Ophelia in a dark dress to play her lute in the scene (Mander and Mitchenson 1952, 115); he, as Roberta Barker points out, managed to garner praise as 'a truly girlish and delightful Ophelia' despite the absence of virginal white (Barker 2008, 62).

Worn by the first Hamlet, the pale white shirt that emerged from his 'unbrac'd' doublet indicated not innocence but the carelessness of social impropriety that comes with madness. The woman's shift is the undergarment which, suggests Carol Rutter, 'tropes nudity' in early modern clothing culture. As Rutter points out of Desdemona in *Othello*:

> the onstage undressing on the early modern stage is a technical nightmare, and risky stuff for *Othello*'s first actors that pushes right at the limits of performance, dangerously threatening to expose "the thing itself," for on Shakespeare's stage, the body beneath is, of course, male. Even when disclothed and taken down to the smock, however, this actorly male body must persuade spectators of its femininity. (Rutter 2010, 117–18)

It is significant that both Ophelia and Desdemona sing, using the unbroken voice of the boy player to indicate femininity, and that Claudius, Gertrude and Laertes all conspire to infantilise and feminise the mad Ophelia, calling her 'pretty', a term commonly used for children or youths of both genders in early modern English. Laertes insists that she turns the fearsome wildness of the distracted state itself into one of 'prettiness' (4.4.189). Ophelia's singing and the dialogue around her madness might, then, 'persuade[s] the spectators' of her femininity here, despite the dishevelled dress that threatens to break the illusion of gender as it becomes unravelled and unpinned.

Audiences are now accustomed to Ophelias who wear very little in their scenes of distraction. Jeremy Lopez's analysis of reviews of *Hamlet* in the journal *Shakespeare Bulletin* from 2003 points to the trope of sexualised semi-nakedness as a sign of her madness: the reviews mark Ophelias who pull up their skirts, appear in underwear or transparent clothing (Lopez 2012, 42–3). An example from Shakespeare suggests that the trope of madness and nakedness might not have been an alien one to early modern audiences: King Lear threatens to strip himself of the 'lendings' that are his clothing in the midst of the storm. However, the idea of the boy playing Ophelia stripped right down to his/her shift is an unlikely one, if only because moments later Gertrude is describing her clothes dragging her down into the water as she drowns. In my reading, drawing on Deanne Williams's study, Ophelia is the female mirror of her own description of Hamlet—an indecorous display of white fabric, partially covered by decorous black mourning clothes. If at the first Globe Hamlet's mourning black, which he refuses to remove, is followed by Ophelia's and then Laertes's as they mourn for the death of their own father, these are all potentially threatening figures to Claudius's regime: repetitive black marks on the colourful couture of a court whose King is pretending that all is well. Claudius has three disconcertingly dark figures wandering about his court at various moments in the play, visually as well as verbally demonstrating that the times are out of joint, followed by a whole stage filling up with dark fabric for Ophelia's burial: as the Ghost haunts Hamlet, so the messy, mistaken deaths of Polonius and Ophelia haunt Claudius and drape his court with black.

'A KING OF SHREDS AND PATCHES': CLAUDIUS

If funeral black in this play contrasts dangerously with the colours of royalty, sartorial signs of that royalty also work to highlight and trouble each other. *Hamlet* stages three contrasting figures of kingship in the Ghost, Claudius and the Player King, and I turn next to how their costumes might have worked as part of the political sign system of the play's first production. Costumes for the Globe's Elizabethan dress production of 2000 (dir. Giles Block, des. Jenny Tiramani) were researched and designed by Jenny Tiramani, who led the theatre's experiments in 'original practices' costumes at that theatre. Here, Claudius stood with his new queen and courtiers in 1.2, upstage centre, dressed in the vivid reds that would have pleased Planché (see below 51), exhorting the darkly dressed Hamlet to come away from his subversive addresses to the audience at the edge of the thrust stage, and become part of the new King's celebratory state tableau. Tiramani researched these costumes in the collections of the Danish castles at Helsingor (Elsinore) and Freidenborg (Bessell 2001, 7), and these may have been what inspired her to design a pair of slashed hose for Hamlet, who, in this production, did finally cast his nighted colour off and conform to the rich, bright colour scheme of this Danish court. Bright, slashed, Danish pludderhose are what Robert Lublin argues Claudius would have worn on the Globe stage in the first years of the seventeenth century: 'It is most likely', he remarks, 'that Hamlet calls Claudius a "king of shreds and patches"' in reference to his Danish hose: 'extra wide breeches with slashed fabric that were stuffed with different coloured materials and ribbons that would peek through the openings in the apparel' (Lublin 2011, 88). Lublin cites Nashe's Pierce Peniless in which typically Danish apparel is

> his apparel is so puft vp with bladders of Taffetie, and his back like biefe stuft with Parsley, so drawne out with Ribands and deuises, and blisterd with light sarcenet bastings, that you would thinke him nothing but a swarme of Butterflies, if you saw him a farre off. (Nashe 1562, 35–6, in Lublin 2011, 88)

Lublin suggests that, for an early modern audience, these brightly coloured and over-sized breeches would have been associated with a Danish, German, Dutch, Swiss and Flemish reputation for drunkenness, a vice of which Hamlet directly accuses Claudius. Lublin also reminds us that 'Danes Hose' may well have been a stock costume item in the early modern theatrical wardrobe: the inventories for the Admiral's men certainly contain a pair (Henslowe 2002, 318, in Lublin 2014, 634). He remarks on what a contrast the figure of the Ghost dressed from head to foot in the armour of past glories would have made to the celebratory figure of the new King in his big, colourful pludderhose, and in turn how different Hamlet, in his solemn black, soberly commenting on his uncle's carousing as 'a custom/ More honoured in the breach than the observance' (1.4.18) would have looked from his uncle (Lublin 2014, 635). This sharp aesthetic difference, as Jean McIntyre remarks, is the 'practical application' that Hamlet's words about his inky cloak and suites of solemn black receives in 'most productions' (MacIntyre 1992, 181).

The 'theatrical precedent' Lublin cites for these 'large baggy breeches' (Lublin 2014, 634), which he implies that only Claudius as chief Dane and chief drunkard would have worn, gives rise to an interesting question of genre. All Lublin's examples of pludderhosed-Danes are comic ones and if he is correct in his assumption about Claudius's 'shreds and patches', then Claudius could have cut something of a comic figure on his first appearance. The full entry in Henslowe, from which Lublin takes his 'Danes Hosse' reads, rendered in modern spelling, thus:

Item, 2 white shepherds' coats, and 2 Danes' suits, and 1 pair of Danes' hose'.

The entry is from an:

inventory of the Clowns' Suits and Hermits' Suits, with diverse other suits, as followeth, 1598, the 10 of March. (Henslowe 2002, 317)

The inclusion of 'Diverse other suits' in the list means that Danes' suits and hose are not necessarily comical or tattered but their inclusion in a list of clothing suitable for clowns and likely raggedy hermits' garments might be significant. Catherine Richardson and Martin Wiggins plausibly link the Danish gear catalogued in Henslowe with the lost play *Hardicanute* (Richardson and Wiggins 2013, 383), probably performed in 1597 and purchased by Henslowe in 1598; it tells the story of the end of Danish rule in England, in which the eponymous king of England and Denmark dies whilst carousing at a feast, suspected of being poisoned. With a narrative possibly derived from Holinshed, Hardicanute was likely a blood-thirsty history play (in an act of vengeance, Hardincanute beheads the dead body of his half-brother); the fact that he dies in drunken celebration supports, more explicitly, Lublin's argument that Danish gear might indeed have been associated with the kind of carousing Hamlet describes Claudius as indulging in (Lublin 2014, 634). An insistence on some kind of consistent tragic costume aesthetic, then, for the staging of Hamlet would be anachronistic, and I can make no argument for why Claudius should not have reminded contemporary audiences of other comical drunken Danes in the early modern canon—or at least, no argument that does not appeal to what is likely a modern desire for consistent tragic decorum. Just as Hamlet's suits of solemn black reflect his inner state, so Claudius's slashed hose construct him as a degenerate king of shreds and patches, within as well as without. Like early modern tragedies themselves, which so often switch startlingly from laugh lines to devastating expressions of psychic pain, costume for an early Hamlet would have allowed for laughter at the comic stereotype, then for Claudius to be revealed as the deadly inciter of the tragedy.

'ARMED AT POINT EXACTLY, CAP-A-PE':
DISAPPEARING ARMOUR

Claudius's costume would have contrasted not only with Hamlet's mourning clothes but with the ghostly figure of the former king, whom the audience have already seen on the first entrance of Claudius's court. When Horatio describes the Ghost appearing to the Watch at Elsinore 'armed at point exactly, *cap a pe*', Hamlet asks him for this detail of dress again:

Hamlet:	Armed, say you?
Marcellus and Barnado:	Armed, my lord.
Hamlet:	From top to toe?
Marcellus and Barnardo:	My lord, from head to foot.
Hamlet:	Then saw you not his face?
Horatio:	O, yes, my lord. He wore his beaver up. (1.2.233–8)

Hamlet wants reassurance that this figure actually looked like his father: how could they be sure it was him if they could not see his face? But the exchange also makes it very clear the military figure the Ghost must have cut on stage.

Head-to-foot armour would have read as archaic to Elizabethan audiences; it had been abandoned in warfare and was only used for displays of jousting and other ceremonies (Foakes 2003, 119; Lublin 2014, 632; Richardson 2011, 72). Full armour would have had a particular ideological value for this period and the Ghost's costume would have served as another visual disruption of the State of Denmark Claudius wants the court to perform in 1.2. Tilts were held each year of Elizabeth's reign to celebrate the Queen's accession to the throne and, as the German tourist Lupold von Wedel described in 1584, were very popular; they included men in full armour on horseback showing tremendous skill at jousting, and some comical gallant speeches given to the Queen by the fighters (von Wedel 1895, 257–9). This nostalgia for a medieval past links the Queen's accession with valiance, chivalry and a historical notion of trial by combat where physical prowess is concomitant with justice. When Hamlet's father's Ghost enters in full armour, he brings with him a past of moral rectitude and upright power to comment on a corrupt present (see also Foakes 2005). However, the Ghost's armour is something of a problem for production today, and this internal costume direction is sometimes ignored and/or the lines quoted above cut. My own experience of a Ghost in full armour cross-ing the stage at the Globe in 2000 was that without the dry ice and lighting technologies to which audiences are now accustomed, the clanking metal and cumbersome appearance of the costume gave rise to something of a comical disjuncture with my notion of what Ghosts should look like.

This very experience is something Aoife Monks discusses, drawing on Dickens's description of the hopelessly comical Ghost in the production of Hamlet attended by Pip in *Great Expectations*. Monks cites Jones and Stallybrass's discussion of modern laughter at ghosts in the theatre; they note that

the clumsy intrusions of body, clanking armour, and the constraints of the-atrical time and space, fundamentally disrupt the possibility that a ghost has appeared onstage (Monks 2010, 120, citing Jones and Stallybrass 2000, 246). These scholars suggest that now, armour has lost its signify-ing power as something ghostly and terrifying (Monks 2010, 123) and has become something that is simply too materially present to represent ghostli-ness for modern audiences. Monks goes further, to suggest that the disap-pearance of the Ghost's armour represents 'a loss of belief in the ability of clothing to resonate with social meanings and remembrance, in the ways that it did in the Renaissance'. (Monks 2010, 123)

In the nineteenth century, as the psychological interiority of character is privileged by the acting conventions of naturalism, the sense that a cos-tume can be adequate to represent a person, let alone the essence of per-sonhood without body that ghostliness now represents, becomes absurd:

Perhaps the biggest problem with the ghost of Hamlet's father for contem-porary audiences is that he renders clothing visibly instrumental in the expression of his past self...Armour no longer works as a ghostly object; it gets in the way of a broader cultural demand for the theatrical means to represent the self in immaterial and interior ways. (Monks 2010, 123; see also Jones and Stallybrass 2000, 245–52)

Exactly this problem seems to be satirised in George Cruikshank's illus-tration of the Ghost coming up from a trap in George Raymond's memoir of the actor Robert William Elliston, published in 1844 and cited by Jones and Stallybrass (2000, 247). In this image, an actor is shown sticking up from the trap looking foolishly glum in his armour, whilst beneath him not only is the labour of a stage hand revealed, winding up a platform so he can emerge, but Elliston and a friend are shown playing a practical joke on him, beating his 'thinly clad calves of his legs' with sticks so that he has to jump and dance below 'like a horse in Ducrow's arena' (Raymond 1857, 280) even as he tries to look like a serious ghost above. As R. A. Foakes notes, the ghost this actor plays is not specified as the one from *Hamlet* in Elliston's biography—it is the cartoonist Cruikshank who makes him a Ghost in armour, presumably because this will readily indicate a very familiar ghost to readers (Foakes 2005, 40). By choosing this armoured ghost for his illustration, Cruikshank draws attention to the materiality of the actor's body (he has calves that can be whipped and tickled despite his attempted appearance of both knightly invincibility and ghostly immateriality, and a clumsy mechanism below stage facilitating his ghostly assent) and draws attention to the theatrical costume worn by that body. This ghost is not entirely armoured 'cap a pie'. He is dressed in a theatrical illusion of armour: the backs of his legs are not covered, presumably because the ghost is going to face the audience on a dimly gas-lit stage. Foakes suggests that well before Dickens's publishers began to serialise *Great Expectations*, a certain scepticism might already have been felt by audiences about ghosts in armour: he cites the hero of Henry Fielding's *Tom Jones*, written in 1750, remarking that 'Ghosts don't appear in such Dresses as that' (Foakes 2005, 40). By the time of Garrick's Hamlet in 1774, the disruptive clanking of full armour had been replaced by a costume made entirely from fabric. Lichtenberg describes a ghost played by Mr Bransby as looking 'in truth, very fine, clad from head to foot in armour, for which a suit of steel-blue satin did duty' (Lichtenberg 1938, 11, in Foakes 2005, 43).

In that it was now only used for nostalgic, chivalric displays of fighting rather than for warfare, full armour in the Chamberlain's Men's *Hamlet* was a 'costume'. But it was still presumably actual armour forged by armourers and it had cultural meanings outside of the theatre; meanings that could, it seems, be brought back from the dead. Although the armour's clanking might not have disrupted the performance of ghostliness as Monks and I argue it does today, it certainly disrupts the early modern scene of contemporary dress and weaponry on stage in *Hamlet*. Both Hamlet and the Ghost appear as determinedly 'past': Hamlet is still in mourning and thus marks visually that he does not accept Claudius's new order; the Ghost wears an armour that more truly denotes the chivalric past than Claudius's criminally pragmatic present.

The early modern Ghost does not appear in armour throughout the play, at least if we accept that Q1 stage directions might indicate theatrical practice. In the Q1 text, the stage direction for the Ghost's interruption of the encounter between Hamlet and Gertrude is 'Enter the ghost in his night gowne'. In his chapter on the significance of this stage direction, Zachary Lesser explains that when Q1 was rediscovered by Henry Bunbury in 1823, Victorian commentators seemed to find this image absurdly undignified (Lesser 2015, 123–6). Goethe, on the other hand, as Lesser notes, decided that the direction is entirely appropriate: in his essay on 'The First Edition of Hamlet', he suggests that whilst we might at first find the idea of the old King Hamlet in his night attire 'incongruous', if we 'think it over' we will consider 'How much more private, homelike, terrible, is his entrance here in the form in which he used to appear—in his house apparel, his night robe, harmless and unarmed—a guise which in itself stigmatizes in the most piteous way the treachery which befell him' (Goethe 1921 in Lesser 2015, 132).

Lesser's chapter draws some fascinating conclusions from the Q1 night gown stage direction, demonstrating that recent historicist sneering at the supposedly Freudian anachronism of putting a bed in Gertrude's 'closet' is in itself something of a historical error (Lesser 2015, 117–23). Whilst the early modern stage might indeed not have included a bed—'closet' means private room, not bed chamber, as many critics irritated by the bed in theatrical practice have commented—the Ghost's night-gown does suggest a husband coming to or from bed. This recalls early modern dramas of adultery, and the adulterate bed of Claudius and Gertrude, suggesting not the Freudian Oedipal reading of *Hamlet* but Gertrude's incestuous desire of a wife for her brother-in-law (Lesser 2015 149, 153–6). Further, the Q1 text does not anywhere mention a 'closet' either for Gertrude or for Ophelia, as Lesser points out (150–2); the location of Hamlet's confrontation of his mother is not made specific until the Ghost enters in his nightgown, suggesting the bourgeois domestic environs of a marital bedroom, not the aristocratic antechamber implied by 'closet' (155). Lesser writes that '…by costuming the Ghost in his nightgown and by not specifying that the room is Gertrude's closet, Q1 shifts the scene subtly away from the markedly aristocratic ideology of the warrior-king in armor' (154); grand aristocratic castles have private closets, familial homes the humbler bedrooms implied by the Ghost's nightgown.

A 'closet' is a private, intimate space nonetheless, as is suggested by Ophelia's shock at Hamlet's mad entrance to hers. Does Q1's mentions of a nightgown imply that in Q2 and F the Ghost is still wearing armour when he enters the intimacy of the 'closet'? I contend that Q1's 'Enter the ghost in his night gowne' suggests a theatrical practice of ghostly night-gown wearing, not that there was some Q2 or F performance without one: a Ghost in full amour might have seemed as odd to an early modern audience in either a bed chamber or a closet. As he debunks recent critical outrage at 'Freudian' onstage beds, Lesser asks, 'Why might Shakespeare, or the Chamberlain's Men', have written a version of *Hamlet*, attested in some way by Q1, in which the bed is simultaneously excised as a stage prop from the sources (hence Corambis's "Arras") and called up in specta-tors' minds by another theatrical property, the night gown?' (Lesser 2015, 150). Lesser plausibly suggests that the company might not always have had access to such a large, expensive prop, or found it convenient for touring. But this does not answer the question of why a bed is differently excised in Q2 and F—by the repeated mention of women's closets and not their bed chambers. One might speculate, along the lines of Leah Marcus's somewhat sceptical characterisation of Q1 as a provincial touring version of *Hamlet* (Marcus 1996, 152), as to whether the version was adapted from a fuller text for audiences who might be more attuned to a bourgeois domestic drama than an aristocratic one. But I hope that Lesser's brilliant argument does not lead scholars to conclude that Q1 contains a domestic drama with a husband in a nightgown who hints at the bourgeois bed-room, and that Q2 and F contain something more aristocratic in which a grander 'closet' is entered by a king in full armour.

This all begs questions around the status of Q1 that lie outside the scope of this study and as a theatre scholar I am no doubt demonstrating the inclination Lesser points to in his Conclusion, towards finding theatri-cal provenance and merit in Q1 (Lesser 2015, 216–7). But by interrogat-ing the history of the bed in Gertrude's 'closet', Lesser draws our attention to the relationship between written editions and theatrical practice in new ways. It may be that Q1 offers us insights into theatrical practice across *Hamlet* performances in Shakespeare's time (so the Ghost always wore a night gown, just as Ophelia's hair was always 'down', but it is only the Q1 text that mentions these theatrical matters). Or it may be that Q1's night-gowned Ghost, suggestive of the domestic bedroom, offers us insight into one set of performances, Q2 and F's closets another, where Hamlet's cry of 'my father in his habit as he lived' might not mean armour but civilian day wear: still kingly, less domestic and with less of the effect of vulnerabil-ity than the nightgown, but still not armour in the intimacy of the imag-ined closet. For indeed, why draw attention to the Ghost's costume if it is the same as at the opening of the play? Does Hamlet's mention of his father's 'habit as he lived' serve to emphasise to the audience that this is no new devilish Ghost come to tempt or betray Hamlet as he fears the first apparition might be—it may not be wearing the same armour as the first, but it is still the Ghost of his father? My own bias is towards a Ghost in a night gown, as this offers such an exciting theatrical contrast to the Ghost in armour, with all of the comparative domesticity and vulnerability Lesser—and Goethe—suggest. Significantly for my argument later in this chapter, Lesser points to the fact that the Ghost thus dressed fit perfectly with Henry Irving's naturalistic, domestic *Hamlet*.

A FELLOW IN A CROWN: THE PLAYERS

The third of the three Kings that appear to *Hamlet* audiences is the Player King in 'The Murder of Gonzago', a piece written to sound deliberately archaic in comparison to the play within which it is staged. How might the costumes of fictional players on the Elizabethan stage differ from those of the actual players presenting *Hamlet* before the audience, if indeed they differed at all, and what work does this do in *Hamlet*'s schema of disrupted kingship? Lucy Munro gives a summary of the possible styles that Shakespeare was parodying when he wrote the 'Mousetrap' sequence and points out that 'The Murder of Gonzago' echoes the stiffer and more stylistically retrained mode adopted by Senecan translators and imitators of the 1560s (Munro 2013, 159). She argues that:

> on an aesthetic level, *Hamlet* not only draws on but incorporates earlier texts, creating an intrageneric system in which the debt to earlier generations of tragedies creates its own set of tensions. (Munro 2013, 162)

Munro thus points to how dramaturgical aesthetics match dramatic crisis in *Hamlet*. This is a play in which a hero accused by his mother and step-father of being stuck in the past receives a visitation from the dead, dressed, as we have seen, in the armour of the past, who asks him to enact a violent revenge tragedy of the kind that would have been familiar to members of his audiences from the recent theatrical past and which he has manifest problems trying to re-perform. Hamlet is a black-clad blot on Claudius's celebratory present but finds it impossible to enact his dead father's demands until he determines that 'the readiness is all' (5.2.152) and resolves to live in an instant and violent present constructed by his murderous uncle. 'The Murder of Gonzago' is in a style from the past which precipitates Hamlet into a present that could be said to imitate that past, by engaging in the cycle of unquestioning violence that is revenge.

What might the actors speaking this archaic text have been wearing? They are a 'contemporary' theatre company, the celebrated tragedians of the city—albeit somewhat down on their luck and forced to tour away from competition with the fashionable children's companies. In production today, they are often plausibly performed as somewhat peeved to receive instructions on avoiding outmoded jokes and old-fashioned, over-emphatic acting from Hamlet and there is no reason to suggest that they would have been costumed in an outmoded theatrical style in early performance. Because of their expertise in the classics and because of the pseudo-Senecan nature of the play it could be argued that Peacham-like Roman details might create the costume aesthetic for 'The Murder of Gonzago'. Roman details were chosen by Shakespeare's Globe in 2000 for Gonzago, after a tapestry of a Roman-costumed performance in Hardwick Hall (Bessell 2001, 7). But the play has been supposedly translated from 'choice Italian' rather than Latin, and Arthur McGee has suggested that it was based on an Italian play which tells the story of a sixteenth century rather than an ancient Roman murder (McGee 1987, 107).

I propose that *Hamlet's* fictional tragedians of the city wore Elizabethan dress just as the actual tragedians playing Hamlet did, perhaps with crowns and rich cloaks over plainer garb for their royal roles, to indicate the practicalities of touring. Their theatrical crowns would not have been unlike those the audience would have seen Claudius and Gertrude wear earlier in 1.2 and which they might still have been wearing to watch the play. If Claudius and Gertrude wore crowns in all public scenes, then the stage in this scene is full of pretend crowns: a theatrical pair of crowns that the audience is supposed to accept as real within the fiction, and another, doubly theatrical pair for the players, one of which is removed by the usurping Lucianus in the dumbshow:

> *Anon comes in a fellow, takes off his crown, kisses it, and pours poison in the King's ears, and exits.* (3.2.112 s.d)

Thus, royalty is rendered startlingly fragile by the meta-theatricality of costume and it is again significant that the other king in the play—the dead one—appears not in a crown but in armour. Here, the early modern bricolage of stock clothing, actors' clothing, inherited clothing and commissioned clothing that makes up the early modern stage wardrobe is rendered particularly visible and significant. *Hamlet*, as MacIntyre suggests, creates a series of stages for the performance of social decorum in the society of the play, and clothing is foregrounded as both constructing and reflecting that performance. However, clothing already signifies in early modern culture in ways that it no longer does so explicitly today: it is an essential, constructive component to the theatrical subjectivity of the Elizabethan body, creating as well as reflecting social role and status. In *Hamlet*, the decorum of social role and status is repeatedly breached, like Hamlet's unbraced doublet. In the 'play within the play', the crown is stolen from the king as he lies dying, and is taken by another to make him king. The crown is a clear symbol of power and authority in an archaic play where everyone's roles are clear, demonstrating starkly how, within the wider narrative of *Hamlet*, no-one's appearance stably refers to an essential self.

What I aim to demonstrate here is that although 'costumes' on Shakespeare's stage were 'real' clothes and thus obviously reflected the clothing codes of social life in 1600, clothing is distinctly visible in *Hamlet* at a theatre like the Globe. Not only does the painted classical imagery that surrounds actors in clothes in the public playhouse lend those live figures their iconicity; the play's attention to disruptive figures in mourning, disruptive ghosts in armour, disruptive mad figures in dishevelled dress, and stolen crowns, would have drawn audience attention to clothing as a maker of political meaning. Next, I am going to consider a moment in the stage history of the play which I read as central to what I am going to call costume's disappearance from *Hamlet*. During the nineteenth century, costume for Shakespeare becomes part of a richly detailed 'historically accurate' *mise en scene*, rather than standing forth as the most costly aspect of the theatre experience, and in *Hamlet*, particularly, the actorly portrayal of Hamlet's interiority is privileged over the conventions of what a Prince of Denmark looks like in his costume. Henry Irving's notably convention-breaking performance of Hamlet is not only key to this theatre historical moment; I suggest that his costume marks the beginning of a long-term demise of costume's political dramaturgy in the theatre.

HENRY IRVING AND THE DISAPPEARING COSTUME

The British theatre maintained the convention of wearing the contemporary dress of its own period for Shakespeare production into the eighteenth century. Mander and Mitchenson's rich 'pictorial record' of *Hamlet* production from 1709 shows not only the familiar image of Garrick at the Theatre Royal Dury Lane in his Georgian black velvet suit (Mander and Mitchenson 1952, 28) with its frock coat and knee-length breeches, but also paintings of David Ross at Covent Garden in 1757 and John Henderson at the Haymarket in 1777, similarly dressed (Mander and Mitchenson 1952, 50). Even more startlingly '18th century' is the image of Ann Barry as Gertrude at Drury Lane in 1778: as Hamlet gazes aghast at the Ghost, she stands with her hand on his arm, dressed in the tall, powdered wig and wide, flat, panniered skirt of the Georgian court. Mander and Mitchenson, and D.A. Russell in an analysis of their collected *Hamlet* images, suggests that it is John Philip Kemble who introduces 'period'—that is to say Elizabethan—costume to the performance of Hamlet (Russell 1956, 54–8) although Mander and Mitchenson include an illustration of Kemble in the role in 1783, just having stabbed Polonius through the arras, wearing the Carolinian-looking 'van Dyck' costume of breeches, collar and cuffs (1952, 96). James Boaden, who published his memoir of Kemble in 1825, writes that Kemble's first Hamlet was performed in dress contemporary to the 1780s:

> a modern court dress of rich black velvet, with a star on the breast, the garter and pendant ribband of an order—mourning sword and buckles with deep ruffles: the hair in powder; which, in the scenes of feigned distraction, flowed dishevelled and in front front and over the shoulders. (Boaden 1825, 104)

Further, in a note in *Theatre Survey*, Raymond J. Pentzell (1972) reprinted a little-known image of Kemble as Hamlet, probably printed in the late 1700s, dressed in just the kind of Georgian suit Boaden describes. By the time Boaden saw Kemble as Hamlet again in 1793, he related that he 'received a complete dressing in the taste of van Dyck, and has ever since been fixed in costume of black satin and bugles' (Boaden 1825, 319). In the painting by Lawrence of 1801,[3] he is wearing the theatricalised Elizabethan garb to be found in images of Edmund Kean's Hamlet at Drury Lane of 1814, albeit only as Elizabethan-looking as can be accepted as properly romantic by his audiences. Few of the nineteenth-century 'Elizabethan' Hamlet costumes include ruffs, and this, I think, is key to an emerging notion of Hamlet as a romantic figure whose interiority is more important than his social or historical identity: ruffs are

---

[3] See Tate, https://www.tate.org.uk/art/artworks/lawrence-john-philip-kemble-as-hamlet-n00142.

likely both too stiff and formal, and too historically alienating, not to be a distraction from a focus on Hamlet's emotional state. Most distinctively in the nineteenth century, images of Poel's first production of *Hamlet* Quarto 1 in 1881 appear to show all the male characters except Hamlet dressed in prominent white ruffs.

It is worth noting here that Ella Hawkins, in her study of the ruff as an icon associated with the Shakespeare 'brand', argues that ruffs were unlikely to have been worn extensively, if at all, on the early modern stage itself. She demonstrates that early modern playhouse inventories have no references to ruffs (Hawkins 2020, 167–8); she also points out that references to these collars in early modern plays tend to be satirical—wealthy figures are described as looking ludicrous in them (170–1)—and that in the single instance that a play by Shakespeare indicates that someone wears one on stage, it is Doll Tearsheet, the prostitute of *2 Henry IV*, and Pistol is threatening to 'murder' it—that is to say, to strangle Doll and in the process to rip a valued article of clothing which, as Hawkins demonstrates using incidents from other plays, prostitutes were satirised for wearing (Hawkins 2020, 169–70). Thus ruffs—hugely time-consuming to dismantle and remake every time they needed washing (Vincent 2002, 32–3)—are a sign of real wealth and status in early modern cultural life, and of mere pretentions to it on the playhouse stage, referred to jokingly rather than worn, or worn in tatters by a disreputable figure. It is Elizabethan and Jacobean portraiture—of the wealthiest members of society dressed in their most fashionable outfits—that give the modern impression of the ruff's ubiquity in this period. The nineteenth-century stage failed to find a late Elizabethan alternative, however. Collars vary from Caroline-style falling band collar, to the small open collar sported by John Philip Kemble in the Rochester Painting which has what looks like small, tousled ruff hanging just beneath it, as if it had come loose in Hamlet's pretended madness, like the play's garters. William Betty, 'the young Roscius', the celebrity child actor who played Hamlet aged only 12, is depicted in several images wearing more ruff-like neckwear as he holds Yorick's skull, and in others with a ruffled collar, possibly representing the later, falling ruff, again rather more Carolinian than Elizabethan (paintings of Charles I and his court show that during the 1620s the ruff begun to 'collapse' thus, until it was replaced entirely by the flat falling band collar). It is as if a child-like actor in ruff is permitted to cut an amusingly archaic rather than a romantic figure.

In the late nineteenth century, a new medievalism in the form of a tunic emerged for Hamlet. This was in line with the move to historical pictorialism, reputedly spear-headed by James Planché, the designer who claimed to have spoken to Charles Kemble of the notion of costuming Shakespeare according to the period in which his plays were set (Planché 1878, 52ff, although see Sillars 2012 36–7, and Baugh 2009, for earlier precedents for Victorian scenic historicism). Richard Schoch points out that *Hamlet* posed something of a problem for Victorian Shakespeare's new historical authenticity:

> Macready and Charles Kean both historicized Hamlet in the 1830s by reference to the period of its action. Unsure, however, just what that period was, they fudged the issues of historical accuracy by opting to wear generically medieval tunics. (Schoch 1998, 153)

Thus Kean 'never produced *Hamlet* with the antiquarian splendour' and detail that he put into other productions (Schoch 1998, 153).

Planché's introduction to his published research for *Hamlet* costumes suggests that 'it would be ridiculous to consider *Hamlet* as an historical play'; it is rather 'perfectly fabulous', as evidenced by the fact that Saxo Grammaticus's tale sets it in a distance past when 'The wild shores and rude rocks of the Baltic…were inhabited by mere barbarians, clothed in skins, and living in caves and woods' (Planché 1823, 3). However, he goes on to refute the argument that the designer might therefore just as well continue to costume the play in the early nineteenth century's vaguely Elizabethan style (Planché 1823, 4):

> My answer is—that in that case, it would be better to play it as formerly, in full-dress suits of the fashion of the day, as that could deceive no one, whereas the habit of the Elizabethan age is a deception of the grossest description, as the tragedy itself will suffice it to shew. (Planché 1823, 4)

Planché's evidence that Shakespeare's setting for *Hamlet* was 'obviously the close of the tenth or the commencement of the eleventh century' is based in its references to Christianity and the fact that the English in the play are still paying tribute to the Danes (Planché 1823, 4). His argument that the anachronisms of '…the players, the assut d'armes, and the repeated allusions to cannon' need not 'destroy the illusion of the scene as fixed in this period' (5) demonstrate that it is precisely an 'illusion' of 'period' that is being sought after here. It is not only the theatrical convention of the early nineteenth-century theatre that Planché finds disruptive to this sacred illusion: he is also irritated by what he considers the historically inaccurate demands of the play itself. His illustrations include a Danish King in red tunic and purple cloak held with a clasp at the shoulder, a 'King of Denmark Armed' from head to foot in chain mail and a crown, a Queen dressed in similar colours to the King and wearing golden bracelets (on the authority of Beowulf), then a Hamlet in collarless black tunic and short black cloak. A black costume for Hamlet himself is an unfortunate necessity of the play, explains Planché: medieval Danes did not go into sartorial mourning, black was a more generally worn colour in Denmark, and Hamlet should really be wearing royal Danish red.

What annoys the designer most, though, is the comedic 'point' apparently insisted on by his own theatrical contemporaries, whereby the First Gravedigger observes 'the absurd and uncalled for practice of pulling off half a dozen waistcoats' (32). For Planché, this piece of costume-led business, which Garrick apparently abolished but then was 'compelled to restore' by popular demand, was 'a piece of buffoonery…utterly unworthy of a good play' (32) and 'contrary to good sense, good taste and correct costume' (33). He fervently hopes that his waistcoat-free medieval costumes for *Hamlet* will 'afford an opportunity for the abolition of this practice' (33) and he illustrates the Gravedigger in a modest brown tunic, with a background figure wearing a striped mantle with a pointed hood. To Planché's dismay, then, early nineteenth-century stage costume participated in the convention of actorly points, whereby particular gestural sequences or moments of theatrical business or seemed to have been just as fixed a part of audience expectation as particular speeches in a well-known play like *Hamlet* (Freeman 2002, 31–2; Roach 1993, 111). The Carolinian falling band collar and wide cuffs seem to have formed one such costuming point, albeit not as active in stage business as the Clown's waistcoats: a number of medieval-style tunics sport them.[4]

---

[4] Charles Kean's medieval-style tunic sports that 'van Dyck' collar in images published as late as 1838 (Mander and Mitchenson 104). Macready's 'medieval' garb had Elizabethan-inflected puffed sleeves and a particularly lavish version of the falling collar and Caroline cuffs. By the time of his Princess's Theatre Hamlet in 1850, Charles Kean's tunic is collarless and much more medieval-looking (51), as is Samuel Phelps's at Sadlers Wells in 1847 (96); but a version of that falling lace collar can still be seen on William Creswick's Surrey Theatre Hamlet costume in 1849 (33) and Barry Sullivan's at the Haymarket in 1852 (51). Macready's 1849 tunic at the Haymarket is collarless, but retains the puffed sleeves and white cuffs that, too, recall the Elizabethan/van Dyck look (29). Charlotte Crampton wore both

Cloaks and gowns for the nineteenth-century Hamlet are largely short and unobtrusive. By 1860, when Charles Dickens first published his celebrated and hilarious account of Mr Wopsle's terrible production of the play in *Great Expectations*, an overly conspicuous funereal cloak for Hamlet gets heckled:

> [Hamlet's] greatest trials were in the churchyard... Mr Wopsle in a comprehensive black cloak, being descried entering at the turnpike, the gravedigger was admonished in a friendly way, 'Look out! Here's the undertaker a-coming to see how you're getting on with your work!' (Dickens 1867, 296)

The very notion of foregrounded costume is the object of satire for Dickens: later, when Pip meets Mr Wopsle's dresser after the performance, the backstage worker gravely reports that

> When he come to the grave...he showed his cloak beautiful. But, judging from the wing, it looked to me that when he see the ghost in the queen's apartment, he might have made more of his stockings. (Dickens 1867, 297)

By the time of Irving's Hamlet at the Lyceum in 1874, the mark of a good medieval costume for Hamlet seemed to be its simplicity and the actor abandoned all sixteenth- to seventeenth-century pieces, according to the well-known painting by Edwin Longsden Long (see Winter 1911, 362), although Elizabethan trunk hose appear in a caricature of the actor by illustrator Harry Furniss (Furniss, National Portrait Gallery). Thus the simple medieval tunic without white collar can be accepted as 'period' in some nominally Old Danish way, then ceases to be a distraction from what becomes increasingly significant to the success of Hamlets from Irving onwards: the performance of Hamlet's tortured mind. The Victorian theatre critic Clement Scott (1900) describing Irving in the role, asks:

> falling band collar and lace cuffs with her decorated black tunic for her populist impersonation of Edwin Forrest's Hamlet (Howard 79), her neck hung with the Order of the Elephant, even though in the extant images of the actor in the role he wears neither (Howard 77); the eclectic mix of the medieval and the Carolinian 'Van Dyke' were, it seemed, so generic that a popular Hamlet impersonation by a woman could not be plausible without them. Even in her supposedly 'archeologically correct' production of 1864 with 'new and appropriate costumes (Howard 81, image 79), Alice Marriott, who Tony Howard argues 'made the female Hamlet respectable in England' (Howard 80) abandoned the collar but made up for it with the lacy prominence of her cuffs (Howard 79).

How is he dressed? How does he look?

and concludes that ultimately, his first question no longer matters as it has done in the past: what audiences were drawn to in Irving's performance were Hamlet's face, his eyes, and ultimately his mind:

> No imitation of the portrait of Sir Thomas Lawrence, no funereal velvet, no elaborate trappings, no Order of the Danish Elephant, no flaxen wig after the model of M. Fetcher, no bugles, no stilted conventionality. We see before us a man and a prince, in thick-robed silk and a jacket, or paletot, edged with fur; a tall imposing figure, so well dressed that nothing distracts the eye from the wonderful face; a costume rich and simple, and relieved alone by a heavy chain of gold; but, above and beyond all, a troubled, wearied face displaying the first effects of moral poison.
> The black, disordered hair is carelessly tossed about the forehead but the fixed and rapt attention of the whole house is directed to the eyes of Hamlet: the eyes that denote the trouble—which tell of the distracted mind. (Scott 1900, 62)

Clement Scott makes his case for Irving as the most pleasingly untheatrical of Hamlets by implying that previous Hamlet costumes have been mere actorly vanity, pompous costume 'points', almost as self-indulgent as the grave-digger waistcoat gag so despised by Planché, whereas this Hamlet 'is thinking aloud as Hazlitt wished. He is as much of the gentleman and scholar as possible and as little of the actor' (Scott 1900, 57). Hamlet's soliloquies, too, cease to be 'points' in and of themselves and become precisely this performance of the character thinking aloud: Scott is pleased to report that Irving's soliloquies are 'not spoken down at the footlights to the audience' (Scott 1900, 63). The illusion of the Medieval produces not the Hamlet of the 'much older cosmos' whom Catherine Belsey contends is residual within Hamlet's dramatic subjectivity: 'no more than the consenting instrument of God, received into heaven at his death by flights of angel...' (Scott 1900, 42). This is the unified Hamlet of theatrical naturalism, through whose eyes we can view the troubled mind, undistracted by the performing costumes that Dickens found so amusing.

The Medieval look for *Hamlet* dominated British production of the play into the early twentieth century, with flowing drapery and an Arts and Crafts medievalism of decor in H. B. Irving's production at the Adelphi in 1905 (Mander and Mitchenson 1952, 13) and an Ophelia, Lily Brayton, straight from a Pre-Raphaelite painting (20); Frank Benson (34) in 1900,

Matheson Lang in 1909 (34), both at the Lyceum, and Forbes Roberson at Drury Lane in 1913 (73, 142), having played the role in similar garb in 1897 (98), all seem to have modelled their tunics on Irving's. Tunics varied in length, then during the 1920s and onwards, morphed into something more broadly 'Renaissance': short doublets or tunics covering short hose that often exposed a great deal of Hamlet's leg in stockings, a look immortalised by Lawrence Olivier in his 1948 film. By the mid-twentieth century, Planché's insistence on the turn of the eleventh century seemed largely forgotten. Hamlets such as Robert Helpmann's at the New Theatre in 1944 sported the top-heavy look of extravagantly cut and ruched sleeves and long, black legs that recalled the mid to late fifteenth century rather than anything either Old Danish or Elizabethan, and two years later in Paris, Jean-Louis Barrault played Hamlet in a short, waisted jerkin and stockings of even more literally early Renaissance style. London's New Theatre in 1934 dressed Jon Gielgud's first Hamlet in stylishly unobtrusive black velvet and less unobtrusive huge gold chain; the production featured an Ophelia straight out of the early sixteenth-century paintings of Lucas Cranach. Basil Langton and his fellow actors at the Shakespeare Memorial Theatre at Stratford in 1940, on the other hand, looked more consciously Elizabethan. These styles offered audiences a vague sense of both Renaissance painting and Medieval castle, and dominated the British stage (Barry Jackson's Birmingham Rep and other occasional experiments with modern dress notwithstanding) during the first half of the twentieth century.

Another twentieth-century Hamlet costume trope has been to costume the Prince as plainly as possible within the boundaries of a plausibly Renaissance look, and against a backdrop of colourful court extravagance, emphasizing not so much his defiant mourning as something urgent and modern about his mindset: the paired-down black suit and white shirt of the Hamlet costume has frequently looked less distinctly historical than the designs for the rest of the cast—Poel's ruff-less Hamlet in a stiff-ruffed court can be read in this way (above 49). This historical disjuncture has occasionally been pushed further, in productions where Hamlet appears wholly or partly in modern dress, in an otherwise broadly Renaissance *mise en scene*. David Warner, in Peter Hall's RSC production in 1965 (costumes Ann Curtis, des. John Berry), wore a historically indeterminate long jerkin, black trousers and a distinctly modern, student-style red scarf, in contrast to a Claudius dressed like Henry VIII, and this eclecticism is taken up again decades later: Timothy Walker in Cheek by Jowl's

Elizabethan-dressed production sported something of a mohican to mark his 'antic disposition' (dir. Declan Donnelan, design Nick Omerod); in 1994, the Peter Hall Company dressed Stephen Dillane in a loose modern blue shirt and black waistcoat, against a backdrop of rich, restricting velvet costumes of broadly Edwardian style (des. Lucy Hall); in a distinct contrast to his mother in her wide, red, Elizabethan gown and rebato (Gertrude: Eleanor Bron), Alan Cumming as Hamlet wore a modern black sweater, rolled up black trousers and modern black shoes in Bunny Christie's design for the English Touring Theatre (dir. Stephen Unwin, 1993).

Hamlet costumes such as these draw attention to the historicity of the rest of the court whilst Hamlet becomes visually both distinctive and indistinct in his modernity: he is 'timeless', a rebellious spirit and a tortured mind in black clothes—Irving's Hamlet as described by Scott taken to a logical extreme—where Claudius and Gertrude are stiffly stuck in the robes of the past. In the first performances of *Hamlet*, Hamlet's rebellious funeral wear is to some degree less marked by the history of dress than early modern clothing more generally: a black funeral cloak swamps the detail of fashionable Elizabethan clothing. But the cloak points very deliberately to the past of the play, too, a past of honourable rule and archaic combat, because it represents Hamlet's refusal to stop mourning his father. It reads politically as well as emotionally.

Twenty-First-Century Disappearing Costumes

In 2001, the RSC staged a hyper-contemporary *Hamlet* (dir. Stephen Pimlott, des. Alison Chitty) in which Samuel West's prince wore a hoodie and hung about a royal court that looked rather as if it were hosting the G8 summit, with figures in slick suits and conference badges and Hamlet as an anti-capitalist protester. This was in obvious contract to the Globe's Elizabethan dress production (2000), and the National Theatre's version (2000) in which a predominance of loose gowns suggested a slightly earlier period than that of the play. But as this century has progressed, the predominant London/Stratford *Hamlet* design has been one that allows Hamlet's costume to disappear almost entirely into a sleek, casual modernity. I propose that the relatively simple medieval tunic that so impressed Clement Scott when worn by Irving's Hamlet can be seen as one point on a theatre historical trajectory which ends in Jude Law or Andrew Scott wearing stylish but barely memorable black cardigans, shirts and trousers. Andrew Scott's Prince, on whose set at the Almeida Dickie

Beau first performed *Re-member Me* was dressed, for the first part of the play, in the plainest possible modern black collarless shirt and trousers ensemble. If fans want to see Benedict Cumberbatch in a pair of hose, they must look to pastiche: images of his performance in Tom Stoppard's *Rosencrantz and Guildenstern are Dead* show him as Rosencrantz in short, paned trunk hose and dark brown doublet, 'unbraced', Hamlet-like, to show the traditional white shirt. But as Hamlet himself, at the Barbican Theatre, (dir. Lydnsey Turner, costumes Katrina Lindsay, des. Es Devlin) Cumberbatch wore a dark corduroy jacket as his 'customary suit [...] of solemn black', and a lightweight grey waterproof of the kind to be found in high street outdoor shops for his return to England, like Rory Kinnear (*Hamlet* NT 2010, dir. Nicholas Hytner, des. Vicki Mortimer) and Sam West (RSC 2001). For his performance of an 'antic disposition', Cumberbatch's Hamlet changed to a bright red, nineteenth-century soldier's costume, found whilst rummaging in a children's dressing up box with Ophelia: a kind of hiding in plain sight in a ceremonial military wear that might have allowed the 'mad' Hamlet to carry a sword whilst planning the assassination of his uncle. This only served to highlight just how plain and unassuming the generic London Hamlet costume, including Cumberbatch's own in other scenes, has become. Had Dickie Beau wanted to dress one of his dummies in the most current possible Hamlet costume, he would have had to choose clothes from a high end chain store that looked as little 'like a costume' (see above 2) as possible.

The barely noticeable black Hamlet costume of the modern dress production helps to foreground *Hamlet* as a play about the central character's psyche rather than about his social world. This disappearance of sartorial surface into psychological depth might be said to have begun with Hamlet himself and his statement about 'that within'. Unlike a number of other Shakespeare plays, including those we will examine in the next two chapters, *Hamlet* has not generally been seen as a play that lends itself to the kind of social commentary produced by costuming it in periods between Shakespeare's and our own. Whilst it has recently been considered possible to comment on the social mores or class and race politics of, for example, the nineteenth century using *Much Ado About Nothing* or *The Tempest*, *Hamlet*, the theatre industry seems to suggest, should generally be set either in a nominal Medieval-to-Renaissance Denmark, or in some version of now. A few noticeable exceptions have used nineteenth-century dress to suggest a Chekhovian family drama or the corruption seething beneath the strict morals and repressed sexuality of an Edwardian court—for example the RSC's 1992 production in which Kenneth Branagh played the role for the fourth time (des. Bob Crowley, dir Adrian Noble). I suggest that both the modern and Medieval-to-Renaissance settings figure Hamlet as existing outside of any explicit historical period. He is eternally fixed in doublet/tunic and hose, a figure striving for authenticity against an oppressive backdrop of grey castle walls in a costume so familiar as to simply mean Hamlet/*Hamlet*, rather than anything specific about either medieval or early modern Europe. Or, as the tortured introvert full of twentieth-century existential angst, he speaks to a contemporary, psychotherapeutic moment. Scott's discussion of Irving tells us that whilst Hamlet must be 'well dressed' according to his status, dressing well invites a focus on face, eyes, mind, not clothes. His (relatively) simple medieval tunic, the simplified Elizabethan costume, and the modern simplicity of black shirt and trousers do the similar work here. Hamlet's clothes focus less on political culture, more on 'that within'.

In the next section of this chapter, I am going to consider a twentieth- and a twenty-first-century *Hamlet*, both of which are distinctive in the absorption of the Ghost into the mind/body of Hamlet. One of these productions (Royal Court 1980) dresses Hamlet in twentieth-century Elizabethan version of the Disappearing Costume: a modern, stripped-down iteration of black doublet and hose. The other costume design (Young Vic 2011) performs a distinctive history of insanity, in a production wherein the whole of the plot of the play appears to be taking place in Hamlet's mind. The 'disappearance' of the Ghost seems to be the logical conclusion to the modern 'psychologising' of Hamlet: the Ghost himself, once a visual and aural material presence in armour or night gown, has become part of the mind of Hamlet. However, I am going to suggest that whilst the Young Vic *Hamlet* might be the ultimate staging of *Hamlet* as the new psychoanalytic Everyman, Jonathan Pryce's costume in 1980 reflected not simply Hamlet's inner turmoil, but the conflicting, historically marked versions of subjectivity contained within the figure.

HAMLET AND THE DISAPPEARING GHOST

In order to solve the modern problem of stage ghostliness considered above (40–42), Hamlet ghosts of the nineteenth and twentieth centuries have dwindled into a variety of immaterial forms, from the celebrated shadow voiced by Gielgud for the Broadway production starring Richard

Burton in 1964, to disembodied voices from behind the audience (RSC 2016), to appearances on CCTV (Almeida 2017). Another solution to the ghostly plausibility problem has been to cut 1.1's sighting of the Ghost by the Watch and Horatio, and to stage its later appearances as if Hamlet were either possessed by the Ghost, or imagining it. For the Royal Court in 1980, Jonathan Pryce researched 'voodoo' possession and spoke the Ghost's lines as if violently physically and mentally tortured by its presence. Thirty years later, at the Young Vic, a London theatre well known, like the Royal Court, for its innovative contemporary theatre work rather than its Shakespeare production, Michael Sheen's Hamlet appeared to have invented a paranoid conspiracy around the death of Old Hamlet, enacting possession by the Ghost in front of his friends in his father's leather greatcoat. In this production, Hamlet's mind had become so much the key to the play that not only was the Ghost an invention of his disturbed imagination, the whole plot was too. I want to consider these disappearing Ghosts as examples of how the materiality of costume has been made to conspire in its own disappearance in recent production.

The 1980 Royal Court production of *Hamlet* directed by Richard Eyre, designed by William Dudley and with costumes by Sue Plummer had a broadly late Medieval/Renaissance design. Polonius's green doublet and hose were recognisably Elizabethan. Gertrude's flat bodice and Spanish farthingale skirt recalled early Tudor costume, whilst Claudius sported a gown with a striking, giant cross-hatching on its huge, late medieval sleeves. Jonathan Pryce's Hamlet wore a paired down version of the more obviously historically inflected costumes worn by other characters. The lower part of his white shirt, its sleeves and subtly ruffled collar peeking out from a black jerkin, was short enough to recall an Elizabethan doublet but in distinctively modern reconstruction. The black sleeves were tied to the jerkin, so that again, the white shirt peeked out at the shoulders. This both recalled the tying and pinning together of Elizabethan dress and, simultaneously, might have given the impression that Hamlet is quite literally falling apart, were it not for the fact that Ophelia (Harriet Walter), too, wears a kind of deconstructed generalisation of Tudor dress from her opening scene: bands that hold together her sleeves at the shoulder and elbow let her shift protrude and produced both an impression of Elizabethan puffed sleeves and slashing, and a deliberate revelation of the costume's architecture.

Whilst Ophelia's costume was historically detailed in such a way as to suggest the deconstructed sleeves were part of the dress's style—her undershirt was gathered at the neck, for example, in the style of an Elizabethan partlet—Pryce's read as more consciously 'timeless'. It comprised the bare minimum of white shirt and black doublet that such a Hamlet must wear to register as Hamlet and yet it was modern in its cut too, particularly compared to the more historically inflected costumes of the other characters. Thus Hamlet read once again as a transhistorical figure trapped within a historical narrative. This 'doublet and hose' were so paired back as to resemble rehearsal gear, or a martial arts outfit. Hamlet became a new Everyman in this costume, the actor or martial artist who can imitate anyone, or give self up to craft. When Pryce's Hamlet was possessed by the Ghost and tore in agony at his loose black jerkin, he became the vessel for a struggle between his own will and that of the vengeful Ghost, and his transhistorical, 'generic' Hamlet became a container for an inner struggle between good and evil. Hamlet's subjectivity is broken down by the force of possession by his father's vengeful spirit and a battle between an 'older cosmos' of vengeful spirits, as Catherine Belsey (1985, 42) has put it, and Hamlet the contemplative modern individual, took place within the body that wore the clothes that marked the actor as Hamlet. His tragedy became that of a modern mind being literally taken over by an older set of understandings of the self. Significantly, though, the past here was also recalled by the court's more obviously historically inflected costumes. Unlike in early production of the play, where the Ghost entered in full, archaic armour, Hamlet's father was not made visually and morally distinct by his costume; he did not appear at all. Pryce's Hamlet thus becomes the sensitive, philosophical modern young thinker pitted against the world of the play; it was not the Ghost that represented the past, but everyone on stage except Pryce. At the same time, Pryce's tearing at his costume as he ventriloquised the Ghost, a sequence which can still be viewed as a Youtube clip at the time of writing,[5] drew attention to costume as it simultaneously suggested its erasure. It reads as an 'Off, off you lendings' moment, to cite *King Lear* (3.4.89–90): it suggests there is something more significant and more real in the otherworldliness of the Ghost than the mere social constructions of the self produced by clothing.

In the Young Vic's *Hamlet* of 2011 (dir. Ian Rickson, costumes Nicky Gillibrand, des. Jeremy Herbert), Michael Sheen's Prince operated within a paranoid fantasy world produced either by mental illness, the brutality

---

[5] From an episode of the television culture show, the South Bank Show: https://www.youtube.com/watch?v=MrMoWcHyw9c.

and corruption of enforced psychiatric incarceration, or the exacerbation of the latter by the former. For this *Hamlet* was set in a secure psychiatric unit and was partly inspired by the anti-psychiatry of R. D. Laing: Sheen's Hamlet appeared to be responding to the violence of his incarceration in the hospital with understandable paranoia and violence. In an interview for *Time Out*, Sheen remarks: 'Laing said that if you take mad people on their own terms then maybe they're just talking in a sort of heightened language about their lived experience' (Sheen in McGinn 2011). However, an intensely engaging naturalistic acting style, particularly a nervily detailed and highly convincing performance by Sheen, was potentially undermined by a scenographic and costume frame which teetered between exploring and reiterating stereotypes and clichés of mental illness and incarceration.

A pre-set sequence saw Hamlet steal his father's heavy leather greatcoat from where it lay on top of the old King's coffin; Sheen put it on to prepare for 'possession' by the Ghost. Here, not only did the Ghost seem to be Hamlet's invention—Hamlet seemed deliberately to be putting on the Ghost as a costume—but the Prince, it seemed, might have imagined his father's murder by Claudius, too. Indeed, the whole plot of *Hamlet* appeared to be taking place in Hamlet's disordered mind: Claudius's speech in which he admits to the murder of Hamlet's father and finds he cannot pray was virtually cut, by placing Claudius in a glass-walled office where Hamlet and the audience could not fully hear him. Finally, when Fortinbras arrived to claim Denmark at the end of the play, Sheen entered in a fencing mask similar to the ones in which he and Laertes had been fighting, and removed it to reveal his face and show that the figure that the audience had thought was Fortinbras was in fact Hamlet—returned, presumably, to take over the asylum (whether for real or in Hamlet's disturbed imagination was not clear).

In terms of period setting, the *Daily Telegraph* reviewer read the secure psychiatric wing setting as from the 1960s or 1970s (Spencer 2011) and, albeit somewhat disparagingly, made the link between the production and Laing's theory of madness as a logical reaction to society's insanity; Julie Carpenter for the *Daily Express* also asserted that this was 'a psychiatric unit circa 1970'. One blogger links set to costume via the set's technologies: 'It's all located somewhere in the early 70s, with clunky dictaphones, big old open-reel tape recorders, bad suits with flared trousers' (Viney 2011). However, whilst a number of reviewers mentioned the period of Claudius's seedy-looking suit, what is striking about published responses to this performance was the lack of comment on the period eclecticism of the costumes. This speaks, perhaps, to a wider desire amongst newspaper critics to fix production to a particular historical period. Whilst the afore-mentioned suit was certainly 1970s in style, the production and publicity referenced not only that decade, but Victorian imagery of the asylum from early photography. The wide-eyed publicity photograph of Michael Sheen, still on the Young Vic's website at the time of writing (Young Vic), with its painterly sepia tones and red left hand glare, looks like a romantically rendered version of early photographic images of asylum inmates from the mid nineteenth to early twentieth century. Hamlet's rough-hewn, smock-shaped shirt and his striped jacket with its visible stitching recall the hardy garments worn by Victorian and Edwardian psychiatric patients; his thick, off-white vest and braces recall the 1950s. Horatio, played by a woman, Hayley Carmichael, wore Edwardian coat tails. Ophelia's fitted, ticking shirt created an Edwardian shape, albeit accompanied by a more modern, wide-pleated skirt. Sally Dexter's Gertrude wore a bustle-like design, his-toricised further, like Ophelia's shirt, by the striped ticking from which it was fashioned.

These ghost-less Hamlets are two of the few productions cited in this book for which there were separate costume and set designers. Nicky Gillibrand designed the costumes for the Young Vic, Jeremy Herbert the set. Gillibrand's approach to design is made clear in her notes for the RSC's web pages on their 2006 production of *The Tempest* (dir. Rupert Goold), a production set, to some degree of critical controversy, in the Arctic:

> So I looked at Eskimos, yes, but I was more interested in Eskimos from very early photographs (1890s), seeing exactly how they would cut up furs to make clothes. In that way, you can update it so it's not just a period costume which would be dull and limiting for an actor on stage.
>
> For other things, like the mariners' clothes, I researched old army things, again because the way they're cut is interesting. Various things lead me on. I love 'working-clothes', you know, things that are made for working in. It's very interesting when you find for example, a Second World War overall. I can relate that back to the Eskimo clothes. (Gillibrand in RSC 'Rupert Goold 2006 Production')

The cut and the workaday practicality of the asylum clothes for *Hamlet* were much in evidence too, as was Gillibrand's lack of interest in pro-ducing 'just a period costume'. Scenography and costumes presented a visual history of the treatment of mental ill health and recalled historically specific cultural fears of the asylum: the costumes staged stereotypes of both a brutalising mid- to late nineteenth-century psychiatric regime and a cash-strapped 1970s one.[6] Gertrude was kept sedated by Claudius with pharmaceuticals to which she was clearly addicted. Claudius, as the asylum manager, or perhaps the consultant psychiatrist, represented all that is nightmarishly worst about the asylum from a Laingian perspective: his relationship with the patients was one of abusive power, however benevolent he seemed in 1.2., a scene that was wittily staged as a therapy session or case conference which ended in Laertes's release and Hamlet's continued confinement. The robust materials of the costumes recalled the canvas of the strait jacket, though one never appeared on stage; the striped ticking and late Victorian shapes of the women's costumes recalled Hugh Welch Diamond's Ophelia-like women asylum inmates (see Addonizio 1999) without having to adorn Ophelia with flowers and herbs: Vinette Robinson was confined, catatonic, to a wheelchair for Ophelia's mad scene, and she failed to notice her fingers bleeding as she strummed her songs.

Whilst this *Hamlet* staged Claudius as the villainous, controlling medic, by the end of each performance the play had been turned into Hamlet's, not Claudius's, fantasy of control, and Hamlet returned from the dead as the conquering Fortinbras. Thus, a potentially interesting visual critique of a set of historical mental health stereotypes was in danger of reiterating a current one. Whilst visually, Sheen's Hamlet rebelled against the anonymity imposed by his Victorian/Edwardian asylum gear by stealing a costume with which to impersonate the Ghost and thus instigate the whole plot of the play, he was in a sense cast back into generalised stereotypes of madness by this production's dramaturgy of interiority: the power politics of the play seemed, finally, only to have existed in his mind. In this production, Hamlet got to punish a doubly old and repressive regime—a regime of mental health care simultaneously from the nineteenth and twentieth centuries—by taking over the world of the play entirely. But the moment in which he revealed himself to be the conquering Fortinbras beneath his black fencing mask turned Sheen's detailed, interiorised performance into that of the stereotypical 'dangerous madman': he imagined the whole murder plot and had now come back to take over the asylum— or imagined he had done so in his disordered mind. The Royal Court and Young Vic Hamlet productions appeared to stage a respective spiritual and

---

[6] See Turner, Hayward et al. (2015, 616–7, for an analysis of the challenges of researching the history of mental health resourcing in the UK.

psycho-political battle for Hamlet's subjectivity, but I suggest that the Young Vic closed this reading down in its sinister denouement, and the conscious theatricality of the costumes veered into the historical macabre.

Before leaving this production, I want to consider the leather coat Sheen donned to 'become' the Ghost. As we have seen, he stole it from the top of what was presumably his father's coffin at the opening of the play, so that his intention to 'become' the Ghost seemed completely conscious (it was not clear what his father's coffin and coat were doing in the asylum; nor whether the idea that they belonged to his father at all had also been dreamed up by a deluded Hamlet). It was a large garment and it swamped Sheen, its material presence foregrounded on stage by the fact that the audience understood that the Ghost was not actually present in this new Hamlet narrative: Hamlet's lie that in the coat he became the Ghost powerfully drew our attention to the coat and staged costume as a powerful liar itself.

Staging Hamlet as a figure whose mind is so open, plastic and fragile that it can be taken over by the Ghost, in the case of Jonathan Pryce, or so disturbed that it can imagine the whole plot of *Hamlet* in response to a brutal psychiatric regime, in the case of Michael Sheen, led to the disappearance of the Ghost as a material reality in both these productions, and to a momentary focus on costume as a material denial of ghostliness. Pryce's costume was, like others I have mentioned here, somewhat effaced by its generic style but was foregrounded again as he clawed at it whilst possessed by the Ghost. Pryce's Hamlet read as a mind trapped in a costume and overtaken by a spirit. Costume figured histories of confinement very literally in the Young Vic production and the coarse, striped clothes were more clearly foregrounded throughout, partly and simply because costume was so distinct from the familiar Elizabethan and modern tropes of costuming the play explored in this chapter. But the Young Vic design finally served to privilege the mind of the protagonist even further than the disappearing Hamlet costumes discussed above, by suggesting that that disturbed mind had invented the whole action of the play and used a huge leather coat to trick the rest of the characters into the belief that clothing can construct reality.

MARKING THE COSTUME, MARKING THE BODY: PAAPA ESSIEDU AT THE RSC

The last 'modern dress' *Hamlet* I will discuss here is the RSC's first starring a black performer as Hamlet: Paapa Essiedu (dir. Simon Godwin, des. Paul Wills). The production was not cast 'colour blind' but set in an imagined West African country. As I have suggested elsewhere with reference to an Othello set in a Yorkshire pub (Escolme 2017, 37), settings for Shakespeare that suggest a modern environment outside of white Western ruling class society can, on the one hand, produce an exciting sense of contemporaneity and recognition for modern audiences and lead to more diverse casting. On the other hand, setting the actions of a 400-year-old play in class- or ethnically-specific communities outside of the privileged norm for tragedy can also produce a worrying primitivism, suggesting, to use the relevant examples here, that people in Yorkshire pubs or African states today behave just like people did in Europe 400 years ago and all have similarly violent, power-driven cultural values. As Monika Smialkowska marks in her critique of the RSC's 2012 *Julius Caesar*, setting a play by Shakespeare 'in an unspecified, nameless African country' begs some uncomfortable questions: 'Are we to assume that Africans in general are like the figures represented here? Are we...dealing in stereotypes and objectifying Africa as an exotic 'other'?' (Smialkowska 2012). My own preference over setting *Hamlet* in an imagined African state would be to see more performers of colour in leading roles on the RSC stage more generally. However, the West African setting for this production allowed for an experimentation with the materiality of colour that produced excitingly different meanings from the grey Denmark in which *Hamlet* is more commonly set, and I use it as a final case study here, partly because it completes a chapter that has discussed black clothing at such length with a meditation on a more literally colourful production: West African-print fabrics and a suit splashed with coloured paint dominated the aesthetic. More importantly, I want to argue that the production managed to avoid a superficial elision of an imagined Africa with colour and violence and produced a detailed reading of the political and personal relations in this play, in a non-white setting. It also explicitly foregrounded costume as a maker of meaning: when this Hamlet had taken on his 'antic disposition', he wore a costume which he had very literally marked with meaning himself.

The African state staged by this *Hamlet* read as a modern, post-colonial one: Hamlet had been sent to a 'Wittenberg' university that dressed its graduands in traditional Western mortar board and gown; his father's funeral service was accompanied by both African drummers and by relatives in Western mourning suits. One strong cultural influence was Ghana: Essiedu himself had Ghanaian parents and visited the country to discuss its traditions of ghosts, conjuring and music for the production (Essiedu 2016b). In the production's programme, a link is made between Hamlet, who returns from university to find his world turned upside down, and Kwame Nkrumah, Ghana's first president, who was beset by thoughts of mortality after returning to Ghana from a period of study in London, in 1949.

This was a Christian state that appropriated Western formal wear but also drew on African traditions of dress and decor for its ceremonies and formalities. Gertrude (Lorna Brown) wore a golden choker adorned with a prominent cross; Claudius (Clarence Smith) found he could not pray before a crucifix with an African-styled Jesus. When Hamlet put on his 'antic disposition', the court called upon white students from Hamlet's university days[7] to surveil him: James Cooney and Bethan Cullinane as Rosencrantz and Guildenstern looked as though they might have taken this opportunity to take a late gap year in Africa: they made an awkward show of touching the floor before Claudius and Gertrude, a tradition everyone who actually lived at court seemed to have abandoned; they brought the King and Queen cringe-worthy presents of Scottish shortbread and a tea pot in the shape of a red telephone box from the UK. As an invited audience member to the play within the play, Rosencrantz wore a Western blue and white striped shirt that he clearly thought appropriate to the formality of the occasion, with an African print tie in yellows and browns, no doubt to demonstrate his sympathy with indigenous culture. In a pre-set sequence, 'Hamlet, Prince of Denmark' was named in a graduation ceremony, received his certificate and turned for a photo, only to be plunged into black out and find himself, in the next moment, accompanying his father's coffin. The pre-set illustrated what the programme notes suggest is the inciting incident for the play and the production: Hamlet returns from the open, nurturing environment of his university to find bewildering regime and family change at home.

---

[7] In a later touring company, the pair were replaced by one black, one white actor: Romayne Andrews as Rosencranzt, Eleanor Wyld as Guildenstern, respectively.

I suggest that the production's Christian West African setting worked to produce a coherent set of meanings for *Hamlet* and that Paul Wills's 'African' design drew attention to fabric in productively readable ways. This is not to say that there were not culturally insensitive moments in the production. It suggested that this state was a Christian one, but Ophelia was carried to her grave by Laertes in a white shroud rather than a coffin. This certainly created a painful intimacy between brother and dead sister in the funeral procession, although it rather took away from the moment in which Laertes declares that he is jumping into the grave to hold Ophelia in his arms, as he had already been doing just that. The lack of a coffin for Ophelia's body was also perhaps intended to emphasise the swiftness and lack of ceremony with which she was buried. But given burial in a plain shroud is an actual Islamic tradition, the moment was in danger of suggesting that production decisions about cultural setting were not being followed through and that anything that might look vaguely African to Stratford-upon-Avon audiences would do.

The use of Kente-style cross-hatched fabric for elements of set and costume was more consistent. A few simple hangings made from this material created the backdrop for the court scenes, against which a double throne was set—a throne which Hamlet later jokily vandalised with male and female toilet icons. One of the hangings created an arras for Polonius (Joseph Mydell) to hide behind, which tumbled to the floor as Hamlet shot him through it. Significantly, the Ghost of Hamlet's father wore a traditional Ashanti-style robe in Kente fabric and his appearance was accompanied by ritual calls and two wildly beaten drums; the drummers were dressed in bright red shirts, also worn by a praise singer/drummer to Claudius in 1.2. Thus, on the entrance of the Ghost, the fabric and the drumming are re-staged as part of a tradition of reverencing family and ancestors which Claudius had, of course, brutally desecrated by killing his brother. Suddenly the visual continuity with tradition that Claudius's post-colonial court had created by its choice of fabric and furniture was exposed as inauthentic and hypocritical by the appearance of the Ghost, who was the true representative of that history and tradition. The Ghost in armour may have reminded Elizabethans of a past set of traditional morals and ethics, now evoked only for ceremonial purposes; the Ghost in his Kente garb emptied out Claudius's uses of tradition and continuity.

Paapa Essiedu's Hamlet appeared to recognise this inauthenticity and sought new artistic expression for his rejection of his Uncle's rule and values, artistic expression which departed from the historical traditions of his father and nation. His 'antic disposition' was marked by a turn to the subversive art of the political graffitist, and to contemporary theatre design, as he vandalised the formal court painting of his mother and uncle with a tag of spray-paint and created new backdrops and floor cloths for his production of 'The Murder of Gonzago' in a rough, colourful, graffiti style. Having seen the Ghost, Hamlet changed his sober black and white gear (funeral jacket and tie with white shirt for 1.2, black blouson jacket and white t-shirt for the battlements of 1.4 and 5) for a pale jacket and rolled-up trousers, all over which he had evidently painted in splashes of bright colour and deliberately crude shapes of crowns and a skull. The 'words, words, words' that Hamlet tells Polonius he is reading were from a book he had decorated in similar fashion. A dominant design on his new clothes was a crown insignia, a graffiti tag with which he also sprayed across a formal portrait of his mother and uncle hanging in the court. A crown shape adorned the breast of his t-shirt beneath which, as we will see, he was revealed to have a tattoo of his father, the man who should still have been wearing the real crown. The crown image marked his jacket cuff, and there was another on his trouser leg, crowning a sinister looking crow, presumably representing Claudius. On his back was daubed a crowned skull, which also dominated backdrop he had evidently made for the play within the play. Even Hamlet's face was splashed with coloured paint.

This costume made a striking publicity icon for the production. See Hamlet daubed and dressed thus on the poster before you see the show, and it is clear that this is going to be a differently coloured production from the mainstream in all senses: actors of colour have the leading roles; bright, African colours replace grey Northern Europe; brightly painted clothing replaces black and grey garb. I suggest that the use of literal colour did not merely represent a conscious change from a range of tired conventions, or a potentially touristic version of African culture. This Hamlet seemed to be struggling for a mode of expression that was outside of the ways in which both his uncle's corrupted court made visual sense of the world, and outside of the visual traditions of his father and nation. Paapa Essiedu, when asked whether his would be a new interpretation of the role (Essiedu 2016a), modestly suggests that the fact of his own youth might work to create a new Hamlet; sure enough, his graffiti, his wildly painted clothing, and the set he makes for 'The Murder of Gonzago', read as the artistic expression of youth. The subversiveness of his art to an older generation was referenced by Gertrude, who, when she spoke to Ophelia of her hopes that the younger woman's 'virtues/ Will bring him to his wonted way again' (3.1.44–5), nodded exasperatedly towards the scrawls and splashes of Hamlet's theatrical preparations when she referred to his 'wildness'. This student art finally became politically intolerable and led to Claudius's plan to send the young artist off to England and have him killed there.

This production also made creative visual use of the tragedians: the Players (Kevin N. Golding: Player King; Maureen Hibbert: Player Queen; Patrick Elue: Lucianus) wore a ragbag of colourful Western clothing for touring, but the Pyrrhus speech was enacted using wooden West African masks, not covering the actors' faces, but gracefully held in the hand like puppets, in a manner that complemented the distancing effect of the third-person speeches in the scene. The masks successfully created the impression of a contemporary theatre company drawing on a traditional narrative and aesthetic, as the Player in the play draws on Europe's Classical heritage. For the play-within-the-play itself, Player King and Queen wore costumes that mixed African prints with satirical clowning tradition: the King was dressed in a heavily-braided military jacket, a parody of Claudius's sartorial militarism in 1.2, offset by the Britishness of bright yellow wellingtons, plus a colourful Zimmer frame to indicate his senescence; the Queen wore fabric of African design mixed with references to Elizabeth I: a curly red wig and brightly coloured ruff-like collar. Lucianus then appeared in a plainer African robe and dreadlocks, disrupting the clownish gaiety of this post-colonial parody as if he had stepped in from a more realist drama: this was a serious villain and Claudius, of course, took him seriously, calling for lights and the play's halt.

In answer to the aforementioned question posed to Essiedu about a new interpretation of the play, I might have suggested that it was in Mimi Ndiweni's reading of Ophelia and her relationship with Polonius that offered the audience one of the production's most original readings. Cyril Nri managed to make Polonius's long-windedness and conformity both funny and sympathetic. The modern habit of having Ophelia and Laertes exchange weary glances during Polonius's lists of fatherly advice was adhered to, but more affectionately than in many productions, and this neatly dressed Ophelia accepted her father's advice to sever her relationship with Hamlet in a way that suggested a mix of obeisance and closeness: father and daughter had been joking together about Hamlet's home-printed T-shirt (the 'honourable fashion' of the text (1.3.115)) and other love tokens; then, when it came to Polonius's actual prohibition of the relationship, it was clear that Ophelia was disconcerted, but ultimately trusted her father; she had, after all, known and trusted him far longer than she had Hamlet. When she came to Polonius with her account of Hamlet's crazed entrance to her closet, she wore night attire that suggested ease and a lack of formality in this family rather than her own incipient madness and Polonius did not register shock at seeing his daughter thus dressed. This Ophelia was far from a weak, submissive figure, as was made clear by her lively reactions to her brother's advice; but she loved and obeyed her father, and this made the angry distress of her madness at his violent death all the more plausible.

In one of the production's most disturbing visual moments, Ndiweni's Ophelia drew attention to the significance of a black woman's hair to her identity and self-image. Prior to the scenes of her madness, she wore it in a neat bun clasped at the top of her head. Indeed, the whole visual impression she created was one of a relaxed but fairly conventional tidiness: her costume was crisp white jeans and a relatively sober mustard and black print shirt, then an elegant silk block-print shirt for attendance at the Play. When she entered 'distracted' she, like Q1's Ophelia, did so with her 'hair down': down from its bun, locks springing from pins that now only loosely held it from her face. The herbs she gave out to Claudius, Gertrude and Laertes were locks of that hair, which she pulled from her head with an agonised cry. On her return after Laertes's entrance, she entered with Polonius's grey Nehru jacket over her nightwear and took off her trousers, momentarily recalling a recent history of half-naked Ophelias (see above 36–37) but switching the focus back to her dead father as she sung 'And will he not come again?' (4.4.190) by laying the trousers and jacket on the floor to represent his dead body, and tenderly kissing the cuff as if it were her father's hand. On exiting, Gertrude lay the lock of hair Ophelia had given her on this forlorn 'body' and echoed Ophelia's pained state when she re-entered to tell of the girl's drowning with her own hair down.

Act 5 brought together all of the costume elements described here. Like the touring Players, the gravediggers (one man, one woman) wore colourful, casual clothes in Western shapes. Tracy-Ann Green's Second Gravedigger wore painted socks in bright splashes of colour, reminiscent of Hamlet's palate for his 'mad' costume, and Ewart James Walters's First Gravedigger wore a pale jacket, also similar to Hamlet's, but daubed with the earth of his trade rather than with paint. By this point in the play, Esseidu had donned a traveling outfit of grey sweater and red beany hat for his trip to England, more like the Hamlet of the disappearing modern costume. The sweater and hat were a practical reflection of the fact that he had just been off to chilly England, of course. But the costume choice also visually recalled critical readings of the play that note Hamlet's verbal disappearance as the play's commentating clown in Act 5 and the fact that the gravedigger—probably played by the dark, dry clown Armin in early production—takes over that clowning role over by Ophelia's graveside. Hamlet's transgressively satirical garb was now being worn by the gravedigger.

For the final fencing match with Laertes, traditional African stick fighting was the martial art of choice, staging simultaneously tradition and the appropriation of tradition by Claudius's corrupted court that we have observed throughout the production. The two young men were stripped to the waist for the fighting bouts and, over modern fencing boots, wore loose pants in a deep pinkish-purple that had already been part of the court's colour palate—Claudius wore a suit in similar colour earlier in the production, Gertrude a dress in the same hue, Osric an ostentatiously bright version with clashing shirt and hat. That the tradition of stick fighting was made to seem somewhat ersatz thus costumed—a pose of traditional, bare-chested warrior in fashionable martial arts pants—read appropriately, because although the fighting style appeared, on the one hand, as a martial art passed down the generations, the purple pants made its display look like one of Claudius's contrivances as, in the play, it is: an exploitation of traditional skill to the usurping King's own ends.

Paapa Essiedu appeared bare-chested in two scenes of *Hamlet*: once in 3.4, for the confrontation between Hamlet and his mother, and once in this fight scene. In 3.4, he revealed that beneath his subversive, homemade t-shirt with the crown on its breast, Hamlet kept a picture of his father much closer to his heart: a tattoo on his skin of the old King's narrow, solemn face. The image of Claudius with which he compared it for the benefit of his mother was a photograph on the cover of *World* magazine: Claudius in a Western suit with a fat, yellow, businessman's tie. This encapsulated the work that costume was doing in this production to highlight the tensions between the old and the new, between tradition and the hypocritical exploitation of tradition in *Hamlet*—and these were not easily either binarised or reconciled in this production. On the one hand, Claudius was obviously a usurping murderer, posing as a benevolent modern leader for the world to see on the magazine cover. However, Hamlet's tattoo did not simply suggest that he was, in diametric opposition to Claudius, authentically dedicated to his ancestor and the true king. The tattoo marked Hamlet permanently with the tradition of revenge that finally leads to his own death. The wild painting of his clothing and set designs represented neither modern capitalism nor generations-old tradition: they were the artistic expression of youth trying to find its own cultural and political purpose. This purpose was obliterated by both Claudius's plotting and Old Hamlet's demand for revenge.

There are questions to be asked here about the aestheticisation or sexualisation of the half-naked black body on stage in the production. At the Hungarian Society for Drama in English conference of 2018, Jana Wild gave a paper on the Slovak tradition of slender Hamlets, a tradition which contradicts Gertrude's description of him as 'fat and scant of breath' (5.2.227) during the fight. On first seeing images from this RSC production at the same event, Professor Péter P. Muller of the University of Pecs remarked that it was rare to see Hamlet bare-chested and with a muscular physique. The stereotype of Hamlet as a fragile, skinny, white intellectual was, it could be argued, being replaced here by another stereotype, more obviously racially marked when a company of predominantly black actors plays to a predominantly white audience at Stratford upon Avon: that of the physically powerful, energetic young black man, who graffitis the court and whom the audience get to see half-naked. Just as we have seen Hamlet's costume 'disappear' in modern production in order to privilege his mind, so Hamlet's body, played by the slender white actor in a black sweater, is presented as a dwindling sign for his restless intellect rather than a notable physical presence. I want to suggest, though, that Paapa Essiedu managed to hold the aestheticization of his own half-naked torso in productive tension with a performance of vulnerability and open weeping in the first scene that was a long way from the machismo of the potential stereotype. Moreover, the tattoo of Hamlet's father's head on his chest drew focus to a body marked with that father's traditional legacy, in opposition to Claudius's opportunist political exploitation of that legacy. This 'African' production made sure that costume did not disappear from the stage of Hamlet: fabric and clothing, and the lack of it, constructed tradition and its uses, its violence and the violence of its appropriation.

Conclusions

In this chapter, I have argued that the first *Hamlet* foregrounded mourning wear as his subversive difference to Claudius's court and his relationship with the past. From the second half of the nineteenth century, not only Hamlet's long black mourning cloak but his costume more generally is erased by the theatrical convention of dressing the figure in a medieval tunic, and Hamlet's mind is privileged over his political position, as signals of his inner turmoil are emphasised over visually evident social construction. Twentieth-century British *Hamlet* designs indicate a generalised medieval/Renaissance pastness, with the occasional burst of modern dress, until we reach the present day, when in British production, the casual modern dress Hamlet in his cool, black shirt or sweater reflects the need to make Hamlet not a prince, but a modern psychological Everyman, and erases the significance of mourning altogether. By setting their latest *Hamlet* in a 'colourful' West African state, the RSC has lately re-emphasised clothing as a site of subversion and conflict in the play. Essiedu's Hamlet obeys his mother's request that he cast his nighted colour off and dons a suit of his own design, angrily graffitied in defiance of his Uncle's appropriation of more traditional colours and fabrics.

Discussing these productions, I have not wanted to privilege any particular mode of costume design over another. However, in the tradition of Catherine Belsey and the late twentieth-century cultural materialists, I think of *Hamlet* as a play that stages the emerging social and interior 'selves' of early modern culture in ways that can reengage audiences with questions of personal will, agency and self-fashioning today. Costume design that draws attention to Hamlet's social self and the systems of power that produce him is design that makes the most of the play for an audience now. It draws attention to the material presence of clothing and thus to all of the gendered, political and racialised hierarchies in which dress is bound up, rather than effacing clothing and insisting that what matters most in drama is 'that within which passeth show' (1.2.85). In this chapter, I have disagreed with Hamlet himself and his privileging of his own interiority here. I have rather argued that the 'show' of costume can reflect, produce and exceed the psychological subject. Hamlet consciously marks his depth of thought in his big black cloak, in contrast to the superficiality of Claudius's court; he also marks his theatrical roles as revenge hero and malcontent, his humoral typography, his attachment to the past. A key question for the designer today is how costume might open up the construction of this multi-faceted dramatic subject to the contemporary audience.

PRODUCTIONS DISCUSSED (ALL PRODUCTIONS ARE OF *HAMLET*)

Barbican Theatre/Sonia Friedman Productions. 2015. Lindsay Turner (director), Katrina Lindsay (costume designer), Es Devlin (designer), Barbican Theatre, London.

Cheek by Jowl. 1990. Declan Donnelan (director), Nick Omerod (designer), Theatre Royal Bury St Edmunds, then touring. https://www.cheekbyjowl.com/productions/hamlet.

English Touring Theatre. 1993. Stephen Unwin (director), Bunnie Christie (designer), Lyceum Theatre, Crew, then touring; Donmar Warehouse, London.

Lyceum. 1874. Henry Irving as Hamlet, Hezekiah Bateman (manager), Lyceum Theatre, London.

National Theatre. 1999. John Caird (director), Tim Hatley (designer), Lytellton Theatre, National Theatre, London.

———. 2010. Nicholas Hytner (director), Vicki Mortimer (designer), Olivier Theatre, National Theatre London.

Peter Hall Company. 1994. Peter Hall (director), Lucy Hall (designer), Gielgud Theatre, London.

Royal Court. 1981. Richard Eyre (director), William Dudley (designer), Royal Court, London.

Royal Shakespeare Company. 1965. Peter Hall (director), Ann Curtis (Costumes), John Berry (Designer, John Berry), Royal Shakespeare Theatre, Stratford upon Avon. https://www.rsc.org.uk/hamlet/past-productions/peter-hall-1965-production.

———. 2016. Simon Godwin (director), Paul Wills (Designer), Royal Shakespeare Company, Stratford upon Avon. https://www.rsc.org.uk/hamlet/past-productions/simon-godwin-2016-production.

Shakespeare's Globe. 2000. Giles Block (director), Jenny Tiramani (designer), Shakespeare's Globe, London.

Young Vic. 2011a. Ian Rickson (director), Nicky Gillibrand (costume designer), Jeremy Herbert (designer), Young Vic, London.

WORKS CITED

Shakespeare, William 1998. *Hamlet* (Quarto One). In *The First Quarto of Hamlet*, ed. Kathleen O. Irace, New Cambridge Shakespeare, The Early Quartos, Cambridge: Cambridge University Press.

All other references to *Hamlet* and other plays by Shakespeare are from the *RSC Shakespeare: Complete Works* (2007). Ed. Jonathan Bate. Houndsmills, Basingstoke: Palgrave Macmillan.

Addonizio, Shari. 1999. Portraits of Madwomen: Another Look at Dr Hugh Welch Diamond's Photographs of the Insane Female in Victorian England. *Athanor*, 17.

Apfelbaum, Roger. 2004. *Shakespeare's Troilus and Cressida: Textual Problems and Performance Solutions.* Newark: University of Delaware Press.

Aubrey, John. 1962, first published 1681. *Aubrey's Brief Lives.* Ed. Oliver Lawson Dick. London: Penguin Books.

Barker, Roberta. 2008. Acting Against the Rules: Remembering the Eroticism of the Shakespearean Boy Actress. In *Shakespeare Re-dressed: Cross-gender Casting in Contemporary Performance*, ed. James C. Bulman. Madison: Fairleigh Dickinson University Press.

Baugh, Christopher. 2009. Shakespeare and the Rhetoric of Scenography, 1770–1825. In *Shakespeare in Stages: New Theatre Histories*, ed. Christie Carson and Christine Dymkowski, 187–209. Cambridge: Cambridge University Press.

Boaden, James. 1825. *Memoirs of the Life of John Philip Kemble Esq: Including a History of the Stage from the Time of Garrick to the Present Period.* London: Longman, Hurst, Rees, Orme, Brown and Green.

Belsey, Catherine. 1985. *The Subject of Tragedy Identity and Difference in Renaissance Drama.* London: Methuen.

Bessell, Jaq. 2001. The 2000 Globe Season: The White Company: *Hamlet*, Research Bulletin 17. https://archive.shakespearesglobe.com/calmview/Record.aspx?src=CalmView.Catalog&id=GB+3316+SGT%2fED%2fRES%2f2%2f5%2f23.

Bulman, James C., ed. 2008. *Shakespeare Re-dressed: Cross-gender Casting in Contemporary Bulman Performance.* Madison: Fairleigh Dickinson University Press.

Carson, Christie, and Christine Dymkowski, eds. 2010. *Shakespeare in Stages: New Theatre Histories.* Cambridge: Cambridge University Press.

Cressy, David. 1997. *Birth, Marriage and Death: Ritual, Religion and the Life Cycle in Early Modern England.* Oxford: Oxford University Press.

Croall, Jonathan. 2018. *Performing Hamlet: Actors in the Modern Age.* London: Bloomsbury, Arden Shakespeare.

Dessen, Alan. 1984. *Elizabethan Stage Conventions and Modern Interpreters.* Cambridge: Cambridge University Press.

Dickens, Charles. 1867. *Great Expectations.* London: Chapman & Hall.

Dillon, Janette. 1994. Is There a Performance in this Text? *Shakespeare Quarterly* 45 (1): 74–86.

Doring, Tobias. 2006. *Performances of Mourning in Shakespearean Theatre and Early Modern Culture.* Basingstoke: Palgrave Macmillan.

'Drawings of Funeral Processions' (1557–1603) British Library Add MS 35324.

Duthie, George Ian. 1941. *The 'Bad' Quarto of Hamlet: A Critical Study.* Cambridge: Cambridge University Press.

Escolme, Bridget. 2014. *Emotional Excess on the Shakespearean Stage: Passion's Slaves*. London: Bloomsbury, Arden Shakespeare.

———. 2017. Shakespeare and the Contemporary: Psychology, Culture, and Audience in Othello Production. In *The Oxford Handbook of Shakespeare in Performance*, ed. James C. Bulman. Oxford: Oxford University Press.

Essiedu, Paapa. 2016a. Interview with Paapa Essiedu/Hamlet/Royal Shakespeare Company. Royal Shakespeare Company. https://www.rsc.org.uk/hamlet/past-productions/simon-godwin-2016-production/video-interview-with-paapa-essiedu.

———. 2016b. Paapa Essiedu on His Ghanaian-Influenced Hamlet at the RSC. Interviewed by Heather Neill, Theatre Voice http://www.theatrevoice.com/audio/paapa-essiedu-ghanaian-influenced-hamlet-rsc/.

Evans, Blakemore G. 1988. *Elizabethan-Jacobean Drama*. London: A & C Black.

Foakes, R.A. 2003. *Shakespeare and Violence*. Cambridge: Cambridge University Press.

———. 2005. "Armed at point exactly": The Ghost in *Hamlet*. *Shakespeare Survey* 58: 34–47.

Freeman, Lisa A. 2002. *Character's Theater: Genre and Identity on the Eighteenth-Century English Stage*. Philadelphia: University of Pennsylvania Press.

Furniss, Harry. 1874. Sir Henry Irving as Hamlet. National Portrait Gallery [image]. https://www.npg.org.uk/collections/search/portrait/mw42176/Sir-Henry-Irving-as-Hamlet.

Gamboa, Brett. 2018. *Shakespeare's Double Plays: Dramatic Economy on the Early Modern Stage*. Cambridge University Press.

Goethe, J. W. von. 1921. The First Edition of *Hamlet*, trans. Randolph S. Bourne. In *Goethe's Literary Essays*, ed. J.E. Spingarn. New York: Harcourt Brace.

Goodland, Katharine. 2006. *Female Mourning in Medieval and Renaissance English Drama: From the Raising of Lazarus to King Lear*. Aldershot: Ashgate.

Hawkins, Ella Kirsty. 2020. *The Significance of Jacobethanism in Twenty-First-Century Costume Design for Shakespeare*. PhD thesis, Shakespeare Institute, University of Birmingham.

Henslowe, Philip, and R.A. Foakes, eds. 2002. *Henslowe's Diary*. Cambridge: Cambridge University Press.

Holderness, Graham, and James Loughrey. 2014. Introduction. In *The Tragicall Historie of Hamlet Prince of Denmarke (Hamlet First Quarto)*, 13–29. Abingdon, Oxon: Routledge.

Howard, Tony. 2007. *Women as Hamlet: Performance and Interpretation in Theatre, Film and Fiction*. Cambridge: Cambridge University Press.

Irace, Kathleen O. (Ed.). 1998. *The First Quarto of Hamlet*. In *New Cambridge Shakespeare, The Early Quartos*. Cambridge: Cambridge University Press.

Jocic, Laura. 2008. The Diversity of Black. In *Black in Fashion: Mourning to Night*, ed. Margaret Trudgeon. Melbourne: Council of Trustees of the National Gallery of Victoria.

Jones, David E. 1988. The Theatricality of the First Quarto of *Hamlet*. *Hamlet Studies* 10: 104–110.

Knutson, Rosalind, David McInnis, and Matthew Steggle. 2018. *Hamlet. Lost Plays Database* Folger Shakespeare Library. https://lostplays.folger.edu/Hamlet.

Laroche, Rebecca. 2011. Ophelia's Plants and the Death of Violence. In *Ecocritical Shakespeare*, ed. Lynne Dickson Bruckner and Daniel Brayton. Farnham: Ashgate.

Lesser, Zachary. 2015. *Hamlet After Q1: An Uncanny History of the Shakespearean Text*. Philadelphia: Pennsylvania University Press.

Lopez, Jeremy. 2012. Reviewing Ophelia. In *The Afterlife of Ophelia. Reproducing Shakespeare: New Studies in Adaptation and Appropriation*, ed. Kaara L. Peterson and Deanne Williams, 29–41. New York: Palgrave Macmillan.

Lichtenberg, Georg Christoph. 1938. *Lichtenberg's Visits to England as Described in His Letters and Diaries*. Oxford: Clarendon Press.

Lublin, Robert I. 2011. *Costuming the Shakespearean Stage: Visual Codes of Representation in Early Modern Theatre and Culture*. Farnham: Ashgate.

———. 2014. "Apparel oft proclaims the man": Visualizing Hamlet on the Early Modern Stage. *Shakespeare Bulletin* 32 (4): 629–647.

McGee, Arthur. 1987. *The Elizabethan Hamlet*. New Haven; London: Yale University Press.

MacIntyre, Jean. 1992. *Costumes and Scripts in the Elizabethan Theatres*. Edmonton: University of Alberta Press.

Mander, Raymond, and Joe Mitchenson. 1952. *Hamlet Through the Ages: A Pictorial Record from 1709*. London: Rockliff.

Marcus, Leah. 1996. *Unediting the Renaissance: Shakespeare, Marlow, Milton*. London: Routledge.

Monks, Aoife. 2010. *The Actor in Costume*. Basingstoke: Palgrave Macmillan.

Munro, Lucy. 2013. *Archaic Style in English Literature, 1590–1674*. Cambridge: Cambridge University Press.

Nashe, Thomas. 1562. Pierce Pennilesse, His Supplication to the Devil. *Luminarium*. http://www.luminarium.org/renlit/penniles.htm.

Newman, Lucile F. 1980. Ophelia's Herbal. *Economic Botany* 33 (2): 227–232.

Orgel, Stephen. 2006. Orgel 'The Book of the Play'. In *From the Performance to Print in Shakespeare's England*, ed. Peter Holland and Stephen Orgel, 13–54. Basingstoke and New York: Palgrave Macmillan.

Pentzell, Raymond J. 1972. Kemble's Hamlet Costume. *Theatre Survey* 13 (1): 81–85.

Peterson Kaara, L., and Deanne Williams, eds. *The Afterlife of Ophelia. Reproducing Shakespeare: New Studies in Adaptation and Appropriation*, 119–136. New York: Palgrave Macmillan.

Planché, J.R., Joseph Kenny Meadows, and George Sir Scharf. 1823. *Costume of Shakespeare's King John – King Henry the Fourth – As You Like It – Hamlet – Othello, and Merchant of Venice Selected from the Best Authorities with Biographical, Critical and Explanatory Notices*. London: John Miller.

Planché, J.R. 1872. *The Recollections and Reflections of J. R. Planché: A Professional Autobiography*. London: Tinsley Bros.

Raymond, George. 1857. *The Life and Enterprises of Robert William Elliston, Comedian*. London: Routledge.

Richardson, Catherine. 2011. *Shakespeare and Material Culture*. Oxford: Oxford University Press.

Richardson, Catherine, and Martin Wiggins. 2013. *British Drama, 1533–1642: A Catalogue Volume 3: 1590–1597*. Oxford: Oxford University Press.

Roach, Joseph. 1993. *The Player's Passion: Studies in the Science of Acting*. Ann Arbor: University of Michigan Press.

Royal Shakespeare Company. Rupert Gold 2006 Production. https://www.rsc.org.uk/the-tempest/past-productions/rupert-gold-2006-production.

Russell, R.A. 1956. Hamlet Costumes from Garrick to Gielgud. *Shakespeare Survey* 9: 54–58.

Rutter, Carol Chillington. 2010. Unpinning Desdemona (Again) or "Who Would Be Toll'd with Wenches in a Shew?". *Shakespeare Bulletin* 28 (1): 111–132.

Jones, Ann Rosalind, and Peter Stallybrass. 2000. *Renaissance Clothing and the Materials of Memory*. Cambridge: Cambridge University Press.

Schoch, Richard W. 1998. *Shakespeare's Victorian Stage: Performing History in the Theatre of Charles Kean*. Cambridge: Cambridge University Press.

Scott, Clement. 1900. *Some Notable Hamlets of the Present Time*. London: Greening and Co Ltd.

Sillars, Stuart. 2012. *Shakespeare, Time and the Victorians: A Pictorial Exploration*. Cambridge: Cambridge University Press.

Sheen, Michael. 2011. Interview with Caroline McGinn. *Time Out*. https://www.timeout.com/london/theatre/michael-sheen-interview.

Smialkowska, Monika. 2012. Year of Shakespeare: Julius Caesar at the RSC. https://www.bloggingshakespeare.com/year-of-shakespeare-julius-caesar-at-the-rsc.

Spencer, Charles. 2011. Hamlet, the Young Vic Theatre: Review. *Daily Telegraph*, November 10. https://www.telegraph.co.uk/culture/theatre/theatre-reviews/8879601/Hamlet-The-Young-Vic-Theatre-review.html.

Stubbes, Philip. 2002, first published 1583. *The Anatomie of Abuses*. Ed. Margaret Kidney. Medieval and Renaissance Text Society. 7th series, vol. 27. Tempe: Arizona Center for Medieval and Renaissance Studies, in conjunction with Renaissance English Text Society.

Taylor, Lou. 1983. *Mourning Dress: A Costume and Social History*. London: Allen & Unwin.

Terry, Ellen. 1908. *The Story of My Life*. New York: McClure Company.

Tiramani, Jenny. 2009. Costume – Dressing the Early Modern Actor, a Demonstration by Jenny Tiramani. In *The Chamber of Demonstrations: Reconstructing the Indoor Playhouse*, ed. Martin White, Ignition Films (DVD).

Trudgeon, Margaret, ed. 2008. *Black in Fashion: Mourning to Night*. Melbourne: Council of Trustees of the National Gallery of Victoria.

Turner, John, Rhodri Hayward, Katherine Angel, et al. 2015. The History of Mental Health Services in Modern England and the Direction of Future Research. *Medical History* 59 (4): 599–624.

Vincent, Susan J. 2002. *When I Am in Good Habitt': Clothes in English Culture c. 1550–c. 1670*. PhD thesis, Department of English and Related Literature, University of York.

Viney, Peter. 2011. Peter Viney's Blog. *Hamlet* Young Vic. November 12. https://peterviney.wordpress.com/stage/hamlet-young-vic-2011/.

von Wedel, Lupold. 1895. Journey Through England and Scotland Made by Lupold von Wedel in the Years 1584 and 1585. In *Transactions of the Royal Historical Society 9*, trans. Gottfried von Bülow, 223–270. Cambridge: Cambridge University Press.

Williams, Deanne. 2012. Enter Ofelia Playing on a Lute. In *The Afterlife of Ophelia. Reproducing Shakespeare: New Studies in Adaptation and Appropriation*, ed. Kaara L. Peterson and Deanne Williams, 119–136. New York: Palgrave Macmillan.

Wild, Jana. 2018. 'A Fat Hamlet?' HUSSDE 5 Conference: 'Dramatic Tradition, Nostalgia and Spectatorship'. The Institute of English and American Studies, Pázmány Péter Catholic University, Budapest, Hungary.

Winter, William. 1911. *Shakespeare on the Stage*. New York: Moffat, Yard and Company.

Young Vic. 2011b. *Hamlet*. https://www.youngvic.org/whats-on/hamlet.

CHAPTER 3

Much Ado About Nothing, Restorative Nostalgia and the Costume Drama: Tires and Rebatoes, Corsets and Lace

Take a magical journey through 100 years of theatre-making in Stratford-upon-Avon. On display are stunning costumes and props from our archives as well as a rare copy of Shakespeare's first folio.
(*RSC web publicity: 'The Play's the Thing' exhibition*)

Restorative nostalgia does not think of itself as nostalgia, but rather as truth and tradition. Reflective nostalgia dwells on the ambivalences of human longing and belonging and does not shy away from the contradictions of modernity. Restorative nostalgia protects the absolute truth, while reflective nostalgia calls it into doubt.
(*Sveltlana Boym 2001, xviii*)

DON PEDRO: (to BEATRICE) Come lady, come, you have lost the heart of Signior Benedick.

BEATRICE: Indeed, my lord, he lent it me awhile, and I gave him use for it, a double heart for his single one. Marry, once before he won it of me with false dice. Therefore your Grace may well say I have lost it.
(Much Ado About Nothing 2.1.192-40)

Visitors to the Royal Shakespeare Company's home in Stratford upon Avon in the summer of 2019 are offered three ways to experience the products of its celebrated costume department, in addition to watching the clothes in action on stage. £8.50 for a yearly pass will take you up a back staircase

© The Author(s), under exclusive license to Springer Nature Switzerland AG 2020
B. Escolme, *Shakespeare and Costume in Practice*, Shakespeare in Practice, https://doi.org/10.1007/978-3-030-57149-8_3

at the Swan theatre to 'The Play's the Thing', an exhibition that 'reveal[s] fascinating secrets and stories from the Royal Shakespeare Company' and invites you to 'See priceless objects, hear tales from behind the scenes, explore the ideas of directors, designers, actors and makers and try your hand at performing on stage' (RSC 'The Play's the Thing'). The exhibition is dominated by glass cases displaying a range of Shakespeare Memorial Theatre and RSC costumes, from Constance Benson's Ganymede disguise (*As You Like It* 1894, 1899, 1908) to Paul Robeson's costume for *Othello* (1959), to Beth Cordingly's Elizabethan/*The Only Way is Essex* fusion outfit in the *Merry Wives* of 2018. On a balcony space above the Royal Shakespeare Theatre's main entrance hall, a much smaller costume display is free, albeit accompanied by the invitation to pay much more. This exhibit supports the RSC's 'Stitch in Time' appeal for donations to 'support the restoration and redevelopment of the RSC's Costume Workshop' (RSC 'A Stitch in Time'). Costumes are displayed in the process of construction and labelled with invitations to donate sums as high as £600. Lastly, and again for free, you can, at the time of writing, have a rummage in a costume cupboard, the 'Cabinet of the Lost', placed near the cafe in the RST's ground floor foyer, and try on some costumes for yourself.

These exhibits all testify to the part costume plays in the artistic, cultural and corporate identity of the UK's largest and best-funded production house for Shakespeare. In 'The Play's the Thing', costume, theatre and Shakespeare are conflated in the rhetorics of humanist artistic vision and down-to-earth craftwork; they make claims to both historicity, and artistic and technological innovation. 'The Play's the Thing' is not a costume exhibition per se; it includes props, photographs and digitised interactive displays offering insight into design and directorial decision making. The exhibition also, as the opening quotation to this chapter announces, displays a copy of the First Folio. However, costumes dominate the exhibition; they are what the woman who sells me my ticket to the exhibition talks to me excitedly about and what the woman who takes me up the intriguingly narrow back staircase at the Swan mentions first: 'they've only recently changed the costumes!'.

Touching and not-touching are key to this exhibition experience: it is both 'hands on' and 'hands off', if you like. I spent time at a 'Director's Desk', at which I could click on the titles of various plays and get access to a digital version of a designer's cork-board, where production decisions are displayed, the digital and the tangible held in tension: 'Real materials' and 'Weighty costumes' state the labels in the section on John Barton and

Peter Halls's much-cited Wars of the Roses trilogy of 1963 (des. John Bury). The labels have little shadows at their edges, tantalisingly hinting at what it might be like to be able to pick up and hold real production photos on a real cork-board. Visitors, particularly children, are invited to 'try on' costumes at a 'Magic costume mirror'. Digitally clothed in a suit of armour or a medieval gown, they can then take a photo of themselves as a souvenir. 'What is it like to transform your appearance with costume?' the legend to this exhibit asks; 'How does it help you change your look and movement to become a character on stage?' The technology is at a relatively primitive stage here: I watch a little boy laugh as a digitised suit of armour is plastered rather clumsily onto his body, his appearance not so much transformed as the contemporaneity of his body is heightened by the image of archaic dress.

The actual costumes from the RSC's archive, displayed behind glass, are accompanied by small panels of fabric that you are invited to take between the fingers, rub and feel. One example seems at first to be from a controversial costume made from wire wool that featured in Russian director Theodore Komisarjevsky's 1933 *Macbeth* (des. Komisarjevsky, costumes Lesley Blanch), a 'shockingly modern' production that 'revolutionalised Shakespeare's story' using 'aluminium and wire wool in the scenery and costume and actors covered in oil so they would shine on stage'. 'Touch!' exhorts a little illustration of a hand, pointing to what might be part of 'a crown made of scouring pads?' but which turns out to be a modern plastic example. The 'real' costumes remain under glass, revered and untouchable, even as the mechanics of making them and the stories behind their reception are 'revealed'. The aura of these costumes is enhanced by reminders of their relationship to the now famous skins that did once touch them. One display case announces that it contains the jacket Zoe Wanamaker wore to play Viola; crowns worn by Virginia McKenna as Gertrude and Kenneth Branagh as Henry V; the leather glove of Michael Gambon's Lear; and Jeremy Irons/Richard II's 'white hart' chain. The legend for this case is entitled 'Hall of fame' and explains how the RSC 'rais[ed] the curtain on careers that have since seen them star on stage and screen'. Costume here is both practical and magical, materiality and aura, digitised version of material memory and originary theatrical narrative for later film stardom.

The 'Stitch in Time' costume display on the balcony above the RST's foyer is part of an appeal about which I have also received material in the post and by email. It goes beyond the fund-raising strategy of a Friends scheme or an invitation to donate extra money to the RSC's work on purchasing a ticket. The appeal of costume becomes source of charitable donation and frames costume as key to sumptuous stage illusion and as the result of painstaking craft work. Magic and materiality, artistic inspiration and craft-labour are all once again on display, this time with a price tag, which the woman directing me to the exhibit coyly elects not to mention. What look like literal price tags hang round costume-maker's dummies dressed in partially constructed and complete costumes. At a quick glance it looks as though a woman's costume costs £600 to make—and perhaps it does. But in fact label suggests that the reader 'support with donations from £600'. Here it is its legend in full:

LADIES' COSTUME
SUPPORT WITH DONATIONS FROM £600
We are proud to say we can make stunning costumes from any period.
Each and every costume is tailored specifically to the actor. Gowns, robes, doublets, Roman and Elizabethan dress, and 21st century garments, are stitched by hand in our specialist Ladies Costume team.
Our costumes bring history to life.
Support Ladies' Costume with a gift of £600 or more and help us create stunning costumes for you and audiences around the world to enjoy.
(RSC, 'A Stitch in Time')

The theatrical magic of 'stunning' spectacle, an intimate relationship with the actor's body—'tailored specifically'—and the laboursome pragmatics of craft, are all on display here, along with a suggestion that one might contribute financially to all this. Of course, the average theatre-goer will not be offering a gift of '£600 or more' to any charitable or artistic endeavour, and there are lower donations suggested here and on the 'Stitch in Time' website—'Underwear - £30'; Shoes - £75'—where one can also donate as much or as little as one desires. But I am interested here in costume on display as something of high economic value, and how that value is associated with the work of individual actors and craftspeople, and with a vaguer sense of spectacle and 'bringing history to life'. This display invites the tourist or theatre goer to make a very literal personal investment in the production of the past through costume.

The oddest of the three displays of costume at the contemporary RST complex is the 'Cabinet of the Lost', an open wardrobe designed, painted and labelled in Art Nouveau style, perhaps roughly to coincide with the period in which the Shakespeare Memorial Theatre opened (1879)—though the Alphonse Mucha-derived heads that crown the cabinet are distinctly1890s. The items in the wardrobe that cannot be taken out and played with are displayed and numbered as if in a 'cabinet of curiosities' or museum display case and a conceit used to label some of the items is that they are the lost property of characters from the plays themselves: Prospero's broken staff, Duke Vincentio's crucifix (*Measure for Measure*), Hero's obituary (*Much Ado About Nothing*), Lavinia's glove (*Titus Andronicus*—labelled as unreturnable, in case you failed to get the joke). You are invited to dress up in the costumes hanging in the wardrobe, making costume part of a palimpsest of past-ness. The Art Nouveau style of the cabinet thus recalls not so much the past of Shakespeare but a nostalgic history of childhood theatricals as they might appear in the early twentieth-century novels of E. Nesbit, in which children spend idyllic summer holidays having adult-free adventures in magical worlds.

This chapter considers 'period' costume in Royal Shakespeare Company productions of the comedy *Much Ado About Nothing* and the ways in which costume might reflect or trouble a nostalgic theatrical relationship with the past. I have begun with the above reflection on the ways in which the RSC is displaying its costumes at the time of writing, because these exhibits, in the company's foyer spaces and hidden away up the little back staircase at the Swan, speak to the links the company make with its own past and with a broader notion of 'past-ness'. Nostalgia for past productions that visitors of different ages may or may not have seen; nostalgia around theatrical origins for cinematic stardom; nostalgia for a past of authentic craft; nostalgia for a past in which the rich seemed to have richer and more exciting clothes: the exhibits all speak to a longing for the past whilst, in the case of 'The Play's the Thing', simultaneously insisting on the RSC as a place of artistic innovation and radical re-makings of Shakespeare. As we will see, *Much Ado About Nothing* is a play whose twentieth-century production has been steeped in a visual culture of nostalgia and has proved a particularly productive one through which to examine nostalgia's workings in costume design.

There is one set of costumes on display from a *Much Ado About Nothing* production in 'The Play's the Thing': the matching green and cream, late medieval-styled garb that Peggy Ashcroft and John Gielgud wore for the Shakespeare Memorial Theatre production in 1950. As we will see, newspaper reviews for later productions hark back to this one as containing an ideal version of Beatrice and Benedick's 'sparkling' wit. Part of the legend in the display case reveals that

> Actors John Gielgud and Peggy Ashcroft came together in a sparkling 1950 production of the play. One night, before a show, they drank champagne together and went on to give their best-ever performance.

The actors' decedent champagne-sipping, and their consummate professionalism despite this 'luvvy' naughtiness, maps nicely onto the play and onto characters of Beatrice and Benedick themselves, whose wit both challenges and upholds the values of the upper-class cultures in which production design situates them. Beatrice and Benedick wittily deny that anyone will capture their hearts, then prove the play's best example of the companionate marriage. The theatrical anecdote of Ashcroft and Gielgud is easily intertwined with the play's twentieth-century history, in which nostalgic scenographic and costume depictions of sunny summers in pretty frocks sit nicely with the idea of behind-the-scenes champagne sipping. A wistful longing for the past has been encoded into the performance of Beatrice's lines quoted at the opening of this chapter, a moment in which past, 'feminine' hurt is revealed beneath brittle sparkle. A number of historical settings for the play, as we will see, tap into nostalgic depictions of the past from the film and TV costume drama.

All this sparkling and witty prettiness might lead one to forget that the plot of *Much Ado About Nothing* turns on the violently misogynistic rejection of Hero on her wedding day. In what follows, I revisit a debate that will be familiar to scholars and students of film and television (see Higson 2003, 75–85), about whether the 'costume drama' is essentially a mere exercise in conservative nostalgia, or has something more critically reflective to offer its audience, particularly on the subject of gender. To cite Susan Bennett's seminal study of the collective, cultural nostalgias at work in Shakespeare production, I consider here whether, in productions of *Much Ado*, 'it might be possible to witness strategies of performing the past which demand of their actors as well as their reading/viewing publics an engagement which denies the inevitability of containment' (Bennett 1996, 13). *Much Ado* is a play that can be read as opening up critiques of and alternatives to heteronormativity, only to simply and successfully re-contain them in the final marriage scene. In what follows, I will be considering ways in which costume works for and against that containment. As Andrew Higson optimistically asserts in his exploration of the 'heritage film', a category frequently conflated with the term 'costume drama', '[Nostalgia] can of course be used to flee from the troubled present into the imaginary stability and grandeur of the past. But it can also be used to comment on the inadequacies of the present from a more radical perspective' (Higson 2003, 85). This chapter focuses particularly on what Michael Dobson has marked as a costuming trope in twentieth-century productions of this play: that of setting the play in historical periods between Shakespeare's and our own. Does costume efface the uncomfortable gender troubles of this play in production? Particularly in periods when film and TV dramas have been awash with colonialist fantasies of sunshine and white dresses, can nineteenth and early twentieth settings for *Much Ado* produce anything but a markedly conservative form of cultural longing? The production case studies in this chapter are of RSC productions from the company's inauguration in 1961, at which point, as we will see, reviewers were already reflecting back nostalgically on a golden age of Ashcroft and Gielgud. The chapter considers costume's relationship to nostalgia as a cultural trope, and the UK's largest Shakespeare production company's figurings of costume as a signifier of the past. It analyses costume as a producer of nostalgia and as a potential collaborator with the less conservative strategies and commentaries marked as at least a possibility by Bennett and Higson.

Democratising *Much Ado*?

1961: Desmond Heeley (Designer) and Michael Langham (Director)

Although the press did not make much of its inaugural status, the first production of Shakespeare performed at the newly named Royal Shakespeare Theatre in Stratford upon Avon in April 1961 was of *Much Ado About Nothing*; the play had also opened the Shakespeare Memorial Theatre in 1879. The 1961 version was directed by Michael Langham, and designed by Desmond Heeley, who set the play in the regency period, with military jackets and empire line dresses that will now be familiar to viewers of subsequent Jane Austen adaptations on British television. The TV 'costume drama', of which the Austen adaptation is a popular example, is an object of despairing contempt for some commentators, who regard these shows as central to moribund traditionalism and the hampering of innovation (Loach 2016; McClean 2007). But in 1961, a number of press critiques regarded Langham and Heely's choice of Regency costume as a disturbing modernisation and democratisation of a Shakespeare comedy. Several reviewers linked the RSC's costume design with a destruction of the play's poetry:

> It is set in the Regency period and it follows necessarily that the full music of the Poetry must be sacrificed and replaced by the brisk prose cadences of the Age of Reason. Less of necessity but very much in tune with this change, Beatrice descends a few steps in the social scale: she is no longer a great lady but a squire's daughter—a Kate Hardcastle let us say, but in the clothes and with much of the self-reliant comic sense of an Elizabeth Bennet. (*Daily Telegraph* 1961)

> I am unable to see any advantage in this idea, even though pictorially, Desmond Heeley's work is quite pretty. It does, however, in its prettiness, somehow diminish the play which is the effect also of Mr Langham's direction, at least in his scenes of light, farcical treatment, as opposed to high Shakespeare comedy. (*The Stage* 1961)

> Just because the men are in the uniforms of Wellington's men and the girls are in Jane Austen's dresses and the whole thing is clearly supposed to be the Age of Reason, is not an excuse for substituting prose cadences for the magic of Shakespeare. (*Bristol Evening Post* 1961)

Again, the *Daily Express* remarks of the 1961 production: "For the most part this is a prose Much Ado" (none of these mourners for Shakespearean poetry seem to be aware that this is a comedy written mainly in prose) before going on to reminisce about the glory days of Ashcroft and Gielgud in their stylised late medieval/early Italian Renaissance clothes. One review, in the *Birmingham Post*, does acknowledge the Victorian setting of a 1958 production at the SMT, but this is in order to rail at the un-Shakespearean nature of all post-Elizabethan settings:

> When we last met Much Ado About Nothing at Stratford it had been transferred to the modes of a century ago. Tonight we got as far back as the Regency. If this goes on, we may expect, with luck, to reach the Renaissance. That is where the comedy belongs. (*Birmingham Post* 1961)

For these reviewers, setting the play in the Regency period is concomitant with the loss of the play's status as high art, its class and its poetry, whereas Peggy Ashcroft in flowing late medieval gowns and dalmation sleeves, Jon Gielgud in a belted tunic and tights, supposedly produced a historicity and courtliness appropriate to Shakespeare's poetry and 'high' comedy. The reviews echo what Michael Dobson, in his lecture 'Shakespearean Comedy and the Curse of Realism' marks as Eric Auerbach's (2003) narrative of the 'fall into realism': the trajectory of disenchantment and downward mobility, as Dobson puts it, whereby literature descends from classical poets' tales of the gods and epic heroism, via medieval kings and knight errant, to Cervantes's comic realism and the supplanting of the chivalric by the bourgeois.

So far, so much 'restorative nostalgia', to cite Svetlana Boym, the theorist of nostalgia from whom I have quoted at the top of this chapter. Boym's work differentiates between the conservative cultural phenomenon of 'restorative nostalgia', which effaces its very nature as nostalgia and believes itself to be restoring something eternally true, and a more self-conscious, interrogatory 'reflective nostalgia', which embraces the contradictions inherent in longing for a lost or imaginary past and allows for critical engagement with that past even as the longing is experienced. These two forms of nostalgia can be read at the level of personally experienced nostalgia in the exchange between Don Pedro and Beatrice that also opens this chapter: Don Pedro asks that Beatrice indulge in a sentimental mourning for the loss of Benedick's heart, in which the value of that heart is unquestioned; the actor playing Beatrice may speak her reply as though she does indeed miss Benedick—but is also highly aware of the complexities and contradictions of her feelings. For the above reviewers of the RSC's opening production, costuming *Much Ado* in the early nineteenth century makes it inauthentically prosaic, and spoils an anticipated experience of high culture. The more properly elite aesthetics and tone are never explicitly defined but it is assumed that everyone will remember it with longing when they are not offered it; restorative nostalgia 'does not think of itself as nostalgia', as Boym puts it 'but rather as truth and tradition' (Boym 2001, xviii). In the *Birmingham Post* review, it is essential that some version of 'the Renaissance' in its broadest European sense is staged in order to fulfil high culture's demands for depictions of the past that offer stable and universal insights into the human condition. The *Telegraph* review, which links lack of poetry with a move down the social ladder for Beatrice, suggests that 'Renaissance' dress distances class in such a way as to universalise and deproblematise it: a Renaissance Beatrice is a 'great lady' of long ago; Beatrice as a 'squire's daughter' or a 'Kate Hardcastle' perhaps comes nearer to a social hierarchy that might be recognisable in the present-day environs of Stratford upon Avon. In the case studies that follow, I am going to use RSC costume designs for *Much Ado about Nothing* to open up Boym's questions of nostalgia for Shakespeare production. Boym's 'reflective nostalgia' is self-reflexive in its longings, whilst 'restorative nostalgia' values its imagined past in uncritical and absolute terms, of which the reviews above could almost be read as parodies. To borrow from Susan Bennett's monograph title, this chapter examines costume's role in 'performing nostalgia'.

COSTUMING NOSTALGIA

In research for this chapter, examining the material and documentary traces left by professional costume designers and makers has helped me not only to understand the process of costuming each production I consider here, but also has drawn me both viscerally and critically into the aesthetic pleasures of 'historical' costume design, pleasures which, as the aforementioned RSC exhibitions testify, are essential to the production of different kinds of pleasure and nostalgia in the theatre. Costume bibles, archived by the RSC, one of which is displayed in 'The Play's the Thing', offer practical documentation of every costume design in a production; they contain sketches of each costume, complete with stapled fabric samples and notes by designers, makers and supervisors; they chart every costume change. They are thus invaluable resources for piecing together what a production might have looked like, particularly where production photographs are solely or mainly in black and white, and where even quite recent video recordings fade and distort colour. The bibles' fabric samples also offer the visceral experience of fabric weight and texture, hinting at what it might feel like to wear a particular costume. Consider, for example, the fabric used to make the textured, 1950s, vivid green-flecked-with-black bathing suit worn by Hero in Mark Thompson's design for the languid opening scene of Di Trevis's *Much Ado* in 1988 and compare it with Hero's fuchsia ball gown for the masque in the same production, the shocking pink silk and magenta chiffon overlay of which feels thin, tacky and new between finger and thumb, but which swamps her in hyperfeminine sumptuosity on stage. The vivid, stretchy bathing-suit fabric spoke to me of fifties futurism and naive optimism, new luxuries and conveniences. It also pricked at my own personal nostalgia for an imagined '50s (imagined because I was born a decade later—but nostalgia is always an imaginative construct, of course), a time of relative modesty in beachwear and a feminine aesthetic which was literally a construction of fabric and elastic, rather than the result of a regimentation of the body by starvation diet. On the other hand, the fabric for Hero's enormous ball gown seemed intentionally inauthentic by comparison, a 1980s' pastiche of the 1950s. In the UK, as the music industry and Hollywood revived a number of 1950s' styles (see Dwyer 2015), the ball dress with its wide skirts and fitted bodice seemed also to reflect the mood of the more privileged of Thatcher's youth as they decided it was fun to dress up as figures from the past, wearing the hunting water-proofs on the streets of Chelsea or reviving the style of the debutante for the college dance.

Of course, the fabrics in the costume bibles have likely all been sourced from modern retailers and there is no reason to supposed that the bathing costume material was somehow more authentically '1950s' than the ball gown fabric; as we will see, the costume design for this production eclectically and consciously evoked Elizabethan, 1950s' and 1980s' shapes to comment on history, class and culture. But the costume bible permits a closeness to the material detail of design and fabric and has provoked me to ask questions about how particular effects of gender, the past, and beauty—all key to the multiple nostalgias of the 'costume drama'—have been created and to what purpose. Here is an example from the costume bible notes to Hero's ball gown in the Trevis/Thompson *Much Ado*:

> shocking pint silk-satin dress with light magenta chiffon overlay; Black velvet ribbon and hem and velvet band round strapless bodice and gloves. Black emb[roidered] decoration on CF bodice pannel [sic] + jet drops—CF skirt split to point with under-skirt (separate) of bark-pleated dk. grey organza with CF panel of fine gold thread emb. organza spotted with diamond faceted brilliants—pointed hem and jet drops—floor length under petticoat to floor length of nylon organza with marcasite frills. (*Much Ado About Nothing* des. Mark Thompson, 1988, costume bible, RSC archive)

In the costume archive, reading this detail, touching this fabric, looking at the costume sketches, I am at once in a place of visceral delight and critical interest; my personal desires for clothing and the past are both evoked and productively set at a critical distance. Boym writes, of reflective nostalgia:

> Re-flection suggests new flexibility, not the reestablishment of stasis. The focus here is not on recovery of what is perceived to be an absolute truth but

on the meditation on history and the passage of time. To paraphrase Nabokov, these kind of nostalgics are often "amateurs of Time, epicures of duration", who resist the pressure of external efficiency and take sensual delight in the texture of time not measurable by clocks and calendars. (Boym 2001, 49)

My experience of the costume archive fits this definition. Thumbing a piece of silk from Hero's ball gown might seem like a guilty pleasure, an apolitical indulgence. But it has allowed me to reflect flexibly, to meditate on what the material culture of a performance meant in its historical moment and might mean to readers of this book now; it has allowed me, I hope, to think better about how we might enjoy performances of the past critically. As I have suggested in the Introduction to this volume (above 5–10), this examination of the material culture of costuming has facilitated the cultural materialist theatre criticism that follows.

The RSC productions I examine next have set the play in historical periods other than Shakespeare's from the RSC's founding in 1961. I examine them in pairs that share period and aesthetic resonances rather than offering a chronological account. This is in order to reveal, on the one hand, how costume designs which draw on the same period aesthetic can produce radically different performances of the past, and, on the other, how costume design can evoke and produce quasi-universal ideas and assumptions about represented time. I focus on the much-celebrated 1976 production directed by John Barton and designed by John Napier, starring Judi Dench as Beatrice and Donald Sinden as Benedick, set in India under British rule; in relation to this, I segue into the play's modern Indian of 2012, directed by Iqbal Khan and designed by Himani Dehlvi and Tom Piper. Next, I examine two Carolinian-styled productions, Terry Hands and Ralph Koltai's of 1982 and Bill Alexander and Kitt Surrey's from 1990, followed by two 1950s-inflected *Much Ados*, the aforementioned Di Trevis and Mark Thompson production from 1988, and the more recent version directed by Marianne Elliot and designed by Lez Brotherston, set in 1950s' Cuba, first performed at the Swan in Stratford in 2006. Lastly, I consider the detailed Southern Italian setting of Greg Doran and Stephen Brimson Lewis's 2002 production, and Luscombe and Higget's Downton Abbey-inflected *Much Ado*, first publicised as *Love's Labour's Won*. This last is the most recent RSC production of the play at the time of writing; it opened in 2014 and its design and tone bear comparison to the company's more recent *Twelfth Night* by the same director and designer. Some of these productions have used costumes to draw attention to their own constructions of the past, some signal that, as we sit in the theatre, we are being offered a transparent window onto that past. But although I draw a broad distinction here between realist and stylised costume, the contradictory pull between longing and critique that makes up Boym's notion of reflective nostalgia is present in both.[1]

The British in/and India

1976: John Napier (Designer), John Barton (Director)

2012: Himani Dehlvi (Costume Designer), Tom Piper (Designer), Iqbal Khan (Director)
Much has been said in recent journalism and scholarship about a nostalgia for an imagined and essentially conservative England underpinning cultural phenomena from royal weddings to television cookery shows (see, for example, Whyman 2017) and much late twentieth century and more recent analysis of racism points to the ongoing presence of imperialist histories attitudes and values in British culture (see for example Stuart Hall 1978; Paul Gilroy 1987; Gargi Bhattacharyya 2018). The idea that a socially experienced nostalgia is essential to the reception of cultural products including the 'costume drama' is key to my argument here. In the next section of this chapter, I analyse a production of *Much Ado About Nothing* which might seem to prefigure the 1980s' and 1990s' TV and film obsession with the British 'Raj', an obsession which, as Andrew Higson suggests in his analysis of the 'heritage film', was repeatedly in danger of prettifying the history of imperialism with gloriously shot scenery and lovely white dresses on lovely white people. Here is Higson on the adaptation of novels to 'heritage' films:

> It is important to recognize...that the novels ...which provide the sources for many of these films, have some edge to them of satire or ironic social critique, and the films in various ways try to reproduce this sensibility. But it

---

[1] The exploration of some of these productions of *Much Ado About Nothing* in terms of cultural nostalgia has been developed from Bridget Escolme's (2018) 'Brexit Dreams: Comedy, Nostalgia, and Critique in *Much Ado About Nothing* and *A Midsummer Night's Dream*' in Hirschfeld, Heather [ed], *The Oxford Handbook of Shakespearean Comedy*. Some of the citations used have been reprinted here.

seems equally clear that it is the pictorial qualities of the exotic period settings which have attracted the film makers as much as the moral critiques implicit in their problematic often becomes prettified, elegant and seductive in the films. (Higson 2003, 80)

John Barton and John Napier's 1976 *Much Ado about Nothing* was set in British-ruled India and could be seen as prefiguring both the film industry's obsession with films about the 'Raj' and a host of prettily nostalgic *Much Ado*s. But I am going to argue here that the production and the relationship it staged between costume, nostalgia and imperialism was a complex one, reflective as well as restorative, despite its now unacceptable 'blacking up' of white actors to play an Indian Dogberry and Watchmen.

Iqbal Khan, Himani Dehlvi and Tom Piper's *Much Ado* was set in present-day India. Indian costume designer Dehlvi was asked to join the design team by Khan and Piper when they met her on a research trip to Delhi; the two British theatre practitioners realised that they did not have the cultural reference points to create detailed references to modern Indian class and gender through costume; Dehlvi's work ensured that the costumes represented contemporary urban Indian class structures and style. The production was criticised for using its all-British Asian cast to set the play in Delhi. Claire Cochrane argues that it problematically homogenised a cast with diverse histories and backgrounds (Cochrane 2016, 61–4). For Kevin Quarmby (2012) the production features 'apparently second generation British actors pretending to return to their cultural roots in a decidedly colonial way' and he argues that it did 'little other than cement the comedy caricature of India in the British psyche'. Kathryn Prince compares her experience of watching the British Asian actors' comic portrayal of the Indian watch with the 'queasiness' of contemplating Barton's blacked-up actors (Prince 2018, 60). The critiques are well-made, but I suggest that they also reflect a cultural issue of representation, whereby performers of colour are expected to act as political representatives of their own ethnicity and culture, whilst white people are left to be individuals who can pretend to be whomsoever they choose within contemporary boundaries of cultural taste. Accounts of the Dehlvi/Khan/Piper production criticised the fact that the Asian actors on stage are British (in Stratford) but are pretending to be Indian (in Delhi), whereas no-one seems disturbed by white British actors pretending to be Italians in Messina (or Cubans in Cuba, as we will see). The play's action takes place in Messina but meditates on issues pertinent to Shakespeare's England and I agree with Varsha Panjwani's argument that 'Khan's decision is no more or less contentious than Shakespeare's, who set the play in Messina even as English actors performed the parts' (Panjwani 2017, 97). This production was set in Delhi but, I suggest (as does Panjwani, and one of the production's leading performers below 100), that it allowed for a meditation on issues that are current for the British Asian community, many of whom may themselves have a complex relationship to the styles and fashions of their own heritage. This *Much Ado* differs from the other stage productions in this chapter in that it was set in the twenty-first century present rather than in a period between Shakespeare's and our own, like all of the others I examine. I touch on it here because it suggests ways in which the clothing of the present might produce and critique the nostalgic tropes of *Much Ado* in recent production.

I begin with the Barton/Napier production and a reading of Judy Dench's costume as Beatrice. In his study of three 'Shakespearean' actresses, Sarah Siddons, Ellen Terry and Judi Dench, Russ McDonald remarks on Dench's introverted melancholy in the role of Beatrice in the Barton/Napier production:

> Playing against Sinden's extroverted style, his natural tendency to woo the audience, Dench made her Beatrice an introvert, shy and unglamorous. She looked decidedly plain, wearing an apron and a babushka, as if this Beatrice wouldn't waste her time attending to her physical appearance...[W]here Terry had been glowing and impishly witty, Dench appeared spinsterish, reserved and obviously insecure. This initial reticence magnified the effect of her confession of love. (McDonald 2005, 134–5)

Whilst the archiving of film recordings of RSC productions had not yet begun in 1976, a clear sound recording of this *Much Ado* is accessible from the British Library; listening to it, the description of Dench's Beatrice as 'shy' and 'reserved' are understandable, but this is not how Dench sounds in the role overall. She was certainly a highly emotionally legible Beatrice, confident enough in her interpretation of the role to 'glow' less and emote more than audiences might have become accustomed to. Lines such as 'I know you of old' (1.1.98) at the end of her opening exchange with Benedick, 'I may sit in a corner and cry heigh-ho for a husband!' in 2.1 (221), and in the same scene, responding to Don Pedro's exclamation that she was born in a merry hour—'No, sure, my lord, my mother cried' (2.1.232)—are all spoken softly, wistfully and in this third case very seriously, as if Beatrice is speaking of women's histories of oppression as well as her own backstory. The delivery of her explanation to Don Pedro of Benedick's past treatment of her heart is positively Chekhovian—'marry, once before he won it of me with false dice' (2.1.193) is spoken with great sadness, then 'therefore your grace may well say I have lost it' (194) is uttered as though laughing through tears. But overall her vocal performance is wry and assertive, a tone encapsulated in the exclamation she adds to the play text after Don Pedro has announced the length of his and his followers' stay: 'A Month! Eurgh!' she cries, openly aghast.

Thus, Dench's was a highly realist Beatrice with an emotional past that she emphasised on chosen lines. Her present was marked by her costume as tough work (the apron and babushka mentioned by McDonald); her past, as her wistfully nostalgic delivery suggested, might have led to a quite different present. The women in the production wore high-necked blouses or overdresses and sturdy, un-crinolined, un-bustled skirts suggesting the late Victorian or Edwardian 'Raj'—but also, in their lack of tight-laced corsetry, the fact of domestic work. The production photographs recall the effort it must take to keep the white clothes, worn for Hero's wedding, white in hot weather. What exactly is Beatrice's unmarried woman's status and role in this society, the production seemed to ask? Beatrice, in her apron and headscarf, as an unmarried orphan, appeared to be bearing as much of the brunt of at least the white woman's domestic labour as anyone lower down the social scale (it was the working men in this production that were figured as Indian). What is she being asked to do when she is told by her uncle to 'look to those things I told you of' (2.1.234)? Reviewing the production in the *Educational Theatre Journal*, Carol L Thompson writes:

> Stage furnishings of *Much Ado about Nothing* were stylish and light. Gauzy awnings, rattan furniture, ribboned nosegays, and straw hats combined to evoke a tropical climate. The costumes, particularly in the delicate textures of the white dresses, contributed to the sense of a style of life where there is time for the care and protection of material elegance. (Thompson 1977, 121)

But Dench's plain linen working overdress and apron suggested that Beatrice herself partakes in the time and care taken to produce Hero's beautiful white wedding.

Dench read as the Anne Elliot of this *Much Ado*, although her more comical, assertive lines of dialogue make her a great deal ruder than the heroine of Jane Austen's *Persuasion*. I make this comparison not only because Anne is a heroine who has a past with a returning member of the military but also because Dench as Beatrice produced a strong effect of authenticity in the superficial social world of *Much Ado*; like Anne in the fashionable world of Regency Bath, Dench's Beatrice stands out against a world concerned with mere appearances and 'fashion'. In his article 'Queer Temporality, Spatiality and Memory in Jane Austen's *Persuasion*', Edward Kozaczka (2009) argues that Anne Elliot's melancholy determination to look back at her past love and use it to find a way to find her own pleasure and happiness, rather than look forward to replacing her mother in the Elliot fortune and marrying a man she does not love for money and position, is an example of a queer temporality which she is finally able to share with Captain Wentworth. Kozaczka's concept of queer temporality is comparable to Boym's reflective nostalgia. Although the ultimate heterosexual and economic normativity of the relationship between Anne and Captain Wentworth stretches the limit of what one might plausibly call queer (Wentworth is ultimately accepted by the Elliot family as a marriage partner for Anne not least because he has eventually made his fortune at sea), Kozaczka's argument reinforces my notion of Dench's Beatrice as a carefully drawn, reflectively nostalgic Anne Elliot figure. Her wry wistfulness worked against the determined upper-class English jollity of Derek Jacobi's Benedick; the couple's past is repressed by him, reinvoked by her. The against-the-grain melancholy of Dench's Beatrice set her doubly against her culture: Beatrice is not only a determinedly unmarried woman until the very end of the play, but feels authentically where others are superficial, and enabled in their unfeeling treatment of others, by their positions in the power structures they dominate.

Dench's Beatrice created a wry, wearily knowing, sometimes melancholic centre for the frivolous, spiteful action of the play. As Russell Jackson suggests, she did not let the costumes of the late nineteenth/early twentieth century turn her into a pretty piece of a nostalgic *mise en scene*. Like Amanda Root in the 1995 BBC television adaptation of *Persuasion*, she looked determinedly plain in period dress, until she arrived at Hero's wedding in delicately embroidered white. This sartorial construction of femininity was ultimately critiqued by the speech in which she demands that Benedick kill Claudio: dressed beautifully, she cannot act.

In photographs of the production, when the women's white blouses and skirts and the men's white trousers and jackets glare in the hot light and shine against the natural wood of the set and wicker of the furniture, one recalls that a decade later, a seemingly endless parade of beautiful white clothes would be shown off to best advantage in Indian surround-ings, in film and television series about the 'Raj'. Does this *Much Ado* prefigure this nostalgic obsession with British imperialism? The review of the production in *Punch* magazine recalled Noel Coward's musical joke about mad dogs and Englishmen:

> the timbered balconies of John Napier's permanent Stratford setting, used last week for the declaration of Juliet's love, now become places to hang awnings and sun-shades out in the midday sun. (Morley 1976)

But this is a less glamorously aestheticised Raj than the film and TV ver-sions to which audiences would later become habituated less than a decade later by films such as Merchant Ivory's *Heat and Dust* (1983), David Lean's *Passage to India* (1984) and TV series such as *The Far Pavilions* (1984) and *The Jewel in the Crown* (1984). I contend that this production managed, in its moment, to trouble its own tendencies towards nostalgia and the prob-lem of the 'heritage film' outlined by Andrew Higson, whereby 'that which in the source narratives is abhorrent or problematic often becomes petti-fied, elegant and seductive in the films' (Higson 2003, 80). In Dench's melancholy and hard-working Beatrice, this production staged a woman who gently critiques the heteronormativity of her culture as it appears in the white lace garb she wears for Hero's wedding. Until the wedding scene, the women's costumes for most of the production are relatively drab and work-aday and the wooden set makes this 'Raj' Messina look like a small settle-ment, for whom a visit from Don Pedro and company is a huge amount of work, rather than a centre of imperial government.

The problem with finding this retrospective subversion of a later, romanticised colonialist aesthetic in Barton's *Much Ado* is that Judi Dench has now become a National Treasure, much to her own wry dismay (Dench 2009), whilst Donald Sinden's acting style seems particularly con-servative now, though it was undermined and made strange by Dench's psychologically complex Beatrice at the time. This production may now have faded into a generalised, nostalgic picture of an RSC golden age. Judi Dench and Donald Sinden as Beatrice and Benedick feature in the *Daily Telegraph*'s Top Ten Beatrice and Benedicks, flanked by Giulgud and Ashcroft, Howard and Suzman, Cusack and Jacobi (*Telegraph* 2013). In 2014, Michael Billington also describes the 1976 production as one of his top two *Much Ados* (Billington 2014) paired with Kenneth Brannagh's film, an archetypal piece, I will argue, of restorative nostalgia. Production photographs of the 1976 *Much Ado* offer snapshots of white people in white costumes, comical minor characters played by white people in brown stage make-up as Indians in white turbans, set against raw wood and white fabric. It is now difficult to establish how challenging the performances, particularly Dench's might have been. Furthermore, though I am suggesting that this production did not have the conservative, nostalgic tone that accumulated over later years of costume-drama preoccupation with colonialism, a white-costume-against-bare-wood version of *Much Ado* has recurred to the present day, to the point where I suggest it inevitably evokes colonialism, even where costumes are not Victorian/Edwardian. Of course, in many productions the glare of the sun against white costumes is presumably supposed to signify the Mediterranean heat of the play's Messina. But the essential Englishness of this look became a colonialist one in the 1980s and 1990s after 'Raj fever' hit cinema and television screens, and the nostalgia for English summers has come to recall the colonialist's nostalgia for home. Judi Dench's own 'Empire Line' white dress, circa-1805 production of *Much Ado*, Elijah Moskinski's 1989 production for the RSC, and Cheek by Jowl's 1998 version all feature creamy white dresses; even the Elizabethan and eighteenth-century mix of Mark Thompson's designs for Triumph Theatre in 1989 turns on the White Heat of India against, once again, bare natural wood.

What exacerbates, with hindsight, the sense that the 1976 production is one of a long line of colonially inflected *Much Ado*s is the 'blacked up' figures who represent the Watch; they look and sound disturbingly like the 'Indian' characters in the BBC sitcom *It Ain't Half Hot Mum*, which ran from 1974 to 1981. John Woodvine's Dogberry, particularly, is reminiscent of Michael Bates as the army Bearer, Rangi Ram. Woodvine spoke lines such as 'Those who touch pitch will be defiled' (3.3.38–9) with the solemnity of old saws, rather like Bates's repeated offerings of 'old Hindu proverbs' at the end of each episode of the sitcom. Dogberry's heartfelt 'God Save the Foundation!' recalls the TV 'Indian's references to 'we British', a key difference being that Dogberry's lines seemed to render him uncritically supportive of his white imperialist superiors, whereas the sitcom character's national loyalties shift from native land to colonial power according to his own interests. There was some debate in reviews of the play as to whether Woodvine's Dogberry was sympathetic or offensive; it is certainly difficult to listen to his laboured 'Indian' accent now. Herb Weil's defence of the production, written from the vantage point of 2007, ironically reads like a much older piece of writing than Harold Hobson's contemporary analysis of the degradation of an Asian figure 'wildly applauded by the frustrated Imperialist audience' (Hobson in Weil 2007, 178).

Of course, it was not Woodvine's fault that Shakespeare likes to make unremittingly snobbish jokes about social pretension, and re-listening to the sound recording of this production, it recalls in its performance of ethnicity/nation/race[2] how easily we are invited by the play to laugh at social class in the more common cases where casting does not make race an issue in this play. Perhaps just as troubling as the 'blacked-up' Watch— this time, I assume, intentionally troubling—was the way in which race was marked in the second wedding scene of this *Much Ado*. At other points in the production, colonialism was critically recalled by a musical score that occasionally had Indian-sounding pipe and drum music drowned out by the sounds of an English concert band. For the entrance of the veiled women in the second wedding scene, that 'Indian' music could be heard, and before Hero revealed herself from beneath her swathe of black fabric, she spoke her lines in yet another cod Indian accent, implying that Claudio thinks he is about to be punished for the shaming and death of Hero by being forced to marry an Indian woman. In the space of the two lines spoken before Hero unveils—'And when I lived, I was your other wife:/ And when you loved, you were my other husband' (5.4.60–61)—a palimpsest of racist, colonialist attitudes are unnervingly staged. In this moment, Leonato's brother, whose daughter Claudio thinks he has agreed to marry, must be assumed to have had sex with an Indian woman to produce this niece, and in the same moment, marrying her is presented as Claudio's punishment and means of mitigating the dishonour he has done Hero. He says he will marry Leonato's niece 'were she an Ethiope', then her accent leads him to believe he is being presented with a different woman of colour.

The black fabric in which the women presented to Claudio were swathed did not seem to suggest anything particularly specific in terms of race or religion. It would be odd if they had been meant to read as a Muslim burqa; they do not look as if they are shaped as such, and the

---

[2] I use all of these terms here not because I think they are interchangeable but because the 'Indian' accent, gestural vocabularies and costumes used for Dogberry and the Watch here, and the fact that these seem to be explicitly laughed at in the performance, seem to me to draw on ethnicity, race and nationality: on the one hand there were elements of stereotype in the performances, both ethnic and racial; on the other hand, aspects of the performances were detailed in such a way as to suggest the action was taking place in a particular part of a specific country.

other 'Indians' in the production are dressed in painstakingly realist detail as local men, their turbans suggesting we are in the Sikh-dominated part of the pre-partition Punjab. *Much Ado*'s second wedding, then, was presented as a theatrical construct, with a fragment of disturbing social realism inserted before its happy ending, a happy ending dependent on a swerve away from miscegenation. Uncomfortable issues of race and colonialism here served also to highlight the uncomfortable issues of class and gender that a theatrical determination to read *Much Ado* as witty, sunny and sparkling always seem finally to efface.

At the time of writing, the RSC has produced one other *Much Ado* set in India: Iqbal Khan's production set in Delhi, part of the RSC's contribution to the Cultural Olympiad's World Shakespeare Festival in 2010. The production is an anomaly in this chapter, in that it is not set in a period between Shakespeare's and our own. The production's Delhi was the Delhi of the twenty-first century, its contemporaneity inspired by Khan's own reluctance to 'comment on colonial rule' through the play, or create an exoticised fantasy of India (Khan in RSC 'Iqbal Khan 2012 Production'). But I discuss it here because this *Much Ado*'s ambivalent relationship to the extravagant exuberance of Bollywood complicates and extends the analysis of the tension between the play's violent central incident and its happy ending and relates it to a different 'costume drama' from the other productions considered in this chapter. It offers ways in to considering how a 'modern dress' Shakespeare production might reflect on the nostalgias of performing the past.

Much Ado in RSC 'period' costume is largely a white affair, its ethnic and cultural whiteness heightened at the RSC in the 1970s by white actors 'blacked up' as Indians in the Barton/Napier production, and that production's prefiguration of the lovely white dresses of white colonialists in the Raj costume film. Khan's production cast an entirely British Asian ensemble and RSC associate designer Tom Piper worked with Indian costume designer Himani Dehlvi to produce the look of the piece: a hectic recreation of a Delhi street environment for the foyer, the calmer courtyard of Leonato's 'heveli' for the stage and auditorium (Piper, in 'Iqbal Khan 2012 Production: Videos'). Dehlvi was asked to join the design team when Piper and Khan visited Delhi on a research trip and suggests in an interview that *Much Ado* enables a plausible and complex way into an exploration of aspects of Indian culture today (Dehlvi, in 'Iqbal Khan 2012 Production: Videos'). Actress Meera Syal who played Beatrice agreed. As Sita Thomas relates:

> [Leonato's] violent rejection of his daughter—"Hence from her, let her die" (act 4, scene 1, line 154)—was read widely by reviewers as a threatened honor killing. The contemporary relevance of this scene heightened the impact of the setting for Syal, who is a patron of the Newham Asian Women's Project, which funds refuges for woman escaping violent marriages. (Thomas 2017, 571)

Of course, for white British audience members at Stratford upon Avon, the contemporary Indian setting might simply have served to alienate the misogynistic culture depicted in the play in a similar way to a period setting, and as I have suggested in the previous chapter, using distinct national and cultural settings like this can 'other' the culture depicted by association with 400-year-old cultural tropes and values (above 64). However, Varsha Panjwani's subtle analysis of the production suggests that by setting *Much Ado* in contemporary India, Khan's version 'challenge[d] long-standing orthodoxies in the representation of British-Asian marriage practices' (Panjwani 2017, 96–7), troubling the range of Indian films and British assumptions that she suggests have stereotyped Asian cultures by conflating arranged and forced marriage. The director and actors whose accounts of the production are in the public domain certainly seem happy to link contemporary India and Elizabethan England. In an interview with Nosheen Iqbal in *The Guardian* Iqbal explains:

> I initially resisted the idea of doing something exotic [...] But the more seriously I thought about the themes of the play—chastity and pure blood lines, the rituals of courtship, the arrangements of marriage—I realised all of those things are incredibly vital in India. How does this sit with the country's attempts to rebrand itself as an aspiring superpower? Delhi is about as Elizabethan a place as you could find in the modern-day world. (Khan, in Iqbal 2012)

More significant, though, for my exploration of costume here, is the equally inevitable association of a play containing a complex love plot, marriage negotiations, wedding scenes, and South Asian performers in large-scale song and dance routines, with the romance of Bollywood. For Sita Thomas, it is the RSC's publicity materials that encouraged critics to connect the production with the products of the Indian popular film industry, and she argues that these 'misrepresented Khan's vision for the production; he was keen to avoid the commercialism of Bollywood and aimed to represent a contemporary slice of Delhi culture' (Thomas 2017, 481). Accordingly, in her review of the production, she reads the costumes here as pure social realism:

Beatrice's clothes reflected contemporary Delhi fashion—a stylishly cut suit jacket, pencil skirt, and shiny red heels. In these shoes, Beatrice trod the unstable metaphorical line between this construction of feminine modernity and an adherence to socially ingrained gender hierarchies. (Thomas 2015, 571)

Thomas's point here is supported by the playfully gendered costumes of the masked ball of the play, in which the women are disguised with sun glasses and clothes borrowed from the play's war, the men with women's headscarves. Beatrice's brilliant blue dress here is accompanied by one of men's camouflage flak jackets and blue UN peacekeeper beret. The fact that she can try on a man's clothes here serves to underline the limits of gender equality in the play when we come to the 'Kill Claudio' moment. At Hero's ill-fated nuptials Meera Syal's Beatrice is dressed as a modern female Hindu wedding guest and adorned with the flower garland that both genders wear at the ceremony, a sign of mutual celebration that of course contrasts starkly with the misogynistic rejection of the bride during the scene. However, it is interesting to note that in her online interview for the production Syal herself laughingly remarks 'It's like a Bollywood plot, it totally is' (Syal in 'Iqbal Khan 2012 Production: Videos'). I want to take Syal's assertion seriously and suggest that this production's inevitable association with popular film enables it to work with the play's 'happy ending' in a way that is more productively self-conscious and playful than many others.

The ornate red sari worn by the bride at a Hindu wedding is a focus for the spectacular Bollywood fantasy version of the same—and the Bollywood version has recently inflected the styles chosen by many couples for their wedding. As Jyotsna Kapur explains:

> Whether made in India or abroad, the big fat Bollywood wedding has become a trademark attraction of contemporary Indian culture. A trend started by films such as *Hum Apke Hain Kaun/Can You Name Our Relationship?* (Sooraj Barjatya 1995) *Dilwale Dulhaniya Le Jayenge/Those With Heart Will Take the Bride* (Aditya Chopra 1995), the trend has migrated internationally via films such as Mira Nair's *Monsoon Wedding* (2001) and Gurinder Chadha's *Bride and Prejudice* (2004). In turn, real weddings have become increasingly spectacular egged on by a newly emerged wedding industry into which the Bollywood form has seamlessly merged. (Kapur 2009, 221)

Celebrated Indian Fashion designer Masaba Gupta confirms this connection with an anecdote in which she was given a 'frantic call' by some of her cousins to enlist her help in finding and buying the actual costumes from a recent film for a family wedding (Gupta 2016). Thus one might argue that it is not only that the RSC's 2012 Much Ado had 'somewhat Bollywood textures', as the *Evening Standard* (2012) has it: Indian weddings themselves sometimes do, too.

An on-stage version of the contemporary Hindu wedding at the RSC's then temporary space the Courtyard Theatre was inevitably smaller scale than the screen version, but the combination of magnificent wedding garb and the song and dance that set up Hero's disastrous wedding read as straight from the cinema and served to stage both Bollywood and Shakespeare critically. Kapur makes clear that when she writes about Bollywood, she uses the term:

> specifically to describe a particular genre of glossy "family-centered feel-good films centered on romantic stories" which emerged in the 1990s and crossed over into North America and the UK to become the cultural icons of a globalizing India...
>
> Promoted by both the Indian government and business, its basic commodity/brand is a playful postmodern reinvention of "Indian culture" as an extravaganza of consumer culture often built upon certain familiar Orientalist or nostalgic tropes. (Kapur 2009, 222)

In one sense, this production of *Much Ado* could, too, be described as 'feel-good', its wedding scene 'a playful postmodern reinvention of "Indian culture" as an extravaganza of consumer culture'. But I want to suggest that Himani Dehlvi's costumes for *Much Ado* work with casting and scenography to highlight a society self-consciously staging its own traditions in multiple ways: performers with South Asian heritage were performing Shakespeare, a writer that would have been part of their parents' or grandparents' colonial education; they staged dance routines and a plot that recalled Bollywood; they engaged with a narrative of arranged marriage and a treatment of Hero that recalled the phenomenon of honour killing. One could argue that the Bollywood references served to erase the painful centre of *Much Ado*'s plot with popular film glamour, just as white Victorian/Edwardian costumes are in danger of conjuring an English colonialist fantasy from the play. However, I suggest that the cultural specificity and contemporary references of the costumes and broader design for this production made for a challenging and interrogatory version of *Much Ado* for all but the white audience members most determined to dismiss the production as outside of their experience. The contrast between the contemporary and the traditional in the modern Indian costuming heightened the tensions between individual desires and gendered norms and conventions implicit in the play, inviting a comparison with how these tensions work across cultures.

Cavalier Much Ados: 1982: Terry Hands (Director), Alexander Reid (Costumes), Ralph Koltai (Designer). 1990: Bill Alexander (Director), Kitt Surrey (Designer)

Read the RSC costume bible description of Claudio's wedding outfit and look at archived photos of the same and it seems clear that Alexander Reid's costumes for the RSC's 'Cavalier' Much Ado of 1982 were deliberately foregrounding the vanity of the 'princes and counties' (4.2.307) who are entirely motivated by fashion and appearance. Here are Claudio's costume notes, for the wedding scene:

> Claudio: Trousers. White satin silk. Below knee length worn over boots.
> Jacket. White satin silk. Fitted jacket just below waist length with splits. Long sleeves with splits. Jacket trimmed with white lace, white silver bows and silver points. Stand collar with organdie and lace...lace cuffs. White rosettes with silver points. Cavalier hat; rosettes on shoes.

In comparison to this 'Count Confect' get-up, to borrow from Beatrice again, Hero's gown was indeed the 'fine, quaint, graceful' one of Margaret's description, despite the fact that the underskirt was made of a fabric that glistened under lights in a way that made it look suspiciously like the Duchess of Milan's 'tinsel' (3.4.15). From the first entrance of Don Pedro's men, in lace-cuffed breeches, shoes with huge orange and pink rosettes, and voluminous cloaks which were draped and hooked for a greater effect of conspicuous consumption, the men in this production cut more extravagant figures than the women, whose wide, slub-silk skirts reflected pleasingly in Ralph Koltai's shining floor but who seemed happy to let the men dominate when it came to performances of fashion. Actor Derek Jacobi describes 'these very frilly costumes, rather baroque, with high heels' (Dickson 2016). When his Benedick entered after being gulled into loving Beatrice, the orange silks, rosettes and ribbons he sported for the scene read as an only slightly exaggerated version of his friends' habitual drapes and flounces, rather than something they might legitimately scoff at. They wore dressing gowns for this scene, creating the impression that Benedick has been up for some time choosing his outfit—but this might have been a decision made in order to avoid unfortunate comparisons.

Look at the recording of the production—one of the earliest archived RSC video recordings—and the showing off and showing up of these men in their Cavalier fancy dress reads less critically of the Cavaliers than in archived photographs and costume documentation. I suggest that this is because whilst all of the dialogue seems very slow and carefully pronounced by current standards of Shakespeare performance in the UK, so that the voices of the upper-class characters seem grand to the point of parody, Jacobi as Benedick has rather more relaxed comic timing and a self-ironising relationship with the audience than Sinéad Cusack's Beatrice. It is curious to watch the recording of the production and compare it to Jacobi's account of how the production saved him from a bout of stage fright:

> I was cast opposite Sinéad Cusack, who has this wonderful Irish fire; you have to be on your mettle playing against her. Rehearsals were wonderful— the dialogue between Beatrice and Benedick is so much fun to play. There are huge reserves of energy there: they just keep on chattering away, sparking off each other. It's almost like they're having sex, but verbally. We went for the laughs, quite shamelessly. Laughs and romance. (Jacobi in Dickson 2016)

Jacobi's account suggests a real theatrical equality in rehearsal, but though Beatrice may have looked less ludicrously showy than the surrounding Princes and Counties, her slow, precise diction and rounded vowels in the archived recording suggest that as late as 1982, the women on this stage were meant to look attractive in their Caroline finery here, not ludicrous; when teased, they were rendered vulnerable, not combative or self-ironising. Today, Cusack would perhaps have been encouraged to use her own accent on an English stage and I wonder if what Jacobi experienced as 'wonderful Irish fire' (Jacobi in Dickson 2016) came across more in rehearsal than performance.

It is interesting that one of the few audience laughs in the archived recording of the women's wedding preparation scene was at the following moment of costume business: Margaret's innuendos about marriage, her tactless remarks about the Duchess of Milan's early modern couture, and the teasing of Beatrice about 'cardus benedictus' (3.4.49) move slowly and solemnly in this production, with little vocal audience response evidenced in the recording. However, when it is announced that Claudio, Don Pedro and all the gallants have come to fetch Hero to church, Cusack's Beatrice instantly shrugs off her bad cold along with the warming shawl she has been huddled in and whips out a large, feathered, cavalier-style hat from under the shawl, which she has evidently been concealing to wear for the wedding. At this there is a resounding guffaw from the auditorium, suggesting the audience's relief that they now have something to laugh at. The fact that Beatrice is so blatantly faking a cold when she actually cares as much as the next woman about weddings and finery is the object of the laughter. She does not seem to get much opportunity to be its subject in collusion with the audience, as Benedick does despite his predilection for Cavalier sartorial excesses; she rather seems obliged to present herself before the audience in a series of beautiful, silken, wide-skirted frocks.

The set for the 1982 *Much Ado*, which comprised a reflective metallic floor in warm, coppery tones, and a dark, painted tree, recalled a beautiful story-book illustration. It had no overt social connotations; it reflected the cast back at themselves, highlighting again, perhaps, the vanity of the men, but it was primarily striking for its abstract loveliness. No-one in the recorded performance seems particularly constrained by it, despite the apparent difficulty of moving across it discussed by Jacobi (Dickson 2016), as they did by the topiary hedges that dominated the set of the RSC's next Caroline-styled production, in 1990, directed by Bill Alexander, with design and costumes by Kitt Surrey. This, too, was a beautiful design, against whose green hedges the RSC's second set of Cavalier costumes was pleasantly set off. The topiary here gave an instant impression of nature tamed and of a possible maze stretching out behind the action. This was a space in which hierarchy and convention might be playfully challenged and romantic entanglements laughed at—but it served to remind the audience that the maze of the play's plot will finally reinscribe the likes of Beatrice and Benedick within society's boundaries, and bring us laughingly back to the norms of marriage. Clothing in this production was not the object of satire; costumes were 'period' in a historical realist style now familiar to RSC audiences: authentic-looking but adapted to modern tastes for the beautiful yet subtle.

Susan Fleetwood's Beatrice opened this production with a bout of fencing in her lovely Caroline frock; every bout of verbal fencing she won with Benedick (Roger Allam) was roundly cheered by her female friends.

Her first line to Benedick—'I wonder you will still be talking Signor Benedick, nobody marks you' (1.1.79–80)—was more obviously set up for a laugh against Benedick than is usual in modern production: just after she uttered it, one of his soldier friends had just conspicuously failed to mark him, wandering off rather rudely during his previous line. In this production, masculine self-importance was the object of laughter; costumes were rather a more serious issue. By 1990, performances of femininity seemed to have changed more radically than might have been expected over the mere eight years between this and the 1982 pastiche Caroline *Much Ado*. Fleetwood's was a clearly feminist Beatrice who raised her fencing foil over her head in triumph and strutted back to her female friends on 'you always end with a jade's trick, I know you of old' (1.1.98), rather than speaking that line as though Beatrice had run out of quips, as has frequently been the reading. She spoke her comic lines with the wry knowingness that the 1982 production permitted only to Benedick. Costuming signalled historicity rather than pastiche in this production, and the performers read as part of a real, socially stratified world, which cheerfully tolerates Beatrice's flouting of convention when the stakes are low but which, of course, finally limits her ability act outside of gender norms: she can only play-fight with her fencing foil in her silken dress, she must demand that Benedick is the one to 'Kill Claudio' (4.2.286).

A curious example of this production's costume realism occurred in the first scene, when on Don Pedro's kindly comment to Leonato that he embraces his 'charge too willingly' (1.1.70) in coming to meet them, a horn sounded as if for the Last Post, and Don Pedro's men began to take off their clothes and weapons, as if they had very recently come from the battlefield. With Beatrice viewing him from a half-concealed position by the set's central cypress tree (in which Benedick would finally hide to be gulled into loving her and to send out comical puffs of smoke from a cigar), Roger Allam's Benedick stripped to the waist for a wash in this first scene. This seemed implausibly indecorous, as the women were looking on quite openly, but it drew attention to the materiality of the body and the clothing that covered it: this was practical soldier's wear, albeit in handsome Cavalier style, and the bodies who wore it got sweaty, needed washing. Social reality and the material culture of clothing was again foregrounded through costume in Hero's wedding preparation scene, though here we saw less naked body. The chosen period was close enough to the play's own for tires and rebatos to appear as actual costume items—head dresses and stiff lace collars rather than vague archaisms for 'attire' or 'robe'—and in this production, detailed, historically-accurate-looking pieces were hung conspicuously on a clothing rail for Hero to choose from, offering exquisite detail on a relatively bare set which indicated a domestic interior with a few large curtain swags, the now familiar RSC-realist trope of socially and historically accurate costumes against more abstract scenography. One was reminded, again, of the materiality of costume, this time in its role in constructing the image of feminine perfection that Hero is briefly to become before being shamed at her wedding.

For Svetlana Boym, 'Restorative nostalgia takes itself dead seriously. Reflective nostalgia, on the other hand, can be ironic and humorous' (Boym 2001, 49). I want to suggest that this second Cavalier *Much Ado* provoked a more reflective nostalgia for a past of a beautiful, silken-costumed, highly gendered world than the 1982 version, despite the fact that the earlier production seems actively to be parodying male sartorial vanity, and the latter to be taking costume more seriously as an authentic reflection of the past. The 1990 production offered the spectator a particular kind of realist-historical relish for costume: the lovely clothes were set off against the plainness of the set, where in 1982, pastiche Caroline fashions read as all of a part of the shiny, glowing scenography—literally a part, in fact, as the costumes were reflected in the coppery floor. The 1990 production did not merely inspire gasps at the beauty of a lost age and the skills of the historical costumier, as the RSC's 'Stitch in Time' exhibit suggests is the dual effect of costume, but drew attention to the social prescriptions and proscriptions created by and reflected in Caroline fashion: we see how Hero's doomed bridal persona is constructed by her lovely, starched lace accoutrements, how Beatrice can only play at fighting in a silk dress, and that men in this period register visually as highly interested in appearance—albeit not, as in 1982, to the point of too much hilarity. To cite Boym again, reflective nostalgia 'reveals that longing and critical thinking are not opposed to one another' (Boym 2001, 49–50). I suggest that the 1990 design seduced the viewer into enjoying the costumes, whilst the performances—particularly Fleetwood's feminist Beatrice—provoked critique along with relish. This was a costume aesthetic that signalled historical accuracy. Court costumes were rich but not pastiche-luxurious; they produced a gendered uniform for men and women, reminding the audience that the society of the play demands gender conformity. Audience members may well have thought the costumes beautiful but this production implied that clothing is part of a society which both celebrates and punishes gendered erotic desire, and which tolerates non-conformity only to a degree.

Interval: Kenneth Branagh's *Much Ado About Nothing*, 1993. The Anti-Erotics of Historical Pastiche

Two years after Alexander and Surrey's production, Kenneth Branagh's much-celebrated film of *Much Ado* was released, and I want at this point to create a cinematic interval in my account of RSC stage production to discuss this film, because it throws much of the dramaturgical costuming practice described in this chapter into interesting relief, particularly the two Caroline productions just considered. The film's costumes are a pastiche of pastness, like the Hands/Koltai/Reid production, albeit not a pastiche of a specific historical period and certainly not as intentionally flamboyant. Furthermore, the film uses 'real' locations to produce an intense effect of restorative nostalgia in ways that help to illuminate the design semiotics of the 'realist' designs I am going to discuss later in this chapter. The RSC's 'The Play's the Thing' exhibition claims Branagh as one of its sons by displaying the crown he wore as Henry V in a production later adapted into a film; he is one of the actors on whose career the RSC 'raised the curtain' (RSC 'The Play's the Thing'). Branagh's career references a range of Shakespearean pasts: he has worked as an old-style actor/manager, both directing and starring in *Henry V*, *Hamlet* and *Much Ado*. Costumes for the theatrical and film versions of *Henry V* consciously recalled Laurence Olivier's World War II propaganda version, taking the pageantry of the Olivier colours and styles as a prototype but ripping and muddying them for a more realist portrayal of the conditions of war (see Donald K. Hedrick's 1997 essay on the meanings of mud in this film, which argues that the self-conscious dirtying of imagery from the Olivier version is serves to exonerate both war in general and Henry's part in it more particularly). Moreover, Branagh's *Much Ado* film was released at the beginning of a decade that would see the UK—or at least England—at the height of its obsession with the TV and film 'costume drama', an obsession that can be productively read alongside theatrical productions of *Much Ado*, a play that already brought with it expectations of light wit, sartorial loveliness and summery sparkle, despite its cruel central plot turn.

Branagh's film was a remarkable box office success for a Shakespeare film, grossing over £4 million in the UK and $22.5 million in the US (Sheppard 2017, 45), and a substantial proportion of audiences for any RSC production of the play in the late twentieth century may well have seen it. In fact it was a non-RSC production that has the most direct links to the film: Judi Dench directed Branagh in *Much Ado* for the Renaissance Theatre Company in 1988 and good-naturedly claims in a newspaper interview that 'he stole all my ideas for the film' (Cable 2014; see also Crowl 2002, 111–12). However, whereas the RTC offered another Regency-costumed *Much Ado*, Branagh's film costumes were consciously constructed as 'timeless', borrowing from elements of fashion history over about 200 years. It is this attempt at creating a non-period through costume on which I centre my critique of the film. It has garnered a wide range of scholarly opinion since its release, ranging from its dismissal as a 'lusty, busty romp' (Loehlin 1997, 70), to crediting Branagh with a revival of the Shakespeare film industry (Crowl 2002, 11–12) and suggesting that with *Much Ado* he succeeds in creating 'a utopian green world vision based on the powers of imagination and intelligence rather than on social status' (Crowl 2002, 69). My own reading tends towards the critical end of the spectrum because I read the 'timeless' costume design as key to the whitewashing of sexuality and gender trouble in this play.

In an introduction to the published screenplay, Branagh explains:

> We consciously avoided setting this version in a specific time but instead went for a look that worked within itself, where clothes, props, architecture all belonged to the same world. This imaginary world could have existed almost any time between 1700 and 1900. It was distant enough to allow the language to work without the clash of period anachronisms and for a certain fairy tale quality to emerge. (Branagh 1993, xiii–xiv)

The women in the film all wear short-waisted false corsets over loose white shifts, wide skirts to above the ankle, and sandals, regardless of their rank in the social world of this *Much Ado*. The shape created by wide skirt and short-waisted corset recalls the mid- to late-eighteenth century, whilst the sheerness of some of the white fabric prefigures the later Grecian turn of the Regency: Daniel Defoe meets Jane Austen. The wide sleeves on the women's shifts are 'timeless' indeed—historically unplaceable unless perhaps in the 1970s. The length of the skirts and the footwear—ankles show sandals that read as possibly classical, possibly modern—are perhaps indebted to the Tuscan-ness of the design rather than its past-ness, for Messina here is in fact Tuscany, described by Branagh as 'a magical landscape of vines and olives that seems untouched by much of modern life' (Branagh 1993, xiv). Filming took place in and around the Villa Vignamaggio, which had been opened to tourists in 1987, and is now partly a hotel: at the time of writing, the film features in its online publicity. Thus whilst Branagh wanted to signal a departure from the 'quintessential Englishness' of his *Henry V* film by assembling an international cast for this one, the film itself 'can be seen as part of the invasion of rich and high-profile Britons due to whose arrival...Tuscany is now known as Chiantishire' (Calvo and Hoeneslaars 2016). The women's cosmetic tans (although it is notable that Hero remains alabaster white), wide skirts and sandals offer a touristic version of Southern Europe, where British viewers might indeed imagine the action of the film 'untouched by much of modern life', as Tuscany could well be where the more privileged of them go to escape the stresses of their own lives. A few years after the film's release, the region had become famous in the UK as Prime Minister Tony Blair's holiday destination of choice.

The military men in this *Much Ado* wear dress uniforms in cream and blue, with blue trousers for our heroes and symbolic black for the villains Don John, Conrad and Borachio. As Celestino Deleyto has marked, Don Pedro and Don John's trousers are both in leather—blue for good guy Pedro (Denzel Washington), black for villain John (Keanu Reeves), problematically suggesting that the villain of the piece and the character played by the only black actor in the film should be equally eroticised (Deleyto 2005, 99). The civilian men wear shifts, jerkins and slops in creams and browns, varying in cleanliness according to social status. In the film's opening sequence, in which Emma Thompson's Beatrice sits in a tree reading the song 'Sigh no more, Ladies' to the picnicking assembled company as if it were a poem, there is no obvious distinction of class amongst Leonato's household. As Courtney Lehmann remarks, 'in Branagh's landscape servants and aristocracy are indistinguishable'; on this pseudo-historicised European holiday, 'no one caters to another's pleasure, everyone enjoys and equal share of the bounty' (Lehmann 1998, 7). Jessica Maerz, in her discussion of Deleyto's examination of costume in the film, suggests that rank is subtly denoted in the men's costume, then remarks in a footnote that 'Deleyto does not examine differences of rank as evidenced in the women's garments'. Maerz suggests that whilst differences are 'certainly less encoded in the women's garb', 'some variances of fabric, cut, and hue—are present' (Maerz 2017, 64). On her next page she admits that:

> the social world Branagh constructs is in some sense Utopian: in contrast to his source text, which carefully constructs a hierarchical order of soldiers, gentles, and servants, very few of the films' servant are ever seen *serving* anyone. (Maerz 2017, 65)

The visiting officers arrive at this class-free Utopia, triumphantly crashing over the fields on horseback, in a sequence that, as almost every commentator on the film remarks, references *The Magnificent Seven* (for example Buchanan 2005, 203; Crowl 2002, 66; McEachern 2005, 155; Maerz 2017, 48). Don Pedro is announced, and everyone seems to decide, spontaneously, that they all need a wash. With much girlish squealing, the languid company springs into action and all the women strip themselves of their white clothes, splash each other merrily in a 'primitive shower cubicle' (Branagh 1993, 11–12), then don a set of presumably fresh, albeit very similar, clothes. The men, having just returned triumphant from the battlefield, leap into their own bath and wash too, 'splashing each other with wild abandon' (Branagh 1993, 12). Once dressed, the two companies are presented to one another in a sunny Tuscan courtyard and are socially reinscribed within the etiquette of bows, curtseys and compliments, the pleasant formalities not so much broken as heightened by comparison with Beatrice's acerbic prologue to her and Benedick's 'merry war'.

In this film, homosocial culture, both male and female, is constructed in the bathing sequence as relaxed, sensual, noisy, child-like, free—and free of clothes (also, as a number of critics have pointed out, white, as Denzel Washington's Don Pedro does not appear in the scene). For Samuel Crowl,

> Branagh's approach attempts to stress the democratic tendencies in Shakespeare's comic art with its youthful egalitarian yearnings of emotion and romance. It's part of a stripping away of fashion to bare flesh which begins the film and provides one explanation for Claudio's eventual confusion of Hero and Margaret as both maiden and maid are dressed in identical white cotton dresses. (Crowl 2002, 74)

But I want to suggest that Shakespeare's 'democratic tendencies' are Crowl's own invention here. Clothes are much more of a serious issue in the play than the film acknowledges; in the film they serve to create a relaxed, pastiche historicity but the opening sequence suggests that everyone's true (child-like, asexual) nature is better expressed without them. The idyllic bathing sequence, the 'stripping away of fashion to bare flesh' works against the grain of an early modern understanding that clothing constructs identity and Crowl's comment implies a modern assumption that it is a merely social layer that needs stripping away to reveal human depth.

The film deals with the ambivalent figure of Margaret in *Much Ado About Nothing* by reducing her to the status of a merry, comically sexualised supernumerary, cutting the women's wedding preparation scene and thus Margaret's description of the Duchess of Milan's gown, which might otherwise have drawn attention to this film's determined erasure of period fashion. In a production that includes the wedding preparation scene, the actor playing unmarried Margaret must decide whether she is being blithely tactless or deliberately spiteful when she mentions the cloth of silver and gold and bluish tinsel of the Milan gown. Either way, Margaret is a woman who is excited by dressing up and sex and, as part of Don John's plot, gets to play-act her social superior Hero who is about to experience both. *Much Ado*'s cameo of this waiting gentlewoman fascinatingly foregrounds—and genders—social and sumptuary status; the film's determinedly celebratory dramaturgy erases it entirely. Margaret is played by Imelda Staunton, who seems deliberately not to have been made up to look conventionally attractive; she is the only figure who seems explicitly to relate the women's toilette to potential sex: the screenplay describes her introduction to the viewer thus:

> CLOSE on a pleasing cleavage, which is then dabbed with a huge powder puff and then, by the pull of some strings, is yanked together in an even more fulsome display. We tilt up quickly to see the delighted face of Margaret observing herself in mirror. (Branagh 1993, 12)

The moment in which Claudio witnesses Margaret dressed as Hero talking to Borachio at Hero's window is filmed as a comical sex scene: Margaret and Borachio's 'making love' as the screenplay describes it (Branagh 1993, 56) comprises much comical thrusting by Borachio at/ into Margaret. In the play, the most direct mention of sex is Margaret's in the wedding preparation scene; in the film, it is portrayed by the thrustings of a couple filmed comically as opposed to erotically.

More broadly, the erotic in this film is figured as either comical or as evil and non-reproductive: the film's other obviously eroticised moment is 1.3, the first scene in which it is suggested that Claudio's desire to marry Hero can be used as 'a model' for Don John to 'build mischief on' (1.3.30). Keanu Reeves's Don John is discovered stripped to the waist, but still in his black leather trousers, receiving a massage from Conrad. The tiresome homophobia of suggesting that the villain who wants to spoil Hero and Claudio's wedding day is a resentful gay man is deftly analysed by Celestino

Deleyto, who remarks that the massage scene is 'unequivocally seeking to position the spectator in terms of homoerotic desire' and Don John's lines in an earlier scene, 'I cannot hide what I am' (1.3.8–9) and 'let me be that I am and speak not to alter me' (1.3.24) 'combine with the visual rendering of the scene to reframe his difference as sexual difference' (Deleyto 2005, 100) for a film audience for whom bastardy as an excuse for bitterness and resentment no longer has cultural resonance.

Whilst the erotic is displaced onto a homosexual villain, the troubling erotics of tying and pinning an early modern woman into her wedding dress when she is about to be disgraced in it is, as we have seen, cut altogether. Branagh writes that the wedding preparation scene was shot, but was finally cut as it slowed the plot (Branagh 1993, xv–xvi); it would also have made little sense, as Hero's white wedding dress is so similar to the white clothes all of the women wear throughout the film that there is nothing much for her to change into, and Margaret's comments on anyone's dress would read oddly when she is dressed so similarly herself. Further, the scene eroticises Margaret and Hero, as they get a bride ready and talk about sex, in a way that cannot be contained by this film's mode of restorative nostalgia. The film concludes with the short, companionable kisses of Branagh and Emma Thompson's Beatrice and Benedick, followed by a reprise of the joyous 'Sigh no more' theme as all of the characters dance together in chains and rings around the beautiful Tuscan gardens. As the camera pans away in aerial view, the film audience truly are being asked to sigh no more: any troublesome cruelty, misogyny or sadness in the narrative—and any of its possible erotic 'sighs'—are wiped way in companionate social dancing and a whirl of homogenising white and beige fabric. What the film seems to long for, from the washing sequences onwards, is a 'prelapsarian moment' (Boym 2001, 49) of fairy-tale pastness, untroubled and unexcited by the erotic.

Costumes in this film and the Carolinian costumes of the RSC's 1982 production are historical pastiches of very different kinds but they both serve to de-eroticise the play's serious business of dressing up. The exaggerated Carolinian shapes on the glowing, reflective RST stage in Hands's production suggest that clothing is a silly vanity; the opening sequence of the film, Crowl's 'stripping away of fashion to bare flesh', suggest that beneath the surface prettiness of summer clothes lies a prelapsarian, unerotic sensuality. The semi-stripped erotics of undress is reserved for Don John's plotting scene, in which it is made clear that this kind of thing is only for gay villains in leather trousers. The troubling erotics of the women's dressing scene is cut. On the RSC stage in 1990, on the other hand, a more realist costume aesthetic creates the curious moment described above in which Benedick strips to the waist, centre stage, in mixed-gender company, positing him as the object of the erotic gaze. He has just returned from battle but it is Beatrice who has been seen in action, fencing. In the RSC's 1990 production, attention is drawn to historical specificity the items of clothing in the women's dressing scene and suggest that that the erotics and gender politics of clothes are taken seriously, as they are in the play itself. Branagh's film typifies the restorative nostalgias of the costume drama, removing the film industry's usual appearances of historical authenticity in costume design and replacing it with an avowedly 'fairy-tale' version of generalised pastness. It is not an RSC production but as the *Much Ado* with the greatest number of viewers to date, it inevitably inflects reception of the play in the theatre, reinforcing expectations of the play as merry war rather than gender trouble.

Fifties *Much Ados*. 1988: Mark Thompson (Designer); Di Trevis (Director). 2006: Lez Brotherston (Designer); Marianne Elliot (Director)

I now return to the 1950s-inflected *Much Ado* mentioned earlier in the chapter for another pairing of productions which share a period setting but, like the two Carolinian productions, work with different semiotics of costume. Di Trevis's 1988 production was costumed in multiple layers of pastiche. It was '1950s' in its glamorous full skirts and swimwear; it was '1980s' in that it seemed to be pastiching the 1950s just as 1980s' fashion had done, because it drew on the 1980s' revival of huge debutante-style ball downs, and because the nipped-in waists of the men's jackets had something of a 'New Romantic' flavour to them. The costume design also had Elizabethan elements: the 1950s' shapes of the women's costumes had distinctively pointed waists in the style of Elizabethan stomachers, and the choice of short jackets for men recalled the late sixteenth-century doublet.

These costumes read as pastiche couture, part of the production's critique of the wealthy, decadent society in which the production was set (Smallwood 1988, 85) and recall how fashion itself pastiches its own past. Hero (Julia Ford)'s huge, deep pink ball dress, described above (89), is more than matched by Beatrice (Maggie Steed)'s blue one, whose full skirt emerges from a tight bodice and an enormous satin peplum, like a gigantic bow at her waist. Fashion creates its version of feminine beauty, and these costumes seemed out to critique it, particularly when one compares them to the very different images of fashionable women from the production's programme. The programme images are black shadow prints of model-like figures that fill the fold of each pair of pages from top to bottom, their heads partially cut off so that it is fashion not face that draws the eye. There are no wide dirndls or post-New Look excesses in these centre-folds; the black-on-white shapes are sleek, straight and slender. In comparison to the women's fashions one might peruse whilst looking through the programme, then, the on-stage, mid-calf length fifties-style day dresses with their Elizabethan pointed waists look comparatively bulky and oddly cut off at the calf. Reviewing for the *TLS*, Katherine Duncan-Jones writes:

> The men consistently lack dignity...dressed in tropical shorts, bell-hop jackets or dressing gowns; the women, in a succession of strapless ball gowns, look foolishly over-dressed rather than glamorous. (Duncan-Jones, cited in Gay 1994, 171)

And sure enough, Benedick (Clive Merrison) in his flowered shirt with shorts riding up to the groin whilst he commented on the foolishness of Claudio in love formed part of an overall picture of excessive costume that everyone seemed to be wearing because convention dictated it and which the production seemed to be satirising: women must always be on show, swamped in the conspicuous consumption of fabric; men, when not dressed for formal occasions, are daftly careless of appearances, but sartorially excessive nonetheless. This dramaturgy of sartorial excess culminated in Hero's aborted wedding, for which she wore an enormous white confection with a gigantic train and headdress; it recalled an inflated version of Lady Diana's wedding dress, which was certainly key to the 1980s' reprise of debutante-ball evening wear. If this was the fine, quaint, excellent fashion of Margaret's description, then the Duchess of Milan's gown must have been truly terrifying. The dress enveloped Hero in a cloud of constructed femininity when she fainted at Claudio's accusations.

Providing a counterpoint to this doomed vision of whiteness were the black dresses worn for the final 'wedding' scene; here, it was as if the characters had not changed from the mourning they wore for Hero's pretended funeral. There was even some black confetti thrown, and the production made it clear that the sartorial wedding-day symbols of gender, wealth and heteronormativity are mere ideological constructs: no-one was going to get to hide behind another white wedding veil at the end of this production. In theory, then, costume should have performed interesting work here in drawing audience attention to fashionable superficiality and gender construction. However, I suggest that expectations of stage realism disrupted stylisation in this production, as actors were dressed in clothes that one could not imagine their characters wanting to wear, and the alienation effect of depicting this privileged elite as having terrible taste, in comparison to the figures wearing such attractive couture in the programme, was perhaps too great. The men's pastiche Carolinian costumes of 1982 were comically extravagant too, as we have seen; but a modern audience is likely to regard Cavalier dress as fairly extreme anyway, and 1980s' couture was already pastiching the 1950s in more attractive ways. Some of the designs here—particularly Beatrice's ball gown and Hero's wedding dress—contained an element of parody rather than pastiche and I contend that where fashion is rendered absurd by costume design, its implied opposite is a nostalgia for an imagined, fashion-less world of authentic depth beneath fashionable surface, a trope that irons out the significance of clothing in early modern drama, and which reached its zenith in the flashes of nakedness in the Branagh film bathing scenes.

When director Marianne Elliot and designer Lez Brotherson set their *Much Ado* in the 1950s eighteen years later, in 2006, a similar shift from pastiche to realism seemed to have occurred as in the Carolinian pairing. The action of this *Much Ado* took place in pre-revolutionary Cuba, and one could imagine Tamsin Greig having seen the 1988 production and deciding that she wanted her Beatrice to look more like the svelt models in the theatre programme than the women characters in their bulky full skirts. This Beatrice never dressed in hyper-feminine shapes; her skirts and dresses, and at one point a trouser suit, were all stylishly straight, based on Katharine Hepburn's celebrated style according to the RSC's website. Hero (Morven Christie) and the other women wore fuller-skirted dresses, but simple, knee-length cotton ones in pastel colours rather than silken extravaganzas bulked out with petticoats. There was no visual suggestion of the corrupted wealth of Batista's elite here; the Cuban setting had been chosen, it seemed, for its potential for plenty of Cuban music and dance, rather to reflect Cuban political history. As Charles Spencer writes in his *Daily Telegraph* review, Elliott certainly did not turn the play 'into a Gorkyesque study of incipient Marxist revolution'. Spencer suggests that she:

just fancied the idea of elegant 1950s costumes, an atmosphere of heat, decay, cigar smoke and rum-soaked afternoons, and, above all, a terrific score from Olly Fox featuring old-time Cuban music that recalls the Buena Vista Social Club at its best. (Spencer 2006)

'Just fancying' the elegance of a particular era between Shakespeare's and the present is key to what Michael Dobson, in his 2018 Annual Shakespeare Lecture for the University of Notre Dame in London, pinpointed as a problem with *Much Ado* in realist historical settings (Dobson 2018). In comparison to *Love's Labour's Lost*, which, suggests Dobson, contains its own social commentary on nostalgia and escapism, *Much Ado* is a relatively realist drama with a vicious set of gendered social standards at the core of the society it depicts. These are standards to which a modern British audience for Shakespeare are no longer likely to relate: no matter how deplorable the misogyny inherent in recently revealed sexual harassment cases in the arts and politics, no woman would now expect to be denounced at her wedding for speaking to someone at a window on the accusation of someone notoriously malicious, then to have to pretend to be dead to restore her public reputation. Even Kenneth Branagh's vaguely historically situated film felt obliged to stage a sex scene for Claudio to watch at Hero's window, to render his behaviour at their wedding plausible. It is for this reason, argues Dobson, that *Much Ado* is rarely performed in modern dress. Joss Whedon's 2012 film fails to solve a problem central to setting the play now: why modern young men would behave towards Hero as they do (not to mention, as Dobson remarks, who the people in the film could possibly be in a modern context, with their live-in servants and all-day parties). On the other hand, a beautifully detailed, realist setting in a period between Shakespeare's and the present in a de-politicised, sultry Cuba can be accused of simply shifting the problems of the play elsewhere, to somewhere far enough away not to trouble a Stratford or London audience. Ignoring the fact that 1950s Cuba was an economically and culturally divided society on the verge of revolution, the production suggested that it had a great night life, dance and music culture; the supposedly benighted attitudes towards women of this time and place could explain the actions of the play, whilst ultimately being absorbed into a seductive visual and rhythmic *mise en scene.*

This production was received much more positively than the 1980s'/1950s' pastiche of 1988, and I would argue that this was partly because it looked and sounded more attractive. It also contained some of the inspired moments that can arise when a randomly chosen time and place seems to fit a moment in a 400-year-old play perfectly. The production was full of realist detail, including the casting of a powerful singer, black actor Yvette Rochester-Duncan, as Balthazar. When she ironically remarked there was not a note of hers 'that's worth the noting' (2.3.45), she pronounced the 'th' of 'there's' and 'worth' with a Caribbean accent that reminded us of the pun on 'noting' and 'nothing' that would have been at the heart of the Elizabethan speaking of this play. Dogberry was played by drag activist Bette Bourne in one of the few successfully funny versions of this figure I have seen. His was a comic turn outside of the realist play-world, in a mode appropriate to the role of the Elizabethan clown. His costume, which included a pink girdle bursting from underneath Dogberry's police uniform, seemed more of a statement about Bourne's performance and activist history than an invitation to imagine a cross-dressing backstory for Dogberry himself. As with the early modern clowns Tarlton and Kempe, audiences who knew the performer had a stage history to draw on and look forward to from Bourne's first entrance. Furthermore, Bourne's chosen accent for Dogberry would have been familiar to British audience members of a certain age as that of a class migrant with an ingrained sense of what 'speaking properly' should sound like, as the constable wandered about the stage giving orders with the confidence of someone entirely assured of his position in the world as reflected in his superior vocabulary. It was a perfect example of the comedy produced by a mistaken sense of high status, but with a staged self-awareness that defied the audience's easy patronisation. The drag costume bursting from the uniform gave the impression, on the one hand, of the shambolic holding together of an authority in which Dogberry himself was completely confident, and on the other was a knowing nod to Bourne's transgressive performance history.

Ultimately, as I have suggested and as Spencer's review argues, this production used set, music and costume detail to produce a celebratory vision of, if not a particularly distant time, then certainly a place far from its production in Stratford (it later played Newcastle and London). The agony of a father at his daughter's shame was explained culturally and Beatrice's sophisticated modern style marked her as the feminist who stood slightly outside of this version of Latino, Catholic patriarchy. For the second wedding, the women lined up before the repentant Claudio stood behind a little stone alter laid with a crucifix, a statue of Mary, images of saints and red offertory lights. They wore not veils but identical masks of the Virgin or a Saint from some feast day parade, surrounded with baroque golden haloes to contrast with their plane black widows' day wear, but perhaps also intended to evoke the influence of Roman Catholicism on the Afro-Caribbean cult of Santería. This served to exoticise and distance the play's forced happy ending, whilst Beatrice's 'stylish modern feminist' look and the seductive musical score allowed us to delight in this version of the Latin, to think of *Much Ado* as a place we would love to be. Mark Thompson's overtly stylised designs for the 1988 costumes seemed unable to overcome the broadly realist narrative of *Much Ado*, so that attempts to make costume speak across time periods and comment on gender construction and conspicuous consumption tended to read as the poor taste of the wealthy characters. The stylish realism of Lez Brotherton's 1950s' Cuba, on the other hand, rendered *Much Ado* safely sexy, warm and attractive.

FROM MESSINA TO DOWNTON

2002: Stephen Brimson Lewis (Designer), Greg Doran (Director)

2014: Simon Higlett (Designer), Christopher Luscombe (Director)
I am now going to turn to the two Royal Shakespeare *Much Ado*s with the most detailed realist historical settings, both of which narrowed the play's period setting to an exact year and created, respectively, a vision of Mussolini's Italy, and England at the end of World War I. Both of these productions go even further than the Elliot/Brotherston Cuban *Much Ado* in creating realist period detail whilst distancing the audience from the troubling aspects of the play. I am going to suggest that of all the RSC *Much Ado* productions discussed here, these beautiful, detailed, historically researched costume and set designs best encapsulate Boym's concept of restorative nostalgia, despite the seriousness with which the first of the two tackles the rejection of Hero at her wedding.

Greg Doran's and Stephen Brimson Lewis's production of *Much Ado* was set in Messina, Sicily, much to the approval of reviewer Michael Billington, for whom acknowledging the play's named setting is a mark of respect to Shakespeare:

> Like Zeffirelli before him, Doran pays Shakespeare the compliment of assuming he calculatedly set the action in Messina. Stephen Brimson Lewis

has come up with a pleasing sun-kissed terracotta set, the town square fills with oom-pah-pah bands. (Billington 2002)

Shakespeare's generalised sense of the Italian culture of his own period (not to mention his lack of experience of the 1930s) makes this something of an odd compliment. Costumes suggested the mid- to late-thirties and the programme notes suggest that Don Pedro's troops in this production are actually returning from Italy's campaign in Abyssinia, in 1936.

Doran and Brimson-Lewis's preset sequence was a detailed and convincing depiction of the domestic and communal life of a wealthy Italian household in the first half of the twentieth century. Characters wandered about a square in front of Leonato's lovely, balconied abode in the summer heat, gossiping and wiping sweat from their brows with handkerchiefs, shaking sheets from windows; when the sound of a motorbike was heard, the small-town, unchanging nature of the community was heightened by the degree of excitement with which the women on stage huddled together and looked on eagerly at the Messenger's arrival. There was then some Catholic crossing of chests in relief at the small number of dead, and some squeals of delight at the prospect of Don Pedro and his party's arrival. The Messenger's (real) motorbike was put to use to suggest that Beatrice (Harriet Walter) is something of a rebellious outsider in terms of gender convention: she was the only woman wearing slacks, and she mounted the bike herself to ask if Signior Mountanto was returned from the wars or no (1.1.20).

Interestingly, the costume bible for this production contains a range of twentieth-century period inspirations—a print-out from a website about soldiers' uniforms in Mussolini's Italy keeps company with women's undergarments from the nineteen-teens, and in the wedding preparation scene, Hero (Kirsten Parker) was laced into the corsetry to go under her early twentieth-century simple white wedding dress. The results of this mildly eclectic costume research did not give an immediate impression of eclecticism on stage, however. My own response to the antique lace of Hero's wedding dress and its look of some and no time in the early 1900s, in comparison to the historical specificity of the soldiers' uniforms and women's day dresses, was to think of it as some quaint family heirloom, quite at one with the production's sense of a community taking tender care of both valuable fabrics and outward respectability. The wedding dress suggested that it was designed for the production in order that the corset-lacing, which so obviously speaks to an audience now of women's oppression, could take place in the dressing scene. The dress also conformed to current Western wedding convention, whereby wedding clothes are in and of themselves nostalgic, harking back to some imagined past of beautiful virgins in white dresses; the same applies to a girl's communion dress within the Catholic church, in which small girls are dressed as minibrides. A plethora of Catholic iconography dominated in both the wedding scenes here: for the aborted ceremony, Beatrice and the other women wore white lace mantillas and a statue of the Virgin was carried at the front of the wedding procession. In contrast to the solemnity of the wedding procession, Leonato's treatment of his daughter at the moment of her disgrace was amongst the most emotive I have seen in production.

The website showcasing photographs and design images from past productions, launched by the RSC around the time of the later, 1918-styled *Much Ado*, explains that 'Gregory Doran...deliberately chose Sicily at this time because he felt that it resonated with many of the play's issues, including the place of women in a male-dominated society, the code of honour, vendetta and the role of the church and the law' (RSC 'Other Productions'). To set the play in Sicily at the present time might have problematically suggested that these were still issues in Italy; here, as with Elliot's 1950s' Cuban setting, the play's misogyny is explained with reference to Catholic/ Latin culture, whilst a relatively distant historical period ensured that there were no insulting suggestions being made about those cultures today. One reviewer of the 1930s' Messina production remembered that Mussolini had turned Italy into a one-party state more than a decade before 1936 and seemed to pick up on some of Doran's intentions. Whilst Charles Spencer suggests, in similar vein to his later comment on Elliot's production, that 'Doran appears to have chosen the period for the frocks rather than the fascism' (Spencer 2002), Nicholas de Jongh, perhaps struck by the intensity of the wedding scene, writes:

> ...since this is an Italy where Mussolini reasserted masculine supremacy, male pride, suspicion and jealousy of women run rampant. Wives are place on pedestals yet kept subservient. The unusually vivid anguish of Gary Waldhorn's Leonato for his daughter reflects a Sicilian dread of sexual scandal. (de Jongh 2002)

Local journalists, on the other hand, saw little gender or political history in the production, and did not suggest that as much of the Sicilian heat could be oppressive. 'Bathed in glorious sunshine' writes the *Worcester*

Evening News, 'the troops return from the war triumphant'. The *Heartland Evening News* calls this a 'glorious, sun-kissed production' and the *Birmingham Mail* describes 'the women dancing in the streets, the musicians playing under hanging vine leaves and a few jovial soldiers rolling up on motorbikes'. It is interesting that the RSC website also relates that Doran was inspired to set the play in Sicily when he went on holiday there (RSC 'Other Productions'). For Lehmann writing on the Branagh film, Branagh's chosen Tuscan setting releases the film from the 'construction of...national myths' around Sicily: 'myths of the Mafia, hot tempers, mama's cooking, lovers' intrigue etc' (Lehmann 1998, 7), where Tuscany denotes, to an international audience, a fairy-tale holiday paradise. But however vicious the wedding scene in Doran's production, Sicily can still be figured as a holiday destination: 1930s' Messina's problems are not a Stratford audience's problems and the beautiful sun-drenched set and lovely costumes serve partially to wipe out any unease at the misogyny that bursts out against Hero, to be solved in a moment by a man of the very Catholic church which institutionalises obsessions with women's chastity.

Twelve years later, the RSC produced a *Much Ado* with a yet more detailed realist set and with an equally specific timeframe. Christopher Luscombe and Simon Higlett's production set was in a country house just after the end of World War I—at Christmas 1918 to be precise—and Higlett based his design for this and the *Love's Labour's Lost* which was in repertory with *Much Ado*, on Charlecote Park, a country house close to Stratford. The scenography's lush period detail was reminiscent of television's *Downton Abbey* (see also Potter 2018, 134) and on the RSC's website, Luscombe reveals that they 'turned to Alastair Bruce, Equerry to the Earl of Wessex, and historical advisor on *Downton Abbey* and *The King's Speech*' for 'protocol expertise' on upper-class life in Edwardian Stratford (RSC '*Love's Labour Lost*'). The play was publicised for its Stratford run as *Love's Labour's Won* on the suggestion of the RSC's artistic director Greg Doran (Potter 2018, 135) implying that *Much Ado About Nothing* is the lost play of that name. Extracts from two critics' delighted responses sum up the steeping in restorative nostalgia that this production gave *Much Ado*:

> Conjuring shades of Downton Abbey, Higlett places the action in an imposing replica of the Elizabethan manor at Charlecote Park, just outside Stratford-upon-Avon. Influenced by Coward, Novello and Gilbert and Sullivan, composer Nigel Hess has concocted a treasure-trove of stirring songs that wing us back to a vanished England. (Cavendish 2014)

The sets for both plays [*Much Ado About Nothing* and *Love's Labour's Lost*], by Simon Higlett, based on stately Charlecote Park in Warwickshire, are exquisite; it's a delight to see the RSC lavish money on the design like this. The costumes are a similar treat, as is the cherishable original music by Nigel Hess. Such elements add up to a sumptuously convincing feel—which Luscombe augments with some immaculate patterning of the actors around the stage—and form the perfect backdrop for romantic frolics among the aristocracy. (Mountford 2014)

As in the *Downton Abbey* television series, the social strata of the play were eroded as the servants all enjoyed a dance with their employers in the sumptuously convincing drawing room with its enormous Christmas tree, the perfect set piece from which Benedick (Edward Bennett) could poke his head whilst being gulled into loving Beatrice (Lisa Dillon). Margaret (Emma Manton), though costumed as a servant in black, white and mop-cap, sounded exceptionally dry and blunt in the wedding preparation scene—but then earthy bluntness is de rigueur for a *Downton* servant. The musical score that Fiona Mountford so cherishes closely recalled the kinds of themes used by nostalgic television costume dramas, and the production even added some carol singers, who gave a rendition of 'In the Bleak Midwinter' in the snow, and a West Country police station complete with bobbies on bikes to represent the Watch, to add to the sense of Edwardian rural idyll. For the scene of Hero's shaming, the wedding guests assembled to a hymn about weddings complete with Latin chorus, and the scene seemed to shift momentarily from Downton to Brideshead to complement the seriousness of the moment, with the effect that the spoiling of all this idyllic Englishness could be blamed on some alien set of Catholic values. But what I want to focus on here is the dramaturgy of Beatrice's costume, which suggested a journey from lonely, discontented feminist to heteronormative romantic heroine.

Beatrice and Hero began the play in nurses' uniforms, processing paperwork in the makeshift ward full of hospital beds that has been set up in their family library, reflecting the commandeering of country houses by the war office for the treatment of wounded soldiers in World War I, and recalling the episodes of the *Downton* series in which the same thing happens to the Crawley family home. Lisa Dillon's performance of Beatrice's first encounter with Benedick was highly original in its complete lack of archness: she seemed busy with the work of administering her home's role in the war effort and was genuinely irritated that Benedick had arrived to involve her in the banter that they were inevitably expected to perform. She spoke the line 'Scratching could not make it worse an 'twere such a face as yours were' (1.1.136–7) whilst scratching with a pen at her paperwork. For the masked ball she was dressed rather in the tradition of the Cuban *Much Ado*—in a markedly slimmer, less frivolous red gown than the other women, marking her out as a less fussily feminine dresser than Hero and, for modern tastes at least, as more stylish. It was a conventionally feminine dress nonetheless, and worn at the masked ball, it read as a pretty performance of gender, a disguise to go with the mask. It read thus, I contend because in the opening scene, it was clear that war had made Beatrice a working woman (or a volunteer, at least), one of those whose efforts on the home front had persuaded government to begin to enfranchise women earlier that year. It seemed almost inevitable that at some point in this production, then, she should be wearing slacks and a tie to further emphasise a feminist independence; this she wore for the gulling scene—and this, it seemed, she was gulled out of.

Of course, the scenes following Beatrice's gulling scenes take place before dinner, at a wedding, at a funeral, and at another wedding, so it was perfectly logical that Beatrice did not wear such casual garb again. But she was gulled into falling in love in conspicuously masculine attire, worn by no other woman in the production, then dressed back up for her final clinch with Benedick in her pretty red dress, this time unmasked. Thus it was suggested that her seeming feminism was either an emotional problem that the love of a good man could solve, or perhaps the effect of the war, in which she had played her part in the country house's makeshift hospital, but after which everyone was expected to return to their conventionally gendered roles. Beatrice and Benedick were left alone on stage for a final kiss, the better to assure the audience that the couple's seeming return to banter and Beatrice's feminist rejection of romance (she comically mimed vomiting over his 'halting sonnet') was only a piece of public play.

Scenography and costumes alike were the most sumptuously detailed of the *Much Ado*s considered here. The design did not conform to that common recent trope for Shakespeare production, detailed costumes on a relatively abstract set. This trope is now, perhaps, prevalent to the point of cliché, and the *Standard*'s sigh of 'it's a delight to see the RSC lavish money on the design like this' perhaps suggests quite simply that this was a style no-one had seen for a while. The critical response spoke also, I would suggest, to a desire to see funding and ticket revenues conspicuously consumed on stage. What detailed costumes on a bare set do in the other productions—particularly successfully, I would argue, in the case of the 1976 Napier/Barton production and the 1990 Alexander/ Surrey production—is to foreground fashion, gendered appearances, and the construction of subjectivity through clothing. These are scenographic choices that ask audiences to look at rather than through clothes, to use Stella Bruzzi's analysis of film costume (see above 4, 17, 19), even where the costume designs also signal social realism and historical authenticity. Whilst the spectator might enjoy the beauty of the costumes, they are not invited to consume them uncritically. They are permitted a sigh of restorative nostalgia for a period when there was time for 'the care and protection of material elegance' (above 94) but are also asked to reflect on what cultural work material elegance does when it is worn, and sometimes, who does all this caring and protecting. I suggest, on the other hand, that detailed, historically inspired costumes, on detailed realist sets of the kinds created by Brimson Lewis and Higlett, produced a restorative nostalgia for an imagined past of material beauty and unproblematic social relations and tended to undo the more challenging aspects of the play in the process. Interestingly, both these productions dressed Beatrice in work and/or masculine attire that she later relinquished. One was set just before a world war, one at the close of another. The first staged or erased Mussolini's Italy, depending on which critic's response one reads. The other offered references to national trauma and women's parts in healing it, particularly in the opening scene of the makeshift hospital, and referenced posttraumatic stress in its interpretation of Dogberry (Nick Haverson). It is significant that the one wounded member of the ruling class in the Luscombe/Higlett production was Don John, who used a crutch. This was, perhaps, one source of his resentment: his brother Don Pedro and his new favourite had escaped injury. Anger about war, then, is displaced onto the villain and must be relinquished in the closure of comedy. Ultimately, the beauty and, in the case of Beatrice, the final femininity of the costumes on this lavish set, the presence of Christmas, a festival invented by the Victorians in already nostalgic mode, and the reassuringly pleasant costume-drama musical score, ensured that a restorative nostalgia for a lovely England of clearly marked but beneficent gender and class structures was the 2014 production's ultimate, lavish gift to its audiences.

CODA: *MUCH ADO* FOR YOUNG PEOPLE: HERO'S SHAME IN SHARED LIGHTING

In Michael Dobson's (2018) lecture cited above, he argues that 'the recurrent problem with *Much Ado*' in the productions he explores, set in periods between Shakespeare's and our own, 'is that what once made its context dangerous, serious and worth laughing at, now looks just like one more aspect of its harmless period charm'. However, he warns against simply dismissing theatrical realism in ways that that suggest all will be culturally and politically well if we stage Shakespeare on bare stages and in shared lighting. Whilst I agree that the cultural politics of restorative nostalgia cannot not be undone by replacing historically detailed, non-Elizabethan settings with productions of the play staged in reconstructed Elizabethan theatres—which can of course produce a nostalgia of their own—I have implied in the section above that the more like a lushly detailed film or television costume drama a designer makes *Much Ado*, the more easily conservative its performances of the past become. I want to end this chapter by drawing on a production from a company other than the RSC, played to a very different audience to the majority of those at Stratford, because it demonstrates how the visual inclusion of audience members in a theatre space with shared lighting can productively disrupt the restorative nostalgia that seems to beset *Much Ado* since, as Dobson brilliantly argues in a scathing critique of the Joss Whedon modern dress film of the play, audiences have ceased to sympathise with the duped men who shame Hero. This production (des. Liz Cooke, dir. Joanne Howarth) was created for Year 9 students (13–14 year olds) as part of Shakespeare's Globe Playing Shakespeare (2007) initiative, whose sponsorship by Deutsche Bank enabled the students to attend free of charge.

Penelope Woods was an audience member for this production at the Globe, as part of her research for the thesis 'Globe Audiences' and recalls standing near to the apron stage at the moment of Hero's shaming as a student remarked loudly, 'She's crying now; I'd cry too if I was her'. At a different performance of the same production, I heard a girl cry out 'Shame!' at a similar place in the play. Whilst many of these young people would have come from cultures which had no attitudes comparable to Claudio and Leonato's, they vocalised their experience of Hero's shaming in a way that suggested they understood it. This was a modern dress production in which Natasha Magigi's Hero was dressed to resemble a cute, feathery duckling, in a 1950s-inspired white wedding dress and little down cape. The moment staged the nostalgic, pastiche-period garb of the modern white wedding and young people seemed particularly shocked at the idea that Claudio's misogyny should be revealed at what is still frequently figured in the modern media as the happiest day of a young woman's life. The young people invested in the 'reality' of the theatrical moment, but in the shared light of performer and audience at the Globe were invited not to gaze silently at the beauty of the wedding costumes but to express their feelings about the shaming of Hero vocally. My question as I move to the next chapter's exploration of *The Tempest* in production is whether it is not so much historically accurate periodisation or theatrical realism that renders *Much Ado* easily, uncritically nostalgic so much as the kind of investment that audiences are invited by costume, casting and staging to make in the dilemmas of the play.

As I was completing the work of this chapter, I returned to the RSC's 'Stitch in Time' exhibit, which was designed to encourage charitable donation to the company's costume department, and was drawn to the half-constructed underpinnings of a late nineteenth-century bustle, the kind of structure that so conveniently lends itself to constructing Hero as a victim of patriarchy on the way to her doomed wedding but will no doubt, once covered in folds, drapes, textures and colour, also make audiences sigh over the beauty of historical constructions of the feminine. I came from poring over costume bibles from that very department, excited at the wealth of historical knowledge, craft expertise and sheer organisational labour that go into costuming a Royal Shakespeare production. If I use myself as an example, the same audience members that will be attuned to a feminist critique of gender as staged by costume in *Much Ado About Nothing* will also be enjoying its conspicuous consumption. Costume is a spectacular consumable, a feast for the eyes. A key question for this chapter has been: what kinds of costume designs in what kinds of theatres invite critical engagement with the moment of visual consumption, rather than—or even as well—as a restorative nostalgic longing for the past?

PRODUCTIONS DISCUSSED (ALL PRODUCTIONS ARE OF MUCH ADO ABOUT NOTHING)

Kenneth Branagh, The Samuel Goldwyn Company, dir. 1993. *Much Ado About Nothing*, [film].

Royal Shakespeare Company. 1961. *Much Ado About Nothing*, Michael Langham (director), Desmond Heely (designer), Royal Shakespeare Theatre, Stratford upon Avon.

———. 1976. *Much Ado About Nothing*, John Barton (director), John Napier (designer), Royal Shakespeare Theatre, Stratford upon Avon. https://www. rsc.org.uk/much-ado-about-nothing/past-productions/ christopher-luscombe-2014-production.

———. 1982. *Much Ado About Nothing*, Terry Hands (director), Alexander Reid (costume designer) Ralph Koltai (designer), Royal Shakespeare Theatre, Stratford upon Avon.

———. 1988. *Much Ado About Nothing*. Di Trevis, dir. Mark Thompson (designer) Royal Shakespeare Theatre, Stratford upon Avon.

Royal Shakespeare Company. 1990. *Much Ado About Nothing*, Bill Alexander (director), Kitt Surrey (designer), Royal Shakespeare Theatre, Stratford upon Avon.

———. 2002. *Much Ado About Nothing*, Greg Doran (director), Stephen Brimson Lewis (designer), Royal Shakespeare Theatre, Stratford upon Avon.

———. 2006. *Much Ado About Nothing*, Marianne Elliot (director), Lez Brotherston (designer), Swan Theatre, Stratford upon Avon.

———. 2012. *Much Ado About Nothing*, Iqbal Khan (director), Himani Dehlvi (costume designer), Tom Piper (designer), Courtyard Theatre, Stratford upon Avon. https://www.rsc.org.uk/much-ado-about-nothing/past-productions/ iqbal-khan-2012-production.

———. 2014. *Much Ado About Nothing* Christopher Luscombe (director), Simon Higlett (designer), Royal Shakespeare Theatre, Stratford upon Avon. https:// www.rsc.org.uk/much-ado-about-nothing/past-productions/ christopher-luscombe-2014-production.

Shakespeare's Globe, Playing Shakespeare with Deutsche Bank. 2007. *Much Ado About Nothing* Jo Howarth (director), Liz Cooke (designer).

WORKS CITED

Auerbach, Erich. 2003. *Mimesis: The Representation of Reality in Western Literature*. Trans. Willard Trask. Princeton: Princeton University Press.

Austen, Jane. 2011. *Persuasion*. New York: Harper Collins.

BBC. 1995. Persuasion adapted by Nick Dear, directed by Roger Michell (Film).

Bennett, Susan. 1996. *Performing Nostalgia: Shifting Shakespeare and the Contemporary Past*. London: Routledge.

Bhattacharyya, Gargi. 2018. *Rethinking Racial Capitalism: Questions of Reproduction and Survival*. London: Rowman and Littlefield.

Billington, Michael. 2002. 'Review of Much Ado About Nothing' (Royal Shakespeare Company). *The Guardian*, May 10. https://www.theguardian. com/stage/2002/may/10/theatre.artsfeatures.

———— 2014. Best Shakespeare Productions: Much Ado About Nothing. *The Guardian*, April 17. https://www.theguardian.com/stage/2014/apr/17/best-shakespeare-productions-much-ado-about-nothing.

Boose Lynda, E., and Richard Burt, eds. 1997. *Shakespeare the Movie: Popularizing the Plays on Film, TV, and Video*. London: Routledge.

Boym, Svetlana. 2001. *The Future of Nostalgia*. New York: Basic Books.

Birmingham Mail. 2002, May. Review of Much Ado About Nothing. *Birmingham Mail*.

Birmingham Post. 1961. Review of Much Ado About Nothing. *Birmingham Post*, April 5.

Branagh, Kenneth. 1993. *Much Ado About Nothing* by William Shakespeare with Screenplay, Introduction and Notes on the Making of the Movie by Kenneth Branagh. London: Chatto & Windus.

Bristol Evening Post. 1961. Review of Much Ado About Nothing. *Bristol Evening Post*, April 8.

Bruzzi, Stella. 1997. *Undressing Cinema: Clothing and Identity in the Movies*. London: Routledge.

Buchanan, Judith. 2005. *Shakespeare on Film*. London: Routledge.

Cable, Simon. 2014. Branagh Stole My Ideas for Shakespeare Movie of Much Ado Claims Dame Judi. Daily Mail, April 11. https://www.dailymail.co.uk/tvshowbiz/article-2602918/Branagh-stole-ideas-Shakespeare-movie-says-Dame-Judi-Much-Ado-About-Nothing.html.

Calvo, Clara, and Ton Hoeneslaars. 2016. Shakespeare Uprooted: The BBC Shakespeare Re-Told (2005). In *The Shakespearean International Yearbook: Special Section, European Shakespeares*, ed. Clara Calvo and Ton Hoeneslaars. Abingdon: Routledge.

Cartmell, Deborah, Peter J. Smith, Andrew Hiscock, and Lisa Hopkins, eds. 2018. New Directions: Much Ado or Love's Labour's Won – Does It Matter Which? *Much Ado About Nothing: A Critical Reader*. London: Bloomsbury, Arden Shakespeare.

Cavendish, Dominic. 2014. Love's Labours Lost/Love's Labours Won, Royal Shakespeare Theatre: 'blissfully entertaining'. *The Telegraph*, October 16. https://www.telegraph.co.uk/culture/theatre/theatre-reviews/11167470/Loves-Labours-LostLoves-Labours-Won-Royal-Shakespeare-Theatre-review.html.

Cochrane, Claire. 2016. Shakespeare and the Re/vision of Indian Heritage in the Postcolonial British Context. In *Performing Shakespeare in India. Exploring Indianness, Literatures and Cultures*, ed. Shormishtha Panja and Babli Moitra Saraf, 60–76. New Delhi: Sage.

Crowl, Samuel. 2002. The Marriage of Shakespeare and Hollywood: Kenneth Branagh's Much Ado About Nothing. In *Spectacular Shakespeare: Critical*

Theory and Popular Cinema, ed. Courtney Lehmann and Lisa S. Starks, 110–125. Madison: Fairleigh Dickinson University Press.

———. 2007. Flamboyant Realist: Kenneth Branagh. In *The Cambridge Companion to Shakespeare on Film*, ed. Russell Jackson, 226–244. Cambridge: Cambridge University Press.

Daily Express. 1961. Review of Much Ado About Nothing. *Daily Express*, April 5.

Daily Telegraph. 1961. Review of Much Ado About Nothing. *Daily Telegraph*, April 4.

———. 2013. The Top Ten Beatrice and Benedicks. *Daily Telegraph*, August 20. https://www.telegraph.co.uk/culture/theatre/william-shakespeare/10307341/The-top-ten-Beatrice-and-Benedicks.html.

Deleyto, Celestino. 2005, Spring. Men in Leather: Kenneth Branagh's 'Much Ado About Nothing' and Romantic Comedy. *Cinema Journal* 20: 92–100.

Dench, Judi, Interview with Kira Cochrane. Judi Dench: Does Nobody Ever Believe Anything I Do?. *Guardian* 12, September 2009. https://www.the-guardian.com/culture/2009/sep/12/judi-dench-interview).

Dobson, Michael. 2018. *Shakespeare and the Curse of Realism*. Notre Dame Annual London Shakespeare Lecture. University of Notre Dame London Global Gateway.

Duffell, Peter, dir., HBO, Goldcrest. 1984. *The Far Pavilions*, Based on Novel by M. M. Kaye [Television Series].

Dwyer, Michael D. 2015. *Back to the Fifties: Nostalgia, Hollywood Film and Popular Music of the Seventies and Eighties*. Oxford: Oxford University Press.

Escolme, Bridget. 2018. Brexit Dreams: Comedy, Nostalgia, and Critique in *Much Ado About Nothing* and *A Midsummer Night's Dream*. In Hirschfeld, Heather, ed. The Oxford Handbook of Shakespearean Comedy

Evening Standard. 2012. Much Ado About Nothing, RSC Courtyard – Review. *Evening Standard*, August 2. https://www.standard.co.uk/go/london/the-atre/much-ado-about-nothing-rsc-courtyard-review-8001453.html.

Gay, Penny. 1994. *As She Likes It: Shakespeare's Unruly Women*. London: Routledge.

Gilroy, Paul. 1987. *There Ain't No Black in the Union Jack*. Chicago: Chicago University Press.

Gupta, Masaba. 2016. Masaba Gupta on India's Obsession with Bollywood Costumes. *Hindustan Times*, January, 14. https://www.hindustantimes.com/fashion-and-trends/masaba-gupta-on-india-s-obsession-with-bollywood-costumes/story-VDbEEbbGLtq7CcwHvWGzEN.html.

Hall, Stuart. 1978. Race and Poverty. In *The Inner Cities*, ed. T. Blair. London: Central London Polytechnic Papers on the Environment.

Heartland Evening News. 2002. Review of Much Ado About Nothing. *Heartland Evening News* [Nuneaton], May 11.

Hedrick, Donald. 1997. War Is Mud: Branagh's Dirty Harry V and the Types of Political Ambiguity. In *Shakespeare the Movie: Popularizing the Plays on Film, TV, and Video*, ed. Lynda E. Boose and Richard Burt. London: Routledge.

Higson, Andrew. 2003. *English Heritage, English Cinema: Costume Drama Since 1980.* Oxford: Oxford University Press.

Iqbal, Nosheen. 2012. Much Ado about Delhi: RSC's Indian Shakespeare. *The Guardian*, August 1. https://www.theguardian.com/culture/2012/aug/01/much-ado-rsc-indian-shakespeare.

Ivory, James, dir., and Ishmail Merchant, producer. 1983. *Heat and Dust*, Film Based on Novel by Ruth Prawer Jhabvala [film].

Jacobi, Derek, interviewed by Andrew Dickson. 2016. Derek Jacobi: "Much Ado Saved me from Stage Fright". *Guardian*, July 25.

Jongh, Nicholas de. 2002. Mature Love Wins the Day (Review of Much Ado About Nothing). *Evening Standard*, May 10. https://www.standard.co.uk/go/london/theatre/mature-love-wins-the-day-7434408.html.

Kapur, Jyotsna. 2009. An "Arranged Love" Marriage: India's Neoliberal Turn and the Bollywood Wedding Culture Industry'. *Communication Culture and Critique* 2: 221–233.

Kozaczka, Edward. 2009. Queer Temporality, Spatiality and Memory in Jane Austen's Persuasion. *Persuasions On-line* 30: 1. http://www.jasna.org/persuasions/on-line/vol30no1/kozaczka.html.

Lean, David, dir. *Passage to India.* 1984. Based on Play by Santha Rama Rau and Novel by E. M Forster [film].

Lehmann, Courtney. 1998. Much Ado About Nothing? Shakespeare, Branagh and the 'National-Popular' in the Age of Multi-national Capitalism. *Textual Practice* 12: 1–22.

Lehmann, Courtney, and Lisa S. Starks. 2002. *Spectacular Shakespeare: Critical Theory and Popular Cinema.* Madison: Fairleigh Dickinson University Press.

Loach, Ken. 2016. Ken Loach bemoans TV's 'fake nostalgia' of Period Dramas. https://www.bbc.co.uk/news/entertainment-arts-37679158.

Loehlin, James N. 1997. "Top of the World, Ma": Richard III and Cinematic Convention. In *Shakespeare the Movie: Popularizing the Plays on Film, TV, and Video,* ed. E. Boose Lynda and Richard Burt. London: Routledge.

Maerz, Jessica. 2017. *Metanarrative Functions in Kenneth Branagh's Shakespeare Films: Strange Bedfellows.* Cambridge: Cambridge Scholars Publishing.

McClean, Gareth. 2007. What Is the Appeal of Costume Dramas?. *Guardian*, December 17. https://www.theguardian.com/culture/garethmclean-blog/2007/dec/17/whatistheappealofcostume.

McDonald, Russ. 2005. *Look to the Lady: Sarah Siddons, Ellen Terry, and Judi Dench on the Shakespearean Stage.* Athens, GA; London: University of Georgia Press.

McEachern, Claire. 2005. *Introduction to William Shakespeare Much Ado About Nothing.* London: Bloomsbury, Arden Shakespeare.

Morahan, Christopher, and Jim O'Brien, dir. 1984. Granada TV *The Jewel in the Crown*, Based on the Novels *The Raj Quartet* by Paul Scott [Television Series].

Morley, Sheridan. 1976. Review of Much Ado About Nothing. *Punch*, April 21.

Mountford, Fiona. 2014. Review of Love's Labours Lost/Love's Labours Won. *Evening Standard*, October 22. https://www.standard.co.uk/go/london/theatre/loves-labours-lost-loves-labours-won-much-ado-about-nothing-royal-shakespeare-theatre-stratford-9809883.html.

Panjwani, Varsha. 2017. Much Ado about Knotting: Arranged Marriages in British-Asian Shakespeare Productions. In *Shakespeare, Race and Performance: the Diverse Bard*, ed. Delia Jarrett-Macauley. Abingdon, Oxon: Routledge.

Potter, Lois. 2018. New Directions: *Much Ado* or *Love's Labour's Won* – Does It Matter Which? In *Much Ado About Nothing: A Critical Reader*, ed. Deborah Cartmell et al., 133–154. London: Bloomsbury, Arden Shakespeare.

Prince, Kathryn. 2018. Performance History: Landmarks, Tendencies, Outliers, Recursions and Riffs in the Performance History of *Much Ado About Nothing*. In *Much Ado About Nothing: A Critical Reader*, ed. Deborah Cartmell and Peter J. Smith, 39–66. London: Bloomsbury, Arden Shakespeare.

Quarmby, Kevin. 2012. Review of *Much Ado About Nothing*. *British Theatre Guide*. https://www.britishtheatreguide.info/reviews/much-ado-about-rsc-courtyard-t-7732.

Royal Shakespeare Company 'Iqbal Khan. 2012. Production. https://www.rsc.org.uk/much-ado-about-nothing/past-productions/iqbal-khan-2012-production.

Royal Shakespeare Company (RSC). Other Productions. https://www.rsc.org.uk/much-ado-about-nothing/past-productions/other-productions.

———. The Play's the Thing. https://www.rsc.org.uk/the-plays-the-thing/about-the-exhibition.

Royal Shakespeare Company. A Stitch in Time. https://www.rsc.org.uk/stitch-in-time.

Sheppard, Philippa. 2017. *Devouring Time: Nostalgia in Contemporary Shakespearean Screen Adaptations*. Montreal: McGill-Queen's University Press.

Smallwood, Robert. 1988. Shakespeare at Stratford Upon Avon 1988. *Shakespeare Quarterly* 40 (1): 83–94.

Spencer, Charles. 2006. Bursting with Life, Wit and Feeling. Review of *Much Ado About Nothing Daily Telegraph*, May 22. https://www.telegraph.co.uk/culture/theatre/3652588/Bursting-with-life-wit-and-feeling.html.

Stage, The. 1961. Review of Much Ado About Nothing. *The Stage*, April 6.

Thomas, Sita Chandra. 2015. Much Ado About Nothing Dir by Iqbal Khan (Review). *Asian Theatre Journal* 32 (2): 570–572.

———. 2017. In Search of a New National Story: Issues of Cultural Diversity in the Casting and Performance of Shakespeare in Britain 2012–2016. PhD, *English and Comparative Literary Studies*, University of Warwick.

Thompson, Carol L. 1977. Review of Romeo and Juliet, Much Ado About Nothing, The Winter's Tale, Troilus and Cressida. *Educational Theatre Journal* 29 (1): 120–122.

Weil, Herb. 2007. Whose Dogberry? Or the Afterlife of John Barton's 'Raj' Much Ado. In *Shakespeare's Local Habitations*, ed. Krystyna Kujawinska-Courtney and R.S. White, 177–189. Lodz: Lodz University Press.

Weiss, Tanja. 1999. *Shakespeare on the Screen : Kenneth Branagh's Adaptations of Henry V, Much Ado About Nothing, and Hamlet, Frankfurt am Main.* New York: P. Lang.

Whyman, Tom. 2017. Theresa May's Empire of the Mind. *New York Times*, July 15. https://www.nytimes.com/2017/02/15/opinion/theresa-mays-empire-of-the-mind.html.

Woods, Penelope. 2011. Globe Audiences: Spectatorship and Reconstruction at Shakespeare's Globe. PhD Thesis, Department of Drama, School of English and Drama, Queen Mary, University of London.

Worcester Evening News. 2002. Review of Much Ado About Nothing Dir. Greg Doran. *Worcester Evening News*, May 11.

CHAPTER 4

Masks of Whiteness: Race, Costume and Casting in the Post-colonial *Tempest*

The cover image on the programme for Leeds Playhouse's 1974–1975 production of *The Tempest* is of a calm sea stretching to the horizon and a sky of hazy purplish pink. The image is a watery blank canvas, disrupted by no play title or company name. This is the calm after the storm, perhaps, when the sun has set on the action of the play. There are no words on the cover and this empty seascape prefigures the programme's chosen quotations from nineteenth- and twentieth-century literary critics, all of which suggest that *The Tempest* is an open, infinitely interpretable text. Samuel Taylor Coleridge is cited first, insisting, in 1836, that the 'complicated scenery and decorations of modern times' are a dangerous distraction in productions of *The Tempest*, '[f]or the principal and only genuine excitement ought to come within from the moved and sympathetic imagination' (Coleridge and Coleridge 1836, 56). Next comes Jan Kott, remarking, in 1965, that *The Tempest*'s magical island has no explicit geographical location (Kott 1965, 308). Lastly, a paragraph from Anne Barton (nee Righter)'s introduction to the 1968 New Penguin edition warns critics against a tendency to consider their own reading of *The Tempest* as the only legitimate one, and says of the play:

> Troubling, complex exasperating, the original is infinitely greater and more suggestive than anything that can be made out of it… Like an iceberg, it conceals most of its bulk beneath the surface. (Barton, nee Righter 1968, 22)

© The Author(s), under exclusive license to Springer Nature Switzerland AG 2020
B. Escolme, *Shakespeare and Costume in Practice*, Shakespeare in Practice, https://doi.org/10.1007/978-3-030-57149-8_4

In the theatre, it is quite possible to create a physical environment for the action of *The Tempest* that does not refer to a particular geographical location; as we will see, a pale, bare set with a trap door for Caliban and some flying equipment for the spirits has become the non-specific site for a number of performances of the play. However, designers, actors and directors cannot work day-to-day with the idea that *The Tempest* is 'infinitely greater and more suggestive than anything that can be made out of it'. They have to make something out of it, and that something will say something about both the play's and the production's historical moments.

In this chapter, I discuss moments in *The Tempest*'s twentieth- and twenty-first-century production history when the play has been made to speak to issues of race, power and colonialism. The idea that this is what the play might be 'about' is now a very familiar one. In the second half of the twentieth century, intellectual debates emerged around the identification of Prospero as a white colonialist, Caliban and Ariel as colonised people of colour. As Chantal Zabus relates in *Tempests After Shakespeare*:

> As decolonization proved an absolute necessity by the 1960s, African and Caribbean postcolonial writers as well as European and Latin American dissenting intellectuals came to use the counter-hegemonic idea of Caliban in order to destabilize colonial sets of ideas and call for the deprivileging of Prospero-qua-colonizer. (Zabus 2002, 8)

The play was remade and written back to by Caribbean artists, making it speak clearly to the post-colonial experience (e.g. Aimé Césaire's play *Une Tempete* (1969), George Lamming's novel *Water with Berries* (1971), Kamau Braithwaite's poems 'Caliban' (1973) and 'Letter SycoraX' (1973, 1993)). In 1970, the British theatre began to explore the play's possible post-colonial resonances.

As we will see, the first British post-colonial *Tempest*, directed by Jonathan Miller, received some enthusiastic, some outraged notices. The more negative responses suggested that a colonially inflected version of the play somehow closes down its Shakespearean openness and plenitude. The implication here is that the play is 'really' about Prospero and his emotional and moral journey, whereas referencing the histories of colonised peoples gives rise to a restricted set of historical meanings, spoiling the play's infinite, timeless significance as depicted in the Leeds Playhouse programme. Some designers, actors and directors of *The Tempest* have made decisions which imply that some costumes, some clothes, some colours reflect broad, universal meanings that have nothing to do with the politics of imperialism, race and power. Here I endeavour to uncover the politics of whiteness in what is ostensibly essential, universal Shakespearean, and to distinguish the part that costume plays in upholding and challenging that politics. I discuss twentieth- and twenty-first-century productions of *The Tempest* in which a white Prospero has controlled, punished, claimed and freed black Ariels and Calibans. I then move to consider British productions of the play from 1988 onwards, to explore how costume contributes to how blackness and whiteness signify on stage in *The Tempest* when the play is cast outside of the consciously post-colonial tradition: with a black actor as Prospero, for example. I ask how costume has produced and reflected post-colonial identity in relation to black and white bodies in this play. What role has costume played in producing race and power in recent productions of *The Tempest?*

The chapter's title puns on Ben Jonson and Inigo Jones's first masque collaboration, *The Masque of Blackness,* a piece of court theatre that now strikes the reader as ludicrously racist. It tells the tale of some beautiful Nigerian women who, on discovering that whiteness is a more fashionable kind of beauty than their own, travel round the world trying to find a country where they can be transformed into white people (this country turns out to be Britain). Its published account is fascinating in its description of what was technically possible for artists who had access to the extraordinary budgets available for court celebrations of this kind. Its reception is also significant for histories of race and racism in performance, as a contemporary letter describing it suggests that court women appearing in black make-up courted negative responses—not, as would be the case now, because the notion of a white actor 'blacking up' was offensive in itself, but because seeing white aristocratic women pretending to be black was so disconcerting to white commentators (Hall 1995, 130; Curran 2009, 33–34), even if the masque did follow their attempts to get whitened.

The Tempest famously contains a masque scene, conjured by Prospero to celebrate his daughter Miranda's wedding, and the public performances of the play that likely took place at the Blackfriars and the Globe might have offered audience members who did not get to take part in court masques a glimpse of what these extravagant productions were like. However, whether the court masque itself was an homogeneous presentation of 'the triumph of an aristocratic community' with 'a belief in the hierarchy' at its centre' (Orgel 1975, 40), or whether it was more ideologically fragmented, a 'diverse expression of conflicting arenas of interest within the court culture' (Bevington and Holbrook 1998, 8), the one in *The Tempest* is brought to an abrupt close rather than finishing in a dance affirming court cohesion, as Prospero remembers a challenge to his own power is approaching in the form of Caliban, Stephano and Trinculo. When framed by the action of the play, the masque certainly draws focus to power's precariousness. In some of the twentieth-century productions I consider here, the spirits of the island who perform the mythic masque goddesses are played by actors of colour. But the reason for entitling this chapter 'Masks of Whiteness' is that I think a number of these productions draw attention to whiteness as precarious performance, whilst others unintentionally assume it as a dominant cultural norm. In her introduction to *Staging Whiteness*, Mary F. Brewer asks:

> What has been theater's role in reinforcing the cultural capital accruing to Whiteness in British and U.S. society by reproducing White hegemony? When and how has it worked against it? (Brewer 2005, xii)

I want to ask comparable questions of *The Tempest* in recent production, paying explicit attention to costume's role in staging and troubling race and power. In considering whiteness and costume I am drawn to think about the literal use of white clothes and white cloth in production, and what they mean for the staging of whiteness in racial and cultural terms. When does white cloth mean whiteness and when does it, can it, not? The casting of actors of colour as Ariel, Caliban and the island spirits foreground the politics of racial identity in some productions, whereas in others, whiteness becomes abstracted, aesthetic, philosophical in ways which suggest that only whiteness can represent the abstract, the aesthetic, the philosophical. As Ruth Frankenberg states in her introduction to the collection *Displacing Whiteness*, '...whiteness makes itself invisible precisely by asserting its normalcy, its transparency, in contrast with the marking of others on which its transparency depends' (Frankenberg 1997, 6). Arthur F. Little has pointed to the hegemonic workings of white invisibility in Shakespeare and early modern studies themselves: his 'Re-historicizing Race, White Melancholia' demonstrates that even in attempting to historicise categories of race in early modern culture, New Historicist and cultural materialist critics have figured the early modern period as pre-racial, thus 'obviat[ing] the presence of race and attenuate[ing] the corrosive power of racism' (Little 2016, 100). Kim F. Hall's *Things of Darkness* documents repeated moments in early modern discourse that testify to anxieties about the assumed stability of whiteness. Twentieth- and twenty-first-century Shakespeare production and its reception uses costume both to assume the stability and invisibility of whiteness and to trouble it. A significant number of British productions have used white—white sets, white costumes, white make-up and particularly a range of white-painted or transparent-looking Ariels—in ways that suggest they are not connected with race and power. But once race, racism and colonialism have been foregrounded in production, as they were by Miller in 1970 and again in 1988, whiteness is frequently thrown into ideological relief by the casting and design of a production, even where an exploration of race and power is not conscious or intentional.

THIS ISLAND'S MINE: DRESSING THE FIRST CALIBAN

Caliban's claim that 'This island's mine' (1.2.389) has been the starting point for many colonially inflected readings of the play. What might he have looked like in the first stagings of *The Tempest*? The question is significant because the answer has been assumed across a significant part of the play's stage history: Caliban should be clothed and made up as a monster, because he is called 'fish', 'monster', 'mooncalf', 'half a fish and half a monster' by other characters in the play. Trevor R. Griffiths's performance history 'This Island's Mine: Caliban and Colonialism' traces 150 years of Tempest performances in which Caliban has featured as a 'comic wodwo' after the Dryden-Davenant version of the play (Griffiths 1983, 159), an ape-like personification of the evolutionary 'missing link' (163–174), and a more distinctly fishy monster (172–174), through to Miller's 1970 production in which a fully human Caliban is most explicitly a colonised black man. In discussing what an early Caliban might have looked like, I do not mean to suggest that research into early production should somehow offer a blueprint for the costuming of this figure today. But I do contend that an exploration of Caliban's first costume offers further insight into the power relations at work in *The Tempest* and suggest that the twentieth century's literary and theatrical readings of the play as 'about colonialism' are not mere modern impositions, any more than the assumption that *The Tempest* is essentially 'about' the moral and emotional journey of a white patriarch is timeless and universal.

In an article for the British Library web pages, Martin Butler suggests that the meanings of *The Tempest* cannot be pinned down, insisting of Caliban that:

Shakespeare is careful to leave [his] appearance and origins enigmatic. Prospero says he is the child of an Algerian witch and the devil, but we never learn quite what he looks like or where he comes from, and he cannot easily be pigeonholed. (Butler 2016)

But the King's Men would have had to make a decision about Caliban's appearance and Shakespeare's audiences would have learned 'what he looked like' the moment he walked onto the stage. How might costume have directed audience reception of Caliban, '*a salvage [savage] deformed slave*' according to the First Folio dramatis personae? One meaning of 'mooncalf', a name repeatedly given to Caliban in the play, is a lump or growth in the womb; so Caliban might be a human figure with a 'deformity' similar to Shakespeare's Richard III's 'bunch-back' (*Richard III* 1.3.247). This might explain Prospero calling him a 'misshapen knave' (5.1.302) and even a 'tortoise' (372), though it should be remembered that when Prospero insults Caliban thus, he is upbraiding him for his slowness. However, 'deformed' according to the entry for the word in Robert Cawdry's *A Table Alphabeticall of Hard Usual English Words* published just a year after *The Tempest*, could simply mean 'ill shapen, ill favoured' (Cawdry 21) that is to say, merely ugly. Was Caliban an extraordinary grotesque with a specially designed, monstrous costume, as in a court antimasque? Or did he essentially look like a ragged, log-bearing man, dirty and stooped with work in ways that earn him the nickname 'monster' and 'mooncalf' from Stephano and Trinculo?

A number of scholars have taken literally those characters who refer to Caliban has half-man half-fish. I tend to accept, with Alden T. and Virginia Mason Vaughn, that the central joke of the passage in which Trinculo initially mistakes Caliban for a fish, and the ensuing fishy insults thrown at Caliban, are jokes about his smell (Vaughn and Vaughn 1991, 7–14). Let us imagine first, then, that the first Caliban was a human figure, deformed from birth or by the back-breaking work Prospero forces him to do daily, as he often appears in modern production. In suggesting this, I am indebted to Patricia Akhimie's brilliant analysis of the trope of 'pinching' in the *Tempest*. As she demonstrates, in *The Tempest*, 'stripes, spots, and pinches' physically transform their victims and 'serve to distinguish Caliban both as a base, nearly inhuman creature and as an upstart'. Caliban is a monstrous man, but he has been literally made so by Prospero: 'Pinches in fact can change the shape of men and Prospero's oddly specific punishments would transform bodies by degrading musculature and bone in much the same way old age would' (Akhimie 2018, 172).

An enslaved, human Caliban's costume might have been a ragged loin cloth and cloak, worn for the sake of modesty and protection from the weather. Or, he might have worn more substantial working garments, which could have registered to the Jacobean audience as hand-me-downs from Prospero. Caliban has, Prospero claimed, been treated with 'humane care' in the past (1.2.405) and been 'lodged' in Prospero's 'own cell' (406); he has been taught Prospero and Miranda's language and treated like a human child or, perhaps a Jacobean apprentice as Andrew Gurr has argued (Gurr *passim*) until he makes his attempt on 'the honour of [Prospero's] child' (1.2.408). So one version of Caliban's costume is the fuller set of clothes Prospero might have given him when he lodged in his cell, left to become ragged and dirty when he falls out of favour. This reading situates Caliban in a social reality: however 'deformed' he is, he looks like an human slave rather than a fantastical monster, and when the servant figures Stephano and Trinculo meet him, perhaps with their own servants' livery as pristine as the clothes of the masters they've been shipwrecked with, he is visually the most wretched of the three, the most clearly disconnected from the material trappings of power, and potentially, then, the most desperate and dangerous to Prospero's rule. This makes the fact that he is not distracted by the gaudy clothes set out by Ariel to foil the assassins' plot visually highly significant: he is perhaps dressed in ragged, broken-down versions of what such frippery becomes. In modern production where a black actor is cast as Caliban and white actors as the Italians, this social reality is sharpened as audiences are asked to consider race, colonialism, and slavery as intrinsic to the Island's social hierarchy—imposed by Prospero, then again in grotesque comic form by Stephano and Trinculo.

Can a fully human reading of the King's Men's Caliban incorporate any 'fishy' elements? If we take the fish insult literally it might lead us to Inigo Jones's designs for *The Masque of Blackness* (1605), which show water-related figures in blue make-up; half-man, half-fish figures appear in that masque, described here:

In front of this sea were placed six tritons, in moving and sprightly actions, their upper parts human, save that their hairs were blue, as partaking of the sea-color: their desinent [i.e. lower] parts fish, mounted above their heads, and all varied in disposition. From their backs were borne out certain light pieces of taffata, as if carried by the wind, and their music made out of wreathed shells. (Jonson 2001, 33–40)

Theatre historians Michael Saengar and Gabriel Egan have claimed documentary evidence for Caliban as a visibly piscine monster, albeit one with legs. Saengar's article in *Notes and Queries*, and another that draws on Saengar's, by Gabriel Egan, use as evidence Antony Munday's description of two figures, Amphion and Corinea, that Shakespearean actors Richard Burbage and John Rice played in a pageant that sailed up the river Thames, to celebrate the inauguration of the Prince of Wales in 1610. An entry in the records of the London Corporation shows that Burbage and Rice were permitted to '...reteyne to their owne uses, in lieu of their paynes therein taken all such Taffety silke and other necessaries as were provided for that purpose' (London Corporation); that is to say, the actors were paid in costumes. Saengar and Egan argue that Burbage and Rice would have taken these costumes for use in *The Tempest*. Whilst Rice might have played Ariel himself, the King's Men's lead actor Burbage would have likely played Prospero, and, according to this theory, passed on his costume to another adult actor playing Caliban. On the side of Saengar and Egan's argument for Rice's costume being used for Ariel are the watery adornments that Rice as Corinea is described as wearing. Corinea, writes Munday, appears as 'a very fayre and beautiful Nimphe', attired in a 'watrie habit yet rich and costlie' and wearing 'a Coronet of Pearles and Cockle shells' (Munday 1610, 14). Saengar suggestively points out that 'If the costume was re-used [in *The Tempest*], Ariel would thus be wearing pearls and sea-shells in a delicately ironic literalization' when he sang to Ferdinand of his father beneath the sea, with bones of coral—'phonetically close to cockle'—and eyes of pearl (Saengar 1995, 335). Rice might indeed have played Ariel in this or an adapted version of this costume; after all, verbal allusions aside, Prospero directly orders Ariel to dress as a sea nymph.

The idea that the whole Amphion costume was used for Caliban is less plausible. Monday describes Amphion as a 'grave and judicious Prophet-like person' (Munday 1610, 14) and it seems unlikely that this is how the log-carrying Caliban, insulted as slave and monster, would have appeared.

It is just as likely that the 'taffety silk' Burbage obtained in payment for the pageant was cut up for his own or the company's use in other ways. However, Rice and Burbage do get to keep the 'other necessaries' from the pageant, as well as the fabric, so perhaps Burbage did sell or pass on Amphion's wreath of sea-shells and other marine-inflected decorations, rather than a full costume, to the actor playing Caliban in the King's Men. In my more 'human' reading of the Caliban costume above, Caliban is forced to wear Prospero's rags for his daily enforced labour. Might he also have worn the shells as the last vestiges of his free island life? We see above that on the backs of the tritons in the *Masque of Blackness* 'were borne out certain light pieces of taffeta, as if carried by the wind, and their music made out of wreathed shells'. Might such shells have rattled triumphantly in memory of that freedom as Caliban sings his song of rebellion?

A common modern costume choice for characters on *The Tempest*'s island is to give the impression that they have had to improvise clothing out of natural materials from the island. This is not, I should say, how the first Prospero and Miranda would have looked; they would likely have worn costly Jacobean dress, and this is, interestingly, something that Shakespeare is at pains to explain: Prospero mentions to Miranda that the good old counsellor Gonzalo ensured not only that the father and daughter had Prospero's books to take with them when they were dispatched from Naples in their rat-abandoned ship, but that their clothes were packed too (1.2.190–195). Further, whereas the sailors on board ship in the storm enter 'wet' in the Folio stage direction, Prospero's shipwrecked enemies are surprised to find that their clothes are untouched by the storm (2.1.59–60); there is no reason to suppose that Ariel has not performed this magical laundry service for Prospero and Miranda too. The nobles' wonder at the cleanliness of their clothes speaks to a practical issue for early modern stage companies, who could have ill afforded to dirty and dampen the expensive clothes worn by upper class characters.

A costume made up from shabby human clothing and marine-inflected objects and fabric, to contrast starkly with the rich dress of his master, is a plausible costume for an early modern Caliban. If, on the other hand, his 'salvage and deformed' state was fantastically, visually monstrous, what might that have looked like, and how might a monster Caliban have been received? One assumption might be that the more monstrous the Caliban, the lower the moral and ethical stakes in his relationship with Prospero and Miranda. The more furry or scaly, the more outlandishly fish-like in colour he is, the easier it might be to dismiss him as an animal with uncontrolled animal appetites, whom the father and daughter mistakenly tried to tame. The line 'This island's mine by Sycorax my mother' (1.2.389) has potentially less ethical force if a monster speaks it to a human being than if one human being speaks it to another. As we will see, more negative reviews of the first colonially inflected production of the play in the UK, at the Mermaid Theatre, London, in 1970, are irritated by Caliban's lack of monstrousness as played by Rudolph Walker. I suggest that this is because a completely human Caliban, played by a black actor, undermines Prospero's moral authority in the play—the moral authority of a figure that has been linked to Shakespeare in scholarship since the second half of the nineteenth century (see Dowden 1877, 426–427).

Writing on histories of the grotesque costume in her *Costume in Performance*, Donatella Barbieri marks the potentially subversive, Rabelaisian meanings of the grotesquely costumed body. However, she also demonstrates how the carnivalesque grotesque is appropriated by the elite of the French court to render safely comic the subversive threat of the growing bourgeoisie (Barbieri 2017, 62). Similarly, if Caliban is a grotesque half-man, half fish as might have been seen in the anti-masque of court performance, he becomes, perhaps, a comic 'other' to human power: an 'other' that might indicate a degree of anxiety about the stability of leadership and masculinity perhaps, but a safely containable anxiety nonetheless. In this reading, Prospero's acknowledgement of 'this thing of darkness' (5.1.309) becomes a laudable admission of the animal appetites in all of us but hardly threatens the status quo.

Early modern travel writing has been marked as a source for the narrative of *The Tempest*. What might the descriptions of foreign peoples that appear in these works tell us about how the first stage Caliban might have been dressed? Whilst the play's island must literally be situated somewhere in the Mediterranean, scholars have long connected the play's narrative with the long letter by William Strachey which describes the wreck of the Virginia Company-backed expedition off the Bermudas, whilst on its way to Jamestown, circulating in Shakespeare's lifetime and published later (See Malone, who made this connection in 1808; Stritmatter and Kositsky 1958; Nosworthy 1948; Fulton 1978; Vaughan and Vaughan 1993, 83–197). If news of this wreck was likely to be in the forefront of audiences' minds when they watched *The Tempest*, would this have influenced the kind of Caliban, that 'islander…lately suffered by a thunderbolt' (2.2.30), the Kings' Men showed them? Shakespeare and his company could already have seen the images of native Americans printed by Theodor de Bry in Thomas Hariot's *Brief and True Report of the New Found Land of Virginia*, who describes 'people clothed with loose mantles made of Deere skins, & aprons of the same rounde about their middles; all els naked' (Hariot 2007, 34) or those of cannibals in de Bry's *America*. These range from woodcuts of naked cannibals, to a war-painted figure with single head-feathers and fringed skirt, to similarly skirted and feathered figures dancing at a feast with others covered in branches and described by Hariot as 'attyred in the most strange fashion they can devise hanging certain marks on the backs to declare of what place they bee' (Hariot 2007; see also Bloechel 2004, 58). Stephen Orgel's introduction to the Oxford edition of the play points to accounts of the free and open sex lives of native Americans as possible sources for Caliban's behaviour towards Miranda and his lack of repentance for it, as well as for Gonzalo's fantasy of a prelapsarian form of government on the island (Orgel 1998, 33–34). Orgel references a German broadsheet of 1505 which contains an image and a description of feathered, be-jewelled figures. The translated broadsheet tells of New World 'natives' that 'their heads, necks, arms, genitals, feet of both women and men are lightly covered with feathers' (Orgel 1998, 33, citing Hugh Honour's *The New Golden Land*) and the description potentially reads as though the adornments are growing on the people's bodies. It is as if seeing feathers on people is so alien to the writer that he slips to conflating them with birds.

It would be anachronistic indeed to suggest that members of the Kings' Men pored over available images of people living on currently-of-interest, far-away places and 'designed' culturally accurate New World costumes. But a Caliban who appears as a human figure decorated with shells and scraps of fabric might not only fit Saengar and Egan's observation that two of the King's Men had recently been paid in marine-inflected accoutrements, but an audience's expectation that the inhabitants of exotic islands would be human figures wearing clothes adorned with natural and animal materials. This, significantly, allows for a spectrum of audience reception of Caliban, from an empathetic wonder at a human, albeit exoticised, figure, to repulsion at a human being visually associated with the animal and animalistic.

A productive Irish connection to Caliban via the American colonies has also been made, by Barbara Fuchs (1997) in her article 'Conquering Islands: Contextualizing *The Tempest*', in which she describes how describers of native American dress reference Ireland, an older site of colonisation:

> The English often perceived the Americas through an Irish filter. Thus Gabriel Archer described the natives' leggings in New England as "like to Irish Dimmie Trouses," and Martin Pring saw natives with "a Beares skinne like an Irish Mantle over one shoulder." Even Powhatan's dress was described by one of John Smith's companions as "a faire Robe of skins as large as an Irish mantle. (26)

Fuchs argues persuasively that it is possible to read the gabardine episode, in which Trinculo is misrecognised as monstrous under Caliban's cloak, 'as one of the indices' of the British 'colonial adventure' in Ireland, where rebels are easily disguised and telling colonised from coloniser is a potential problem. If Caliban's gabardine is made of skins, his body adorned with shells, then he becomes an amalgam of the early modern imaginary colonised other—wondrous one moment, a monstrous threat the next.

Finally, might the company have taken literally Caliban's Algerian connection through Sycorax his mother, and staged a North African Caliban? Sycorax was deported to the island from Algiers, and it is not necessary to take Prospero literally when he calls Caliban a 'poisonous slave, got by the devil himself/ Upon thy wicked dam' (1.2.376–377), any more than one expects to see furry ears and a wagging tail on a modern dramatic character whom someone calls a 'son of a bitch'. As Caliban's mother was Algerian, so might his father have been. On the one hand, Prospero finally claims Caliban as 'this thing of darkness' but in *Othello* and *Titus*, and across Shakespeare's work, dark and darkness are used in the context of night time and of evil, but never in relation to race. Othello and Aaron are referred to and refer to themselves as black, as does Cleopatra. It is the word 'black', not 'dark' that denotes race, and no-one ever says Caliban is black. If the King's Men were staging the proto-colonial 'other' in Caliban, it could be argued that their audiences recalled accounts of indigenous Americans and Bermudans, or even Irishmen as Fuchs suggests, rather than an African man. However, in following such a line of argument, one might be in danger of erasing blackness from the early modern canon, in comparable fashion to the 'white melancholic' scholars of Little's critique (above 138). In the introduction to Kim F. Hall's seminal *Things of Darkness: Economies of Race and Gender in Early Modern England*, she draws our attention to scholars who remystify 'the appearance of blackness in literary works by insisting that references to race are rooted in European

aesthetic tradition rather than in any consciousness of racial difference'
(Hall 1995, 1). Hall demonstrates that '[t]he trope of blackness' whilst it:

> had a broad arsenal of effects in the early modern period, meaning that it
> applied not only to dark-skinned Africans but to Native Americans, Indians,
> Spanish, and even Irish and Welsh as groups that needed to be marked as
> "other"...still draws power from England's ongoing negotiation of African
> difference and from the implied color comparison therein. Thus the Irish
> may be called 'black' and an English woman may be called 'Ethiopian', but
> these moments always depend on a visual schema that itself relies on an idea
> of African difference. (1995, 6–7)

One powerful visual schema I have suggested is at work through *The
Tempest* is one of clothing, where the once-favoured Caliban is staged in
his ragged livery next to Prospero and his daughter who are wearing fine
Jacobean garments, and later next to the fine frippery he rejects on the
way to Prospero's cell. Caliban also features in Prospero's break-up of the
Masque performance—the ragged revolutionary momentarily breaks up
the ceremony of aristocratic continuity, just as, according to Prospero he
nearly succeeded in breaking the former Duke's line and peopling all the
isle with Calibans. As the on- and off-stage audience enjoy the rich and
fantastical costumes of the masque, Caliban in his rags is once again
recalled. In a play whose inciting incident is a shipwreck on the return
from a wedding of a young white woman to 'an African' (2.1.123), Hall's
analysis on the 'visual schema that itself relies on an idea of African difference' could well be coming into play. In the early modern period, Caliban
cannot be the enslaved black man of eighteenth- and nineteenth-century
history, but he could read on the early modern stage as an enslaved black
man nonetheless.

My citation of Hall here can also be productively linked to costume via
Ian Smith's fascinating analysis of 'The Textile Black Body' in *The Merchant
of Venice*, where he draws attention to the tradition of using textile pros-
thetics—gloves, arm coverings, leg coverings, animal skin wigs—in court
masque performances of Moors. Smith points out that the Prince of
Morocco in the play 'excuses' his physical difference from dominant
Venetian culture with the lines 'Mislike me not for my complexion,/ The
shadowed livery of the burnished sun,/ To whom I am a neighbour and
near bred' (2.1.1–3). Livery is clothing given to servants to mark their
servitude, their place and position within a household. Thus the masque

costumes used to denote blackness become a racialised livery, conflating the black body with servitude, and with merchandise to be bought and sold. It is fascinating to imagine the contrast between the rich clothing of the masque-within-the-play in *The Tempest* (as Hall points out, full of the promise of bounty in comparison to the wedding of his own daughter to an African that Alonso so regrets in Act 2 (Hall 1995, 149)) and a Caliban made black by the textiles used to denote blackness in masque performance. In the end, we cannot know whether the early Caliban—or any figure outside of masque performance—would have worn such a 'shadowed livery'. But I suggest that imagining an 'original' Caliban as a slave adorned with decorations that connect him to a former, free life on the island taps into the possible expectations of the early modern spectator that they will see extraordinary, exotic figures in a play about an island voyaged to by Westerners, and paves the way for the more recent stagings that I explore next, in which the possibility of Caliban as a colonised figure of colour and his claim that 'this island's mine' is taken seriously.

SLAVES AND BUTLERS: THE FIRST BLACK BRITISH ARIEL AND CALIBAN, MERMAID THEATRE 1970, DIRECTOR, JONATHAN MILLER, COSTUMES ROSEMARY VERCOE, DESIGNER JOHN COLLINS

The first British production to cast black performers as Ariel and Caliban, and the first of three in which the actor Rudolph Walker played Caliban, was directed by Jonathan Miller and produced by the Mermaid Theatre London in 1970. Trevor L Griffiths writes that 'In general, the critical reaction was extremely favourable to Miller's conception' (1983, 178) but my own readings of press responses to the casting of Walker as Caliban and Norman Beaton as Ariel, and to the commentary on colonial power with which director Jonathan Miller and costume designer Rosemary Vercoe inflected the play, suggest that critical reception ranged from the awestruck to the patronising and irritable. Vercoe is lauded in her obituary of 2013 as a designer who 'gravitated to the real rather than the romantic' and whose 'period designs were clothes not costumes' (Jays 2013). Jacobean costume on John Collins's bare set for the Mermaid *Tempest* clearly delineates Caliban and Ariel's status in Prospero's colony: Beaton's Ariel is sharply dressed in dark doublet and hose, Caliban in a battered old greatcoat. Thus the *Punch* reviewer tells us:

Norman Beaton's Ariel is the lordly African colonized by European Prospero, impatient for independence. Rudolph Walker's Caliban is the ex-African degraded into the New World slave, used solely for Prospero's profit. (1970)

Michael Billington, for *Plays and Players*, was 'delighted' at the 'fresh impetus' given to the play by the production's interpretation; he reads Ariel as 'a black major-domo' clothed in 'the fashionable Western style of dress but also carrying a fly-whisk to remind us of his origins' (Billington 1970). Walker's Caliban, on the other hand was played, according to Billington as, 'the oppressed primitive with a justifiable grievance'; readers are presumably meant to know what oppressed primitives look like. In most of the positive reviews of the production, the impression is given of Ariel as a calm, dignified, high-status servant biding his time before taking over power from Prospero (Graham Crowden), which he does by reassembling Prospero's broken staff, a final gesture with which Cyril Nri's Ariel also finished the play in the production Miller directed in 1988.

Less positive reviews for this *Tempest* are determined that this is not what Shakespeare would have wanted. Now that the concept of Caliban and Ariel as colonised people of colour is such a theatrical commonplace, their objections read as startlingly conservative. Milton Shulman in the *Evening Standard* upbraids Miller for 'trying too hard to squeeze his imperialist allegory into a story that will obviously resist such an interpretation' and takes a tone of sarcastic incredulity at the social realism that he clearly thinks is the bathetic result:

Ariel, instead of the usual athletic sprite, is a rather sedate, world-weary Haitian butler who goes about his ethereal tasks with a magic whisk and looking for the most part as if his chief concern is overtime. Norman Beaton handles this novel interpretation with the circumspect dignity of an old hand from a domestic agency. The only evidence of Caliban's semi-human proportions is the fact that he wears a soiled, army greatcoat and Rudolph Walker's grumbling creature has the endearing quality of a rasping, grovelling, ingratiating Uncle Tom.

Philip Hope-Wallace in the *Guardian* is equally irritated. For him:

the Caliban (Rudolph Walker) does not get at the pity of the poor oppressed beast of burden one bit and the 'delicate Ariel' (Norman Beaton) as a rather lazy-footed kind of native butler with a fly-whisk also seemed to me to miss the heart of the role: nothing thereat, a big solid house-boy rather, with a certain sly charm.

The discourse here is startlingly racist, as the reviewers read through Beaton's crisp, black Jacobean doublet and hose to later black histories of domestic service and slavery. Caliban becomes an 'Uncle Tom', in the *Evening Standard*; Ariel's status in the colonial power structure of the production is reduced to the denigrating 'house-boy' in the *Guardian*, his pace read as 'lazy footed' rather than calm, measured or dignified as in the more positive reviews and his 'charm', also commented on positively elsewhere, read as 'sly'. The negative reviews are also disappointed that Caliban isn't portrayed as half-monster in his battered great-coat; for Hope-Wallace, Walker doesn't get at 'the pity of the poor beast of burden' and Shulman clearly wants more evidence of 'Caliban's semi-human proportions'.

Significantly, in an interview published in 1989, just after Miller's second colonially-inflected production of *The Tempest* had been performed at the Old Vic, London (in which Walker again played Caliban) Miller cites costume clichés for Ariel and Caliban as his first inspiration for his thinking about the play:

> some of my moves in the theatre have been prompted by revulsion against certain well-established clichés. Now the one that stuck in my gorge was the sequin-spangled, pointed-eared, flitting figures of Ariel...similarly the scaly, web-footed monster of Caliban just didn't tell me anything about anyone, it wasn't a monster which meant anything and it clotted my imagination and stopped it from thinking. (Miller in Berry 1977, 33–34)

Miller goes on to explain how Mannoni's essay *La Psychologie de la Colonisation* offered him a productive alternative reading. As students of the post-colonial critical history of the play will be aware, Mannoni's reading of *The Tempest*, a lengthy section of the English translation of which is reproduced in the Mermaid's programme for the 1970 production, suggests that coloniser and colonised are destructively co-dependent, a psychoanalytic interpretation that was later roundly condemned by Aimé Césaire and the Caribbean scholar Frantz Fanon, for failing to acknowledge the coloniser's primary reason for colonisation: economic power (Césaire 2000, 59–63; Fanon 2008, 71–81; see also Nixon 1987, 564–565). In his interview with Ralph Berry, however, whilst Miller is interested in Mannoni's concept of 'Caliban and Ariel as different forms of black response to white paternalism' (Berry 1977, 34), the director emphasises not so much that Caliban is child-like in his dependency on Prospero, but

Mannoni's idea that Prospero is psychologically immature in his desire for control. Prospero's psychological journey towards relinquishing control—over the island and its people, over Miranda—is a popular reading of *The Tempest*, certainly by actors playing Prospero. What I contend is significant about the *Tempests* directed by Miller is not that they erased Prospero's emotional and moral journey but that they created a political, colonial context for it. Rosemary Vercoe's costume design was essential to the creation of this context in Miller's first production: it demonstrated Ariel's closeness to Prospero and his future as the Island's next colonial power, and the brutality of Caliban's existence at the very bottom of the power structure. As we will see, costumes for Miller's next post-colonial *Tempest*, designed by Richard Hudson, linked Caliban more closely to Prospero, and staged Ariel as part of a more distinct 'island' culture.

'DOWN TO WORK' WITH WALKER, NRI AND MILLER: THE TEMPEST 1988, DIRECTOR JONATHAN MILLER, DESIGNER RICHARD HUDSON

In 1988, a favourite production image for critics writing on the second colonially-inflected *Tempest* directed by Miller, was of Max von Sydow's Prospero gazing seriously out into the auditorium/ocean. Typical is a photograph from the *Daily Telegraph*, in which Prospero's thoughts are so serious he seems to have forgotten that he is holding on to Miranda (Rudi Davies)'s head. Critics commented on the colour-conscious casting (the *Sunday Telegraph*'s headline is 'O Black New World') but their chosen photographs suggest that what they consider *The Tempest* is really 'about' is the older, white man, his emotional and moral journey, and his relationship with his daughter.

A few days before the production opened, a rather different image of a white patriarch appeared in the press in connection with the production: the V&A Theatre Collection hold a clip from the *Daily Telegraph* which shows a photograph of director Jonathan Miller emerging from Caliban's trap door. The photograph is entitled 'Down to Work with Miller' and the legend beneath the image reads:

> A pensive Jonathan Miller, deeply involved in a hole in the stage and his production of The Tempest which opens at the Old Vic on October 11, starring Max von Sydow as Prospero, Rudi Davies as Miranda and with Alexei Sayle as Trinculo.

It is Caliban's trap door from which Miller emerges, looking pensive and studious in the scholarly uniform of comfortable old tweed jacket, and the reader is invited to get 'down to work' with Miller, not Caliban; Rudolph Walker is not mentioned in the legend beneath the photo, despite this being the second time Miller had directed him in the role. Here, 'under the stage' indicates not Caliban's enslavement but the director's depth of thought. The white patriarch, whether he be director/auteur or central character, is at the centre of meaning-making in these images, despite the reviews' persistence in commenting on the significance of Ariel and Caliban and their casting.

The *Observer* appeared to be interested in the 'visually arresting' aspects of what they call, according to convention, Jonathan Miller's *Tempest*, though designer Richard Hudson is of course responsible for the pale set with its rocky outcrop stage right and its modern white box and telescope representing Prospero's cell stage left. In the image published with the *Observer* review, a black actor in a white space is the visual focus: Rudolph Walker wearing a battered jerkin and remnants of 'grass skirt' fringing stands against the uncluttered, pale, textured space. Where Rosemary Vercoe's costumes for Miller's first Tempest were broadly Jacobean (Rudolph Walker's battered greatcoat being a historically less specific exception I would suggest), Hudson produced a more visually explicit reference to colonialism in his costume designs for the 1988 production. Where Cecil Beaton's Ariel in 1970 was sharply and elegantly dressed by Vercoe to indicate his status as a servant close to Prospero, Cyril Nri's Ariel stood in contrast to Prospero and the Italian nobles because much of his costume consisted of a grey, ash-like body paint, inspired, as we will see, by the Nuba peoples of the then Sudan. Ariel and the black bodies of the island spirit figures he controls stood largely naked against the pale set and in contrast to the elaborately dressed European nobles.

Nri himself evidently had a role in designing his own costume here. Talking to Michael MacMillan for the essay "The Black Body and Shakespeare: Conversations with Black Actors", he writes about his movement style and appearance in the production:

> It was set in a fictional African island, though having grown up in Africa it wasn't quite authentic. From my research about animals and people, like the Aborigines, I found that there was lightness of touch that enabled them to survive the intense heat, such as the zigzag movement of a desert snake almost not touching the sand.

I looked at photographs of the Nuba from southern Sudan in *The Last of the Nuba* (1976) by the German photographer Leni Riefenstahl. They used ash and dust from the earth to create, decorate and protect their bodies from the elements. I used these bodily materials in preparing to play Ariel. (Nri in McMillan 2017, 127)

Nri may well not have known that Riefenstahl was the director of the notorious Nazi propaganda film *Triumph of the Will* amongst others. In a review of this book of photography, Susan Sontag suggested that it was part of a project to rehabilitate Riefenstahl two decades after the Nazi era, a project of which Sontag was understandably suspicious. For Sontag:

What is distinctive about the fascist version of the old idea of the Noble Savage is its contempt for all that is reflective, critical, and pluralistic. In Riefenstahl's casebook of primitive virtue, it is hardly the intricacy and subtlety of primitive myth, social organization, or thinking that are being extolled. She is especially enthusiastic about the ways the Nuba are exalted and unified by the physical ordeals of their wrestling matches, in which the "heaving and straining" Nuba men...throw one another to the ground—fighting not for material prizes but "for the renewal of sacred vitality of the tribe. (Sontag 1975)

Startling in their near nakedness and in control of the island's magic, albeit under Prospero's rule, Nri's Ariel and the island spirits could be in danger of colluding with the stereotype that is often recalled in the casting and costuming of actors of colour in Shakespeare production, and one close to the 'noble savage': that of the 'magical negro'. Discussing one black actress's experience of being cast as a witch in make-believe play as a child, then in the theatre in *Macbeth*, Ayanna Thompson writes, in *Passing Strange: Shakespeare, Race and Contemporary America*:

Black witches make sense because of the stereotype of the "magical negro", a stereotypical, stock character employed in many genres of contemporary popular culture, a figure who has other-worldly, unearthly connections, a figure who has no past, a figure who helps to save a white protagonist: a kind of negro ex-machina. (2011, 78)

Were the ash-covered black bodies in this *Tempest* examples of exactly this phenomenon? I contend that Hudson and Nri's design for Ariel, and Nri's performance, were, to borrow from Sontag above, rather more 'reflective, critical and pluralistic', particularly because of the way in which Ariel became as much of an observer of those who are wrecked on the island as Prospero and Miranda. He sat near Ferdinand, curiously imitating his actions, rendering the young Neopolitan prince absurd in the court dress that made sitting on the ground an uncomfortable business. Ariel laughed in conspiracy with Prospero, like Puck with Oberon, but his seeming obedience in the face of Prospero's threats masked a plan to rule the island himself; in the last moment of the production, as in the 1970 version, he reassembled the magician's staff, much to the horror of Caliban. Unlike Thompson's 'magical negro', Ariel has a past in this play and a political present in this colonially inflected production, one that he ultimately controlled himself. He and the island spirits were, moreover, the only figures on stage whose dress did not seem to be controlled by Prospero. Miranda was dressed very similarly to her father; Caliban was dressed in his ragged cast offs with only vestiges of indigenous decoration.

A source close to Miller recalls that he spoke on several occasions during the rehearsal period for the 1988 *Tempest* about the Belgian colonial powers in Rwanda and how they divided the different ethnic groups, designating their relative roles largely on the difference in their appearance and the supposed superiority of the Tutsis (Ariel) compared to Houtis (Caliban). Miller also mentions in his interview with Berry 'this situation only a few years ago in Nigearia, with the skilled civil servant Ibos and the unskilled tribal Hausas' (Miller in Berry 1977, 34). Whilst Nri was using the Nuba as an aesthetic stimulus, the director was concerned with colonial divide and rule. Miller also mentions Zimbabwe (then Rhodesia), as a colonial example that would have been in the forefront of spectators' minds. Miller is explicit that the production is not intended to recall one particular colonial situation but rather than he wanted to 'bring [audiences] into a closer relationship with the whole notion of subordination and mastery which I think is one of the things which Shakespeare is talking about with great eloquence in that play' (Miller in Berry 1977, 34). However, many reviewers read costume in the 1988 production as indicating a specific geographical location. Reviews held by the V&A Theatre and Performance Collections confidently and variously assert that it is set in the Pacific or the Torres strait, somewhere in Africa, or in Papua New Guinea; another informs us that Ariel and the spirits who control the feast scene are aboriginal whilst Caliban is Caribbean. As in 1970, some reviewers were troubled that Caliban appeared to be fully human in Rudolph Walker's performance, and, once more citing Shakespearean authority, put

Caliban's lack of monstrousness down to Miller's determination to sacrifice the play on the altar of his politics. The passing of eighteen years, which had seen three more Black Calibans on the British stage,[1] did not seem to have entirely dispelled critical irritation at the supposed imposition of a colonial reading on the play. Paul Taylor of the *Independent*, on the other hand, is much more sympathetic to what he calls Miller's 'fine tuning [of] ideas with which he experimented in his 1970 production' and, conjuring similar costume clichés to the ones Miller so disliked, sums up the longer-standing versions of Ariel and Caliban that other reviewers seem to be pining for:

> His Ariel is no ethereal androgyne flitting about the stage striking corny balletic attitudes, nor is Caliban a slime-covered, walking midden or scaly evolutionary deviant. Scrapping the notion that Prospero's servants are personifications of air and earth, Miller re-imagines them as black inhabitants of the island whose responses to the white colonialists pointedly differ. (Taylor 1988)

Overall, it seems that more negative reviews seem keen to offer a highly specific geographical location for the production and to suggest that Miller was rather silly to set the play there, whilst more positive reviews were happy to read it as making a more general point about white colonialists and colonised people of colour. There are political problems with both readings: the more generalised one could suggest that Ariel and the Islanders' costumes were making some vague, nativist point about what colonised people might look like. But what interests me about the more irritable, geographically specific readings is that they are never applied to the places the white actors' characters might come from. The shipwrecked Italians' costumes at the Old Vic in 1988 are startlingly pale and clean; Antonio and Sebastian look awkward in their cream doublets, trunk hose and white fitted hose, sitting on the island's rough surface, planning their plot to assassinate Alonso, but no critic remarked that as Italian nobles they would likely have worn darker fabrics, or wondered, therefore, if in this production they were meant to be from somewhere else. Some more negative reviews from press night also suggest that Max Von Sydow did not speak the lines very clearly and a few reviewers tiresomely suggest that

---

[1] Jeffery Kissoon at the RSC's Other Place in 1974; Thomas Baptiste at the Oxford Playhouse in 1976; Rudolph Walker again at Bristol Old Vic in 1980.

this is because the actor is Swedish; no one, however, speculates as to whether Milan in this production has been transposed to Stockholm. It is the black actors on stage whom the reviewers read as intrinsic to Miller's willfully political, colonial interpretation; the white actors maintain, in these readings, a generalised white Europeanness, which does not have to look Italian and which is consistent with an assumption that it is white characters who have universally human emotional and moral journeys—towards forgiveness, redemption, better self-knowledge—whilst black characters bear the burden of representing political and cultural power relations.

I contend that Richard Hudson's costume design did significant work to stage and expose the trope that white 'means' universal emotional and moral journey in Shakespeare production, safely distinct from racialised power relations. White people's clothes became implicated in political and colonial power in this production. The shipwrecked nobles' plotting and scheming was exposed on the island as they sat on the rocks in their pristine, stuffed doublets and white tights. When the play opens, Prospero and Miranda were wearing linen shirts—the undergarments of Elizabethan/Jacobean dress—and looser beige breeches, practical for life on the island. But as the play ended and Prospero prepared to return to Milan, he re-assembled himself as a Jacobean aristocrat, donning a velvet doublet for the wedding masque and then, for his final scene and with Ariel's help, a sword, soft cap and non-magical cloak of baroque design. He looked at himself for a long pause in a mirror held by Ariel. This moment of re-dressing for European power was an interesting one in the stage history of the play, in which Prospero's disrobing, his relinquishing of his magic garment, has more frequently been the more significant costume moment. The more common visual trope suggests that at the end of the play Prospero gives up his magical control over the island and exposes himself as a mere man—one who has taken a universal emotional and moral journey. This production recalled that although Prospero considers himself close to death, he is still returning to a Milan of presumably unchanged court scheming and hierarchy. Thus costume in this *Tempest* produces whiteness as a product of power relations as much as (enslaved) blackness.

Rudolph Walker's second Caliban wore not a dilapidated modern great coat, as in the 1970 production, but tatty slops and a battered version of a Jacobean jerkin, open to a bare chest, which recall the kind of garments I have argued he might have worn in the first performances of the play. This costume suggested that the master had given the slave clothes when he was being treated member of the family, but later left those clothes to wear and tear with labour after he had fallen out of favour. This Caliban also wore the vestiges of an indigenous island culture in the strips of material at his waist, which looked like remnants of the kinds of grass skirts the masque goddesses wore later in the play. The power structure of the comic scenes was played out visually: Stephano and Trinculo were evidently of higher status than Caliban in European terms, with their linen-covered chests, but symbolically on their way downwards whilst they fantasise power over the island: their clothes were stained, they had clearly not had them preserved from sea and storm by Ariel as the nobles had. Of course, clothes are finally their downfall as they are distracted by the garments Ariel lays out for them on the way to Prospero's cell.

The masque goddesses were played by Melanie E. Marshall, Dorothy Ross and Laverne Williams, black performers wearing Elizabethan shapes created from the stuff of the island: grass skirt farthingales and shell neck-laces that framed the head like the Elizabethan ruff. Even Paul Taylor, in his otherwise enthusiastic review, objects to this:

> Decked out in dresses which cross grass-skirts with crinolines [sic] and laden with tribal wigs and jewellery, the Goddesses are three black divas who belt out the verse in an operatic pastiche of Montiverdi. This ... seems to be tak-ing things too far: is Prospero trying to Europeanise the supernatural, one is left wondering? (Taylor 1988)

I assume that this was exactly what was being suggested. Von Sydow's Prospero used costume to make bodies mean he wanted them to mean: he played with his magical cloak in the manner of a bullfighter when con-fronting Caliban, reducing Caliban the figure of a bull to his toreador. He seemed to have designed the wedding masque using Elizabethan shapes and Western musical forms, to Europeanise the supernatural just as Taylor sarcastically suggests. Prospero's masque at once rendered the indigenous materials of the island exotic by means of the alienation effect created by the Western forms, and rendered Western court dress natural and univer-sal by constructing it in natural materials.

My own memories of this production have been sharpened by the recording archived in the Victoria and Albert Museum theatre collection and by a conversation with designer Richard Hudson. I have pieced together a sense of the 1970 production, on the other hand, via its rather more fragmented documentation, including photographer Douglas Jeffry's archive, also in the Victoria and Albert collection, and the memories of those who saw the work. Costume designer Rosemary Vercoe and designer John Collins have both passed. Shakespeare scholar Tony Howard, who led on the production of the Black British and Asian Shakespeare database that has so richly informed this chapter, and who saw both productions, was more excited by the 1970 Tempest, because it rigorously pursued Mannoni's theorization of the colonial mindset, particularly in the relationship between Prospero and Miranda:

> Graham Crowden's Prospero, unlike Von Sidow's, was psychologically maimed by the experience of colonisation (or else he was a colonist because of his psychological inadequacy—cf the debates of Franz Fanon versus Mannoni) and this was even more visibly embodied in his infantalisation of Miranda, whom Angela Pleasance played as almost incapable of speech. (Howard, personal correspondence)

For Howard, 1988 Miranda, Rudi Davies, was more conventional: 'the wild child/free spirit reading', whilst von Sydow's Prospero was more 'relaxed' and, by implication, offered a less compelling analysis of the colonial mindset as a result. However, I suggest that in its very conventionality, von Sydow's performance created not so much a psychological analysis of the colonial as a theatrical and political one. Watching the recording now and reading backwards and forwards into the *Tempest*s that came before and afterwards, von Sydow encapsulates some classic modern theatrical Prospero traits which, I would argue, are heightened in order to be interrogated in this production: he is a warm but controlling father, and a patronizing, sometimes brutal, controller of Ariel and Caliban, who finally, of course, sets Ariel free and acknowledges Caliban 'his'. When he puts his Milanese garments back on, the thoughtful deliberation with which he looks at himself in the mirror suggests that he has 'learned something' on his emotional and spiritual journey through the play. However, when Ariel takes up his staff at the end of the performance to reassemble it, much to Caliban's terror, the production suggests that Prospero has learned nothing of political significance. He is returning to his position of power in Milan, better able to keep it until the death he claims he is going to be musing upon, essentially leaving intact the power structures he has imposed on the island.

Having made this political claim for the production, its aesthetic of over-clothed white bodies and near-naked black may still strike the contemporary viewer of the production photographs as troubling. I have argued that Cyril Nri's nuanced and detailed performance of Ariel goes some way to undoing the stereotype of the 'magical negro' and that the awkwardness of the Italian nobles' crisp white doublet and hose on Hudson's island setting foregrounds white power in politically astute ways. But white still reads as 'artifice' and 'power' in this costume scheme, black as either 'nature' or 'oppressed'. It could be argued that the semantic force of Jacobean dress on the Shakespearean stage was finally in danger of undoing the production's interrogation of colour and power, potentially reiterating the stereotypes Miller and Hudson sought to undo. White actors in beautiful clothes are what audiences may be used to seeing on the Shakespearean stage, after all; they read, like Miller emerging from Caliban's trap door, as the meaning-makers of Shakespeare, as symbols of proto-colonial Renaissance humanity and knowledge, however morally corrupted in the usurping Antonio and his company, however literally corrupted in the dirty costumes of Stephano and Trinculo. Next to all of them, Ariel and the spirit islanders could still be in danger of reading as the exotic, unclothed other. But overall, I contend that Hudson's costume designs put the play's power relations, and the racialised power relations produced by casting in this production, into critical relief, rather than simply reiterating and confirming colonial power.

Post Post-colonial Tempests

As Ralph Berry notes in his early nineties book *Shakespeare and Performance—Casting and Metamorphoses*, 1988 was something of a year of *Tempest*s in the UK: the RSC and the National Theatre produced the play in the same year, and so did theatre company Cheek by Jowl. Where Miller cast eight actors of colour out of a cast of 20, there were only three in the RSC's cast of 26, all in minor roles—and for part of the run that was reduced to two. The production directed by Peter Hall at the National had an all-white cast. Cheek by Jowl cast black British actor Paterson Joseph in the relatively small role of Adrian; the production's other performer of colour was, more prominently, Cecilia Noble as Miranda, who appeared for the wedding celebrations and when playing chess with Ferdinand in a 'traditional' whiter than white wedding dress. Reviews and scholarly accounts of this production make much of the fact that Alonso was re-gendered female and reminded everyone of Margaret Thatcher. However, Cheek by Jowl's *Tempest* is of more interest here for the use of a form of clown-like white-face for the (already white) Timothy Walker as Prospero, who made himself up on stage as the performance progressed, which had the effect of making Miranda look 'natural' and Prospero 'theatrical'; Miranda appeared to be under the control of a sinister white-faced, top-hatted father and theatrical impresario and had to undertake the white wedding ceremony of Western convention to escape him.

Charles Spencer's review of the RSC's 2002 production of *The Tempest* suggests that an awareness of the post-colonial turn in *Tempest* criticism was widespread by the end of the twentieth century, so that no-one was any longer likely to express surprise at the casting of black actors in the roles of Ariel and Caliban as they had at the Miller productions:

> The show is visually thrilling, but doesn't let spectacle stand in the way of hard thought and strong interpretation. In line with current critical orthodoxy, it presents The Tempest as a study of the evils of colonialism, but, though this is a dark reading, it is a continually persuasive one. (Spencer 2002)

Next, I consider what happens to costume in relation to casting for *The Tempest* in the UK after the Miller productions, and contend that whilst some productions seem determined—in one case quite consciously determined—that *The Tempest* should still be about something else, the meanings of white and whiteness in these productions can be read, both productively and uncomfortably, in post-colonial terms. I look at a kind of hyper-white costume for Ariel, a common choice that equates the colour white with the character's spirit nature and can unconsciously reiterate the trope of whiteness as abstract spirit or psyche, blackness as earth and the somatic.

Especially amongst majority white audiences, whiteness-as-race is likely to be assumed as normative and its construction not readable in white costumes. Of course, it would be perverse to suggest that race is always foregrounded when white—or indeed black—clothing is worn on stage, or to always conflate those colours with particular racial groups. White cloth, for example, might in some cases more readily be associated with African culture than with European: Chloe Obolensky designed a 'traditional' white robe for Nigerian actor Sotigui Kouyate as Prospero in Peter Brook's French version of *The Tempest*; for every set of crisp white garments designed by a Richard Hudson (for Miller's 1988 production) or a Luciano Damiani (for Giorgio Strehler's of 1978), there are a numerous

Tempest designs in which a pale stage design sets off the dark Jacobean dress worn by white actors playing Alonso, Antonio and company. However, I contend that whiteness-as-spirit does have a troubling, racially marked history given the colonially-inflected stage history of this play, and I want to spend a moment with one of the twentieth century's white Ariels to support this argument.

I also consider costume in productions that have given major roles to actors of colour in ways that have not suggested the colonial power relations of 'current critical orthodoxy', to borrow from Charles Spencer above, implicit in the casting of black actors for the people of the island and a white performer as Prospero. A modern audience potentially experiences an early modern drama dually, as both familiar and historically alien at different points in a performance; costume design can be part of what produces this experience, rather than a means of erasing historical difference. Ayanna Thompson argues that the 'practice of colorblind casting cannot resolve the larger societal tensions in which they are enmeshed' (Thompson 2006a, 8) and I am not suggesting that the *Tempest* productions I consider do resolve these tensions. I rather contend that costume can foreground them one moment, erase them the next, just as production foregrounds and erases the 'past-ness' of a play.

ARIEL WHITENESS

In a programme note to *The Tempest* produced by the Haymarket Theatre, London, in 2011, director Trevor Nunn insists that 'the moment you are in [a colonial] reading of the play, then 80 percent of what Shakespeare is also exploring gets trampled' (Nunn in Lindley 2013, 79). His assertion echoes the negative critical responses to the 1970 and 1988 productions, according to which Miller supposedly rides roughshod over Shakespearean authority with his post-colonial politics. Nunn's use of the word 'also' in the above does suggest that he accepts colonial power as part of the play's meaning. But the statement reads oddly when one considers casting and costuming choices for the production. As David Lindley points out in his introduction to the *New Cambridge Shakespeare* edition of the play, Nunn cast only one actor of colour in a major role in this production, Black British actor Giles Terera, as Caliban (Lindley 2013, 79). He was costumed naked to the waist, his upper torso bound with ropes. Terera's Caliban was, as Michael Billington remarks, quite gently and easily reconciled with Ralph Fiennes's Prospero at the end of the magician's spiritual

and moral journey, despite the fact that Terera's bound body recalled slavery whenever he was on stage. Ariel, on the other hand, was played by
white British actor Tom Byam Shaw, his swept-back hair dyed blue-white
to match his part-translucent, tight, blue-white costume and blue-white
face paint. The costume recalls Steven Macintosh's white Ariel in Peter
Hall's production of 1988, whose own white face was also whitened and
who also wore a translucent white body stocking decorated with patches
of more opaque white. Hall's was an all-white cast, whereas casting and
costume choices for Nunn's production situate Caliban in the history of
black slavery to the point where the director's claiming the play is not
about colonialism is startling.

White actors playing Ariel dressed in white, or costumed to suggest
transparency, potentially erase the colonial connotations of the play by
privileging spirit over body, theatrical magic over real human cultures, in
the portrayal of Prospero's 'airy' spirit. A white-painted, white actor as
Ariel in pale costume and makeup—particularly, but not necessarily only,
when juxtaposed with a black actor playing Caliban—draws attention to
white skin and suggests, troublingly, that a theatrical representation of
'spirit'; needs to be whiter than white. The costume choice has precedents
and antecedents in addition to the Hall production. Clifford Williams and
Peter Brook's RSC production (1963), designed by Farrah, stages Ian
Holm as a blue-white Ariel in a tight body suit. In the same year as the
Mermaid production directed by Miller, 1970, production photographs
suggest that future Gandhi actor, Ben Kingsley, appeared even more naked
in John Barton's RSC production than Cyril Nri did in Miller's next production of 1988: but where Nri's costume drew attention to blackness
with the grey-white ash-paint of the Numa, Kingsley's Asian heritage
seemed whited out by white body paint in this production. A version of
the white-clothed, white-painted Ariel also appeared in Georgio Strehler's
Tempest of 1978, and although I have otherwise discussed only British
production here, this production is worth mentioning because its sparse
scenography foregrounded the literal and racial uses of black and white in
a way that, with hindsight, reads as a distillation of colonially inflected
casting in *The Tempest*.

This was the second of Strehler's two *Tempests* and one of his most
celebrated productions. Although the director wrote about the work in
ways that suggest he was well aware of the colonial implications of the play
and highly sympathetic to the figure of Caliban (Strehler and Simpson
2002, 14–15), his Calibans were three white Italian actors in succession,

all painted black. A recording of the full production is available online at the time of writing (https://www.youtube.com/watch?v=RyP6CdLSL6Y), and it brings the twenty-first-century viewer up troublingly close to a 'black-face' Caliban. From the familiar Caliban trap door, the painted black hands of Caliban emerge onto the pale set. He moves in a crouch across the stage, like a spider, as Pia Kleber has also noted (Kleber 1993, 148). Jan Kott has remarked that Strehler insisted on the artistry of having a white actor play a black character here (Kott 2002, 115). However, any 'black' figure on stage to whom a white figure, Tino Carraro's Prospero, nearly takes a belt, who moves across the floor like an animal then gets up to confront Prospero with a great deal of deliberate dignity, and who later paints his face with make-up that recalls African tribal war paint, inevitably recalls a range of black histories. When these histories are embodied by a blacked-up white actor, a range of historical and performance stereotypes are also disturbingly invoked. Tina Lazzarini's Ariel, in contrast, is a white-painted white figure in a fluid white garment reminiscent of a Pierrot costume, who twists and somersaults freely on a rope that both enables her to fly and traps her: she pulls at it in performance, drawing attention to it as the symbol and material reality of her servitude. This whiter-than-white figure appears to represent both a spirit world and the art of the theatre. Just as Ariel is freed at the end of the play and Caliban is not, white body, fabric and face-paint here is free to represent the abstractions of spirit and Prospero's psyche or art. Strehler's casting and Luciano Damiani's design produced a distillation of blackness and whiteness in *Tempest* production, whereby blackness represents a set of historical oppressions and Ariel is a white person painted white, even as she is intended to represent an abstract, theatricalised spirit force.

At the RSC in 1982 and again in 2017 Mark Rylance's and Mark Quartley's Ariel costumes showed a system of veins and muscles respectively, as if Ariel was so pale as to be transparent. In the first of these productions, directed by Ron Daniels and designed by Maria Björnson, Rylance and his fellow sprits of the island were costumed as if naked, their bright, white delicateness showing veins through skin. The white actor Bob Peck as Caliban, on the other hand, actually performed partially naked. He wore his hair in beaded braids, as did Alice Krige as Miranda. Three years after Bo Derek had popularised cornrows amongst white people, in the film *10* (1979), this was an interesting but troubling choice: interesting in that it linked Miranda visually to Caliban; troubling in that it linked a black hairstyle that had just been controversially appropriated by white culture to semi-naked white body of Peck, so that he simultaneously recalled Caliban's blackness and erased it.

Mark Quartley's body suit in 2017 was of a bluish colour that shone blue-white in some light; this costume was also a motion capture suit, which produced the movements of an Ariel avatar who could fly anywhere and be any colour. Reviews for this *Tempest*, which was directed by the RSC's artistic director Greg Doran and which played at the RST Stratford and the Barbican Theatre (the RSC's former home in London) focussed on the familiar personal journey of the white patriarch, with a number of reviewers expressing relief that the spectacular digitally-produced imagery of the production did not detract from the play's central performance and emotional and moral focal point, Simon Russell Beale's Prospero. Only one review that I have seen mentioned the casting of an actor of colour as Caliban. As Nunn's aforementioned dismissive remarks seemed to suggest, perhaps this was because this had become such common practice as to be unremarkable. Nevertheless, William Drew, for the online magazine *Exeunt*, waxed ironic about the casting of Black British actor Joe Dixon in ways that are pertinent to my discussion here:

> What about Caliban? Oh dear. How to deal with the mass of racist, postcolonial, Hobbesian mutated mess that is that thing of darkness? Even that line. Thing of darkness. Yikes! It's 2017, guys. What the hell is this play? It's fine, it's fine. Get Joe Dixon. Solid. Give him a hunch-back. Ambiguous. Perfect. We're back on track. (Drew 2017)

The hunch back to which Drew refers is part of a 'fat suit' that Dixon wore for the part, on the back of which a distorted spine was sculpted, and over which the common Caliban costume trope of the ropes of enslavement were fixed. 'Ambiguous. Perfect' jokes Drew, and the costume suggested to me a residual anxiety around the imagery of slavery in the play's stage history. Dixon's fat suit with its external spine recalled the monster-Caliban of earlier stage tradition; it covered his torso so that the ropes the actor wore were not binding an actual black body. Returning to Peck, tropes of blackness (braided hair) and of slavery (a dirty, semi-naked body) also seem to me to speak to a felt obligation and a simultaneous reluctance to stage Caliban as black. Newly staged as monster on a set created from spectacular displays of shifting, colourful technology, Joe Dixon's Caliban also recalled a creature from a computer game, a monster against which the cyber-hero must battle. Thus the stakes in the 'mass of racist, post-colonial, Hobbesian mutated mess' that Walker reads in the play were dramatically lowered and the play's post-colonial history gave way once again to the white male protagonist's emotional and moral journey. As Amy Borsuk (to whom I am indebted for pointing me to Drew's review) discusses in her analysis of the meanings produced by the production's mix of digital innovation and humanist essentialism:

> Dixon's spiky-backed monster costume and his face-paint—as 'ambiguous' design choices—attempts to erase any coding for racial otherness, making his otherness based in being a literal monstrous creature. This monstrous ambiguity neutralises the politics of the character, but arguably makes it more complicated by potentially conflating racial otherness with monstrousness. This attempt at neutralisation also implies a sense of safety in avoiding any engagement with the politics of the play, and of their production. (Borsuk 2020, 185)

Meanwhile, Quartley's Ariel, in his motion-capture body suit, was digitally linked to an Ariel avatar free from the arielist's rope of past production. The binary of air and earth became a focus for the play once more via this digital Ariel, literally abstracted from Mark Quartley's body, and a monstrous, earthbound Caliban who stomped off back to Prospero's cell at the end of the play, after a moment of potential rebellion when Dixon drew himself up to full height and towered over Simon Russell Beale. Caliban's decision to '"seek for grace" rather than kill Prospero' (Borsuk 2020, 184, citing Doran) was supposed to humanise Caliban—the production offers him 'character growth, signified by 'his ability to understand and perform human morality' (Borsuk 2020, 184). The white and black bodies of Caliban and Ariel are differently erased by their bodysuits but are reinscribed as freed spirit and humanised monster in ways that cannot quite neutralise the play's post-colonial performance history.

Recolonising Caliban and Ariel: The Tempest 2002, Michael Boyd (Director) Tom Piper (Designer)

The *Tempest*s I have analysed in this part of the chapter each stage Ariel as unproblematically whiter than white. Costumes have repeatedly effaced the post-colonial narrative for Ariel, whilst still occasionally marking Caliban as a colonialised figure. Before moving to productions of *The Tempest* that have cast actors of colour in other ways than to reflect colonial power relations, I want to examine one more production in which black performers have played Caliban and Ariel, whose costume designs have, I will argue, enabled the staging of wider issues of power in addition to the colonial, but which have not appeared intent on erasing colonial history. The designer for the RSC's 2002 production, which Charles Spencer comments on above (2002, 160), was Tom Piper, long-time collaborator with then RSC artistic director Michael Boyd. Piper's design used a whitish costume for Ariel and, like Strehler, a trapeze rope to both trap and free her—but casting an actor of colour here, and using the rope in multiple ways, shifted the meanings of this familiar image.

Tom Piper confirms that he and Boyd were highly aware of *The Tempest*'s post-colonial life in theatre and criticism (Piper, Interview). They also had other preoccupations. This production was in the RSC's first season at the Roundhouse, when the company had left their permanent London home at the Barbican and before the space had been refurbished as the relatively comfortable London venue it is now. Ladders were used as part of the design; they produced a tower-like cylinder that came apart and left the ladders hanging in the space after the opening storm. Piper relates that in 2002, he and Boyd felt that a cataclysmic storm could not help but recall the attack on the twin towers in New York, so that their *Tempest* had to some degree be a response to it. Moreover, costumes in this production very clearly produced power in additional ways to the casting of black actors Geff Francis and Kananu Kirimi as Caliban and Ariel. In this production, the aerialist's rope appeared in three configurations, producing power and restraint, sometimes at different moments, sometimes simultaneously. The figure of the usurping Alonso was hung in the space by a rope, deliberately recalling, explains Piper, one of Francis Bacon's pope paintings, a series of violent images that connote, simultaneously, power and entrapment. Geff Francis's Caliban was attached to another thick rope, and this one clearly represented a tether. Whilst Ariel was a multivalent figure representing spirit, magic and colonial oppression, Caliban was clearly a slave—a dignified and angry one as reviewers commented (Spencer 2002; Billington 2002). He carried human figures—members of the spirit ensemble—instead of logs, which read against Prospero's line to Miranda that insists they need Caliban's labour (1.2.365-8) and suggested that Prospero deliberately conjures him work to do. Once again, Caliban looked as though he has had to make his own protective gaberdine out of what has been left lying around the island.

Like Alonso, Kananu Kirimi's Ariel hung in the space by a rope; she wore a pragmatic version of male Jacobean garb, a pale doublet and breeches that allowed for free movement. The rope on which she descended reminded the audience that she was tethered to Prospero until he chose to set her free but, like Strehler's Ariel, it also gave her the freedom of the theatre space through which to fly and tumble at will (although the other spirits did rather more tumbling: Kirimi herself is not an aerialist). Unlike Strehler's Ariel, the white-painted white actor Tina Lazzarini, Kirimi is of Caribbean heritage. Kirimi's costume can be read as an amalgam of, and commentary on, a number of traditions for costuming Ariel. She was a slight woman on an aerialist's rope, recalling her nineteenth-century, fairy-like predecessors, and dressed in creamy white like their hyper-white successors; she was a woman of colour in a production with a man of colour as Caliban, so was part of the play's colonially inflected history—but like Norman Beaton, rather than Cyril Nri, she was dressed in Jacobean style like her master and his daughter and so laid claim to Shakespearean authority as they do. She also had facial markings reminiscent of the Madagascan face on Miller's 1970 programme, to draw the audience to the colonial again. Like Strehler's Ariel, she was the theatrical spirit with access to all areas in a consciously referenced performance space. She presided over a group of aerialists, their faces made up in a greenish-blue, who changed from mariners to theatrical spirits after the storm scene. Paul Taylor describes them as 'verdigrised transmogrifications of the mariners' (Taylor 2002) and Ariel controlled them using a mariner's whistle. The magical feast provided by Ariel for Antonio and his cronies turned out to be Ariel herself: the Italian nobles tucked viciously into a feast of swan, only to have it burst forth as Ariel's harpy and spatter them all with blood—'the shipwrecked toffs ending up as bloodied in sartorial fact as they always have been in intent', writes Taylor.

Ariel's multivalent costume and rope helped to make Kirimi one of the more empowered black figures in the *Tempests* I have examined here, without Boyd needing to intimate that she takes over the island after the play ends, as Miller did. This Ariel appeared to have access to all possible meanings for the figure, whilst also seeming powerfully un-invested in the power structures which Prospero imposes on the island and to which he returns at the end of the play. Ariel is bound to Prospero, of course, until the duke/magician decides otherwise. But once this Prospero had broken his magic staff, Kirimi disappeared without visual or musical flourish. Once released, Prospero's world was meaningless to Ariel, and she did not need to perform a theatrical finale in it. The post-colonial connotations were, I think, powerful and liberating.

'Non-traditional' *Tempests* and Their Others

Thus far I have considered production and reception of *The Tempest* in terms of how costume collaborates and colludes with actors' performances, actors' bodies, and directors interpretations, to produce constructions of race and power. I have begun to pay attention to what the colour white means in the fabrics and body paints in which Ariel has been costumed and what it might mean, in terms of costume, to attempt to stage or to erase the post-colonial politics of the play. I look next at the meanings produced by non-traditional casting in twentieth- and twenty-first-century British productions of the play. Ayanna Thompson simply and usefully defines non-traditional casting when she writes that 'In the most reductive sense, non-traditional casting is the practice of casting actors of color for roles that were originally conceived of as white and written for white actors' (Thompson 2006b, 76). She discusses the Non-Traditional Casting Project's four models for non-traditional casting (colorblind, societal, conceptual and cross-cultural) (Thompson 2006b, 76), in terms of the 'four radically different conceptions of the semiotic meaning of racial difference on stage' she argues they connote (2006b, 77). In the last part of this chapter, I explore how costume works with and against the grain of these semiotic meanings, in productions of *The Tempest* where major roles other than the colonised Caliban and Ariel are played by people of colour. How does costume signify when the role of Prospero, together with his emotional and moral journey, is given to an actor of colour? What do the costumes of Prosperos, Mirandas and Ferdinands of colour do to the intersectional politics of race and gender on stage? In the last section of this chapter, I consider costume design in Liverpool Everyman's production of 1984, which was the first British *Tempest* to cast a black actor as Prospero (the African American actor Ricco Ross, who played Prospero as a ring-master in sharp control of a circus setting for the play); Birmingham Rep's production of 1994 in which Prospero, Miranda, Ariel and Antonio were all played by black British actors; the West Yorkshire Playhouse's 'gender-' and 'colour-blind' production; Improbable's 2015 collaboration with Northern Stage and the Oxford Playhouse, in which black British actors Tyrone Higson and Jade Ogugua played Prospero and Miranda on a set created from a mass of modern garments; and Donmar Warehouse's all-woman, multiply cross-cast *Tempest* of 2016.

The first of NTCP's non-traditional casting models is 'color-blind', a term which has recently been criticised for its inherent ableism (by, e.g. Subini Ancy Annamma) and that, as Thompson points out, 'assumes one can and should be blind to race' and that 'an actor's color has no semiotic value on stage unless it is invested in one by the director' (Thompson 2006b, 77). Whilst some of the companies I discuss next have been highly conscious of the potential meanings produced by colour and race when casting their *Tempests*, at least one appears to have attempted to cast 'colour-blind' as a means of diversifying stage pictures and employment practices. This was, as Ayanna Thompson reminds us, the 'initial idea behind color-blind casting' as it was pioneered by Joseph Papp in New York in the mid-twentieth century: 'that neither the race nor the ethnicity of an actor should prevent her or him from playing a role as long as she or he was the best actor available' (Thompson 2006a, 6). But as Thompson also explains,

> the exact significance of an actor's race is perpetually in flux within color-blind casting because we [in the USA and UK] as a society have not been able to pinpoint a stable signification for race. The practice[s] of colorblind casting cannot resolve the larger societal tensions in which they are enmeshed. (2006a, 8)

Significantly for my exploration here, Thompson points to the non-traditional casting convention of exploiting an audience's assumed lack of colour blindness 'by drawing attention to an actor's colour, race, or ethnicity' (2006a, 7). This is partially what happens in Miller's consciously colonial *Tempests*, although here, Ariel and Caliban are transformed into explicitly black characters on an island colonised by a white Prospero, so that colour-consciousness is a given from their first entrances. Colour-conscious casting of this kind can be both progressive and regressive. On the one hand, it might suggest that the black body can be conveniently made to do the work of symbolising oppression of any and every historical kind, thus reiterating racist power relations rather than progressively exploring them. On the other, as I hope to demonstrate, non-traditionally cast productions that assume audiences can read through race for part of a play, but which also draw their attention to race in particular stage moments or via particular aspects of design, can invite the spectator to examine their own subject position with regards to race and power in progressive ways.

REVERSING RACE? *THE TEMPEST* 1994, BILL ALEXANDER (DIRECTOR), RUARI MURCHISON (DESIGNER)

Like Charles Spencer in his 2002 review cited above (160), director Bill Alexander, in an interview with Tony Howard for the British Black and Asian Shakespeare database, suggests that an all-white cast save for a black Caliban, or black Caliban and Ariel, had become the norm for productions of *The Tempest* by the early 90s. I now turn to the costuming of Alexander's Birmingham Rep production of 1994, in which black British actors played a number of major roles, not including Caliban. Bill Alexander came to the Rep as artistic director in 1992, excited at the opportunities that performing Shakespeare in a culturally diverse city outside of Stratford upon Avon afforded for multi-racial casting. In his conversation with Howard, Alexander suggests that the cross-casting practice of the RSC repertory, whereby each director in a season worked with the others' casts, limited the choices he wanted to make there, particularly when other directors in a season seemed uninterested in employing a cast of diverse heritage. Whilst Alexander's *Macbeth* the following year, in which Jeffery Kissoon also played the lead, was cast without the suggestion of a particular, racialised meaning for a black Macbeth, Alexander explains that his casting principles for *The Tempest* were based on an 'internal realism': alongside Kissoon's Prospero, black actors also played Miranda (Ginny Holder) and Antonio (Tony Armatrading) because all of those characters are in the same family; then because Ariel is, suggests Alexander, 'the spirit of the man [Prospero]' (Alexander, interview with Howard), he cast a black actor, Raykie Ayola, as Ariel too. This complicates a critical response to this Ariel by Christine Dymkovski, who suggests that Ayola's was a highly conventional, submissive figure in the tradition of Victorian actresses in the role (Dymkovski 46–47; Billington in Dymkovski). If Ariel is a playful element of Prospero's 'spirit' in the sense of mind or soul, then little wonder there was gentle warmth rather than hierarchical tension between them. Caliban in this production, on the other hand, was played by white British actor Richard McCabe and was, explains Alexander:

> made very white…he was someone who never saw the daylight, like…a creature from…H. G. Wells' 'The Time Traveller', the ones who live underground…and who never see daylight. (Alexander, interview with Howard)

This whitened white Caliban created a new set of connotations for the insult thrown at Caliban by Prospero, 'thou earth!' (1.2.369). Instead of the stereotype that associates a black Caliban with the earth, earthiness, and an uncontrolled id or animal behaviour, it is whiteness that is equated with earth here: Caliban is whitened by a cramped and limited existence underground, whilst Prospero's airy spirit is black, and a materialization of Prospero's own 'spirit'. I want to develop Alexander's idea that this was a kind of colonial *Tempest* in negative by suggesting that McCabe's white-painted face paradoxically and productively recalls the history of racist black-face, a history that the production did not seem intentionally to reference.

Costumes for Kissoon as Prospero and Holder as Miranda recalled a range of conventions for playing these characters which have so much more frequently been played by white actors. Miranda wore a sleeveless cream dress with a flowing skirt, tighter over the bust, of no obvious historical period, whilst the men in the play wore distinctly Victorian dark suits, top hats, stiff collars, stark against the pale sand of the circular playing space of Ruari Murchison's set. Prospero casualised this masculine uniform by removing his jacket on the island but still wore a white dress shirt and braces with his formal black trousers. For his return to Milan, he reassembled the ensemble by donning a formal jacket, complete with the sash, gold braid and military epaulettes of Victorian imperialism, whilst his erstwhile usurper and his friends were reduced to shirts and braces. The relationship between Prospero and Miranda was a close one in this production: father embraced daughter as he told her their family backstory, kneeling as she leant against him. In a number of rehearsal and production images she is photographed in this position, looking up into his face, the picture of childhood innocence in her simple white dress. Prospero and his countrymen's clothes spoke distinctly of the middle of 'Britain's imperial century' (Hyam 2002)—particularly in a period following so much aesthetic reiteration of empire in the heritage film (see above 91–92, 96). Miranda's costume represented a more generalised girlish innocence. The costumes recall Ruth Frankenberg's discussion of tropes of whiteness, whereby:

White Woman is frail, vulnerable, delicate, sexually pure but at times easily led "astray." White Man is strong, dominant, arbiter of truth, and self-designated protector of white womankind, defender of the nation/territory (and here defense of the nation and its honor often also entails defending the White Woman's racial chastity). (1997, 11)

By costuming black actors in these tropes of whiteness, the production both reverses and recalls Miller's colonial version of the play. The imperial patriarch and his innocent daughter are no longer white and the production forces race and power apart.

What meanings does the white-painted white figure of Caliban produce in this context? The etiolated white face of the underground dweller is how Alexander describes it. But there was nothing naturalistic about the way McCabe was made up: the colour of his own flesh showed distinctly at his neck and chest and his lips show dark against the white make up. McCabe wore a dirty, white, open-necked shirt and trousers on his first entrance. Once he had teamed up with Stephano and Trinculo, he donned a black dress suit jacket, stiff collar and bow-tie with the filthy trousers, making a fantasy entrance into the ruling class: his chest was still bare, so that the collar and tie stood out absurdly. Here was a whitened white actor in a fancy-dress of white power. Alexander reflects back over his ideas for the production saying that it 'almost became an inversion and challenge to that [colonial] way of seeing the play', in which Ariel and Caliban represent black, colonised peoples. One could argue that the casting of this *Tempest* simply obliterates the colonial power structures that the play has suggested to contemporary production and reception: black people now have the power on stage and this frees the audience up to think about something else. But the Victorian men's costumes and Caliban's whiteface referenced Britain's colonial century and racist depictions of race respectively; they were permitted a critical presence in a production that was determined not to reiterate them.

A briefer, starker recollection of colonialism in a production that seemed to be attempting 'colour-blind' casting occurred five years later at the West Yorkshire Playhouse. In fact, in Jude Kelly's production of 1999, casting appeared to be both gender- and colour-blind. Again, the colonial century was invoked in the Edwardian-style military formal wear worn by the shipwrecked nobles, but Ian McKellen played Prospero dressed in an old hat and cardigan, as if the trauma of his exile had led him to reject court convention entirely. Black British actor Claire Benedict played not only the masque figure Juno but Prospero's usurping brother Antonio; black British actor Rhashan Stone played Ferdinand whilst his father Alonso was played by a white woman, Susie Baxter. But when Rhashan Stone was made to carry logs like Timothy Walker's white Caliban, was similarly chained and manacled and his chest bared, an effect was produced similar to the one Thompson remarks upon in Hughes's *Winter's Tale* at the Guthrie theatre, Minneapolis, when a black actress playing Hermione 'came out dressed in a burlap sack and shackles when Leontes accuse her of adultery.' (Thompson 2006a, 7). Miranda's love for a figure who cannot but recall an enslaved black man pulled the spectator back into histories of slavery and white cultural anxieties around miscegenation. Prospero's fear of losing control over his daughter's sexuality was magnified by the visual recollection of racist fears of black sexuality; Caliban's desire for Miranda, characterised by Prospero as rape, was momentarily figured in Ferdinand. This was a more predominantly white production than Alexander's, however, and the casting of the celebrated actor McKellen in his shabby cardigan placed it firmly in a predominantly white Shakespearean tradition. Alexander's production suggested that one could both employ a diverse cast in a Shakespeare production with some of *The Tempest*'s most significant figures played by black actors and, by reversing colonial power relations in terms of casting, still produce a critique of the colonial through costume.

THE TEMPEST IN PRISON: PHYLLIDA LLOYD'S SHAKESPEARE TRILOGY, CHLOE LAMFORD (DESIGNER); BUNNY CHRISTIE (ENVIRONMENT DESIGNER)

The most recent British non-traditionally cast *Tempest* at the time of writing drew attention to colour, race and ethnicity using a meta-dramatic frame. This was the Donmar Warehouse's all-women *Tempest*, the last in a trilogy of Shakespeare plays directed by Phyllida Lloyd and performed in a temporary theatre near King's Cross station in London. Brutus in *Julius Caesar*, King Henry in *Henry IV* and Prospero in *The Tempest* were played by Harriet Walter, who has written about the first two productions in her memoir, *Brutus and Other Heroines*. The trilogy was given the fictional frame of a women's prison, in which the inmates were performing the Shakespeare plays, and audience members were dragooned into the four-sided auditorium by an actor dressed as a prison warden at the beginning of every performance. Each of the performers took on the role of a prisoner across the trilogy, figures they devised themselves and whom they imagined playing all of their Shakespearean characters. Walter explains that prison frame was Lloyd's idea and that

The advantages…were that we would be de-sexed by our uniform, it would explain why there were no male actors, the violence and aggression in the play would be more convincing in a prison context, and it is no stretch to imagine prisoners playing Shakespeare as it is now a fairly common practice for actors to do workshops in prisons. (Walter 2016, 159)

Mock interviews with a number of the prisoner characters formed part of the online publicity for the trilogy and some are available to watch at the time of writing. Some of these interviews suggest that the fictional prisoners had been involved in exactly the kind of 'Shakespeare in prison' project Walter references: Jade Onouka, as the prisoner Sade who plays Ariel, and Sophie Stanton, as the one who plays Caliban, for example, discuss drama as part of their rehabilitation.[2] But the production itself did not, I contend, simplistically suggest that 'doing Shakespeare' is a productive or redemptive occupation for prison inmates. Particularly in its use of costume, it invited the spectator to shift their perspective from one reality and location to another—from a prison where women are incarcerated to an island where people are shipwrecked—and to explore the potential for injustice and oppression, rehabilitation and redemption in each.

The prison frame was cast as a realist drama; the refreshingly large number of young women of colour cast in a British Shakespeare production also troublingly recalling the disproportionate number of young black women incarcerated within the British prison system (Prison Reform Trust 2017; Uhrig 2016); the cast evidently drew on their own cultural heritages to form their prisoner personae. The production of *The Tempest* within this frame might be labelled 'colour-blind' insofar as actors/prisoners of different colours were assigned roles without regard to the family relationships within the play. However, a complex colour-consciousness emerged as the narrative of play and prisoners unfolded. The overall aesthetic for this *Tempest* was created by the prison uniforms—the dull grey of joggers and sweatshirts punctuated with bright yellow t-shirts—against which any changes or decorative elements read strongly. Jade Anouka's compelling and energetic Ariel, whose songs she partly rapped, wore flowery shorts and a red hat with her yellow top, as if her spirit role gave her freedom to rebel against prison dress, if not against Prospero. The combination of hat, accent, rap music, and the breakdancing she broke into

---

[2] Anouka/Sade's interview is currently online at https://www.youtube.com/watch?v=lMf1gQFTtw8, Stanton/Andrea's at https://www.youtube.com/watch?v=xsZYuXtK_r8.

when contemplating freedom, foregrounded the black South London heritage of her prison role, a young woman called Sade. The illusion that Ariel (and Mark Antony, and Hotspur) were being played by a young, black prison inmate was reinforced by the aforementioned online 'interview', in which Anouka as Sade talks to camera about how joining the prison drama group kept her away from drugs and other trouble.

Singing along with Anouka to 'Full Fathom Five', the prisoner-cast wore makeshift masks in fishy shapes, seemingly formed from the bits of rubbish it was Andrea/Caliban's role to collect from around the prison. For her wedding, Leah Harvey's Miranda wore white net curtains as a skirt, giving rise to delightful speculation as to whether some prison official had given permission for her office to be denuded for the show. Miranda's wedding bouquet made of tissues and dangling, unused tampons was surprisingly charming. Tampons were used again when Ariel appears to Alonso and his company to condemn them as 'three men of sin': Onouka dressed as a court judge, her wig constructed from tampons. This improvised costume aesthetic was not entirely consistent: imagining too hard that the prisoners had constructed their own *Tempest* costumes left one wondering where Ariel got her flowery shorts, or Ferdinand (Sheila Atim) his/her black net petticoat for a joyously non-binary wedding scene, in which huge white helium balloons showed projected images of prisoners' freedom fantasies of everything from lush natural scenery to McDonald's logos. But the slippage from improvised costumes for a prison drama project, to theatrical fantasy from beyond the prison walls, hinted at a world of freedom, promise and potential to which these prisoners one day might return—a particularly suggestive theme for Ariel/an incarcerated young black woman.

In one extra-textual moment, Alonso and his friends were admitted to the prison dressed in blue suit jackets and fat blue ties. They were told to put on their 'HMP garments' by a warden who sarcastically acknowledged that these clothes might not be up to the nobles' usual standards. Alonso got short shrift when she asked to 'see the governor'; these were clearly meant to read as high-status prisoners who expected special treatment. Prospero's magic garment was a dark green prison blanket, and Harriet Walter in the role was given the same blue suit and tie as her former enemies when she renounced her magic, although she was not permitted to return to 'Milan' because her prison character, Hannah Wake, was a lifer without parole. Walter's character was inspired by Judy Clark, a woman who had been the driver for a robbery in which victims had been killed;

she had received a life sentence despite not having been directly responsible for the violence of the crime, because she refused to co-operate with the criminal justice system.[3] When this *Tempest* ended and Prospero spoke of his/her return to Milan, Hannah broke down in tears at her own fate, and other prisoners were seen leaving the prison and wishing her luck, dressed in their own 'civvies', some of them significantly feminine in comparison to the prison wear: a blue dress for Ariel; a floral dress for Alonso; a pale pink hoodie for Trinculo.

Caliban, Stephano and Trinculo were played by white actors. Sophie Stanton's Caliban wore grey and yellow like the other prisoners, but it was not immediately clear whether the black cap protecting her hair, and the bags of rubbish she wore at her waist, indicated an inmate's cleaning job, a homeless past, or whether her prison frame role was a prison worker rather than an inmate. Her video 'interview' makes clear that she was a prisoner, but even if one read her as having a low-paid job in the prison, she was clearly stuck there, and was left in the prison/on the island with Walter's Prospero at the end of the production. Karen Dunbar and Jackie Clune played rowdy Scottish and East Anglian women respectively, who entered for the 'frippery' episode of 4.1 in Scottish- and Union Jack-flagged boxer shorts as Trinculo and Stephano (the garments that distracted them from the plan to kill Prospero were the white gowns and slippers of a luxury spa). Following the Scottish Independence and EU referendums of 2014 and 2016, the trio of Caliban, Stephano and Trinculo resonated troublingly with discussions in the media about class-divided Britain and the rise of nationalism. Whilst Ferdinand, Miranda and Ariel were played by black British actors with an energy and playfulness that suggested the huge creative potential that might be realised once they were released from the island, from the prison, perhaps even from Shakespeare, the sorry belligerence of the white, working class trio felt appropriate to their pathetic plot to take over the island, but potentially read as a comical sneer at working class figures as imagined by the middle class theatrical establishment. However, whilst the stereotype of working class figures as drunken, nationalist no-hopers was troubling, it was also refreshing to have Caliban, Trinculo and Stephano cast and costumed in such a way as to put the burden of stereotype and political commentary onto white performers, whilst young black women were partially relieved

---

[3] 'Hannah's' online interview can currently be found here: https://www.youtube.com/watch?v=CxBoNnBJ6AE.

of longstanding burdens of representation and able to get on with the dramatic business of falling in love and taking emotional and moral journeys of their own. The Donmar Shakespeare Trilogy production of *The Tempest*, with its deliberately drab, uniform costume base and creative use of rubbish and detritus to emphasise the resourcefulness and creative potential of incarcerated women, could be read superficially as the story of these women performing *The Tempest* as resourcefully as possible, with the best possible actor for each role cast regardless of colour. The aesthetic of the prison frame, on the other hand, potentially reminded the audience that whilst they may not be used to seeing so many actors of colour in classical theatre, there are a dismaying number of people of colour in UK prisons. The continual slippage from play world to fictional frame and back, created through costume and set, and the interference with the plot by the routine of prison and its officers, created a holding form for *The Tempest* that worked both with and against the grain of the play, offering a colour-conscious political critique of the prison system, and of power relations within *The Tempest*.

Theatrical Islands: the Liverpool Everyman and Improbable's *Tempests*: Glen Walford (Director), Susan Mayes (Designer); Phelim McDermott (Director), Becs Andrews (Designer)

Lastly in this chapter, I consider two consciously meta-theatrical design frames for *The Tempest*: the Liverpool Everyman's 1984 version, directed by Glen Walford and designed by Susan Mayes, which used a circus ring setting to represent the island, and Improbable's 2015 production, directed by Phelim McDermott and designed by Becs Andrews, which created the play's island from mountains of clothes. These were highly stylised aesthetic frames rather than realist settings. The Everyman's circus asked the audience to read *The Tempest* through familiar figures from a particular form of popular entertainment. Improbable's mountain of clothes was superficially an entirely abstract setting, but it both took references to clothing as a very literal joke and used them to foreground clothes and their meanings in the culture of the play and beyond. In both of these productions, Prospero and Miranda were played by black actors and I contend that the non-realist settings and their costumes allow for fascinating slippages between different readings of the semiotics of race.

Mayes's design and costumes for the Everyman production created a circus ring for the island in *The Tempest*. The Italian nobles became clown-like figures alongside Trinculo and Stephano; Caliban was dressed both as a joke on his possibly fishy origins and a human figure, pushing up through elasticated green fabric covering the circular stage/circus ring to give an monstrous initial impression, but then emerging as a clumsy, grey and, for most reviewers, sympathetic human figure in large frogman's flippers. Miranda swung above the stage watching her father controlling the island from a trapeze-artist's crescent moon and was wooed by an enchained strong-man Ferdinand. A silvery Ariel was trapped inside an acrobat's giant wheel, pushed around the stage by his master. Prospero himself was, of course, the circus ringmaster, and gave up a whip rather than a magical staff at the end of the play. He was played by African American actor Ricco Ross, to my knowledge the first black actor to play Prospero in the UK; his daughter Miranda was black British actor Cathy Tyson.

The tone of the critical responses to this production was generally one of excitement at the spectacle and the 'colourful' set and costumes, with a few provisos about the distance between fictional frame and Shakespearean drama: 'If the story gets a little lost in the fun-making, no-one seems to mind' writes the *Liverpool Daily Post* critic Philip Key (1984b). Terry Morgan of Merseymart enjoys the production but, in a now familiar critical response, is suspicious that the casting of people of colour in the roles of Prospero and Miranda must mean that someone is trying to slip an un-Shakespearean political agenda beneath the universal humanist radar:

> If [director] Ms Walford is trying to make a particular point by choosing black actors for the Milan family, then it passed me by. Similarly I remain indifferent to any ideas she might have been putting over about colonialism, the power struggle, the noble savage, or any other of the things that commentators insist the play is 'about'. What I was emphatically not indifferent to was the magic, the sensuality, the humour and general aura of the production. (Morgan 1984)

Morgan associates actors of colour with narratives of political struggle (and, disturbingly, 'the noble savage' even though it is not the 'savage' Caliban who is played by a black performer) despite the reviewer's own assertion that the 'general aura of the production' allowed him to experience the performance as being 'about' something quite different, and despite the fact that, as in the Birmingham Rep production years later, this is quite different casting from the post-colonial trope of portraying Caliban and Ariel as the colonised. Several reviewers and a press release remark excitedly that Ross had played Tyler Bragg in Hill Street Blues. This is ironic, given that in an article for the *Daily Post*, Ross relates how he came to the UK to study Shakespeare at LAMDA, in the reverse of the personal story more recently told by a number of black British actors who have left the UK for the US to escape type casting: 'I was always being cast as a street guy and a gangster [in the US]. They were all different parts, but really the same role' (Ross in Key 1984a). Ross's costume signalled Ringmaster in traditional style, with top-hat and whip. However, his black trousers showed white fabric through horizontal slashes, reminiscent of the Elizabethan/Jacobean fashion for slashing; other costumes in the piece also recalled period fashion: the clown-like nobles sported Elizabethan ruffs, for example. The trousers also referenced a post-punk, New Romantic look, a nod to nineteen eighties street fashion.

Ross was a young actor to play Prospero and in images of him as he relinquished his ringmaster's top hat and jacket for the trousers and a sleeveless white top, he appears as both a vulnerable Everyman, and as an actor with many possible Shakespearean leads ahead of him, even as Prospero announced that his third thought at court is going to be death (5.1.346). As this young, black Prospero relinquished the whip of control, it was denuded in one obvious sense of its connotations of slavery by the Circus setting, but it potentially recalled those connotations nevertheless. Ross stood before the audience as the male lead at the end of his emotional and moral journey, so often the privilege of an older white actor. It is significant that this moment of colour-consciousness is one that contradicts rather than reiterates the historically more predictable image of a white ringmaster, or slave owner, holding a whip. I contend that the bold, non-realist theatricality of this design, combined with the production's casting, permitted both a simple shifting of a leading role and its power from white to black body whilst potentially still reminding the audience of the violent racial histories that make such an image unusual.

In Improbable's *Tempest*, designed by Becs Andrews, a collaboration with Oxford Playhouse and Northern Stage, the entire set was created from clothing. Piles of clothes made hills on which rotatory clothes lines serve as trees; clothes line after clothes line, hung with garments in a palate from blue to gold, created a seascape stretching to a sun made of yellow tops, with trousers as its rays. The shipwrecked Italians, dressed in off-white garments, padded like Jacobean-styled duvets, shouted their opening lines over the sound of a washing machine, into which Ariel, with a pun on the washing powder brand, had popped a tea towel bearing the image of a ship. The clothes that distract Caliban, Stephano and Trinculo from their plans to kill Prospero were glistering gold. Ariel was a cross-dressed figure, a male actor costumed as a brightly-coloured version of a suburban housewife in blouse, tank-top and skirt. The masque Goddesses were created from debris: Ceres's garment was made of bottles, Juno's of plastic shopping bags. The majority of the costumes were made from modern garments sewn together in a range of eclectic ways.

This non-realist, theatrically conscious design only momentarily became a 'setting'. It was a fantasy island of fabric, foregrounding how clothing produces and re-produces everyone in structures of power, but it also looked, fleetingly, like a rather beautiful landfill site on which all of the characters were scavenging. The powerful Duke-Magician and his daughter were played by black British actors: Tyrone Huggins was Prospero, Jade Ogugua, Miranda. Huggins's costume created a historically non-specific image of an African patriarch in a pale, loose garment, made out of Western raincoats—a *Tempest* joke—and referencing Western status-symbol clothing: a familiar piece of Burberry fabric crossed his belly, an expensive-looking tie hung from his waist. Caliban, played by white actor Peter Peverley, most clearly referenced the scavenging aesthetic. His costume was decorated with bits of frayed rope, a string vest reminiscent of a fishing net, an old doll and an animal's skull: detritus that he might have picked up as he combed the island's beach for scraps.

This was a rich, allusive, multivalent and wryly funny set and costume design; I conclude with it because its scenographic aesthetic is created from clothing, but also because the collaborative processes of theatre making developed by Improbable has helped me to think about how performers might be empowered to make aesthetic as well as textual decisions, and how this empowerment might enable more diverse and culturally conscious designs for a play like *The Tempest*, freighted as it now is with questions of race and power. In a published interview with Ruska Radosavljević and in conversation with myself, McDermott has expressed something of a frustration with so-called ensemble processes that are more competitive than democratic, rehearsals that are in fact 'disguised arguments' in which the person with the loudest ideas 'wins' and has their ideas realised, and which 'breed a dependency culture in which the director is God and people are trying to please in the rehearsal room rather than trusting their own impulses' (McDermott, interview with Escolme; see also McDermott in Radosavljević 2013, 200). From its 'epic spectacles' to its 'intimate puppetry' Improbable's work, on the other hand, is centred on improvisation: 'a deeply democratic art form', asserts the company website, 'that fosters a sense of community and empowerment amongst its participants and audiences alike' (Improbable website). McDermott explained to me that for *The Tempest*, Becs Andrews created some costume designs that fitted the concept of an island made of clothes, which director and designer had discussed before rehearsals began, but also that piles of clothes were brought to rehearsals themselves, so that actors could experiment with the kinds of shapes and colours they might wear. This, McDermott suggests, allowed black actor Huggins to invent his own version of what their initial idea of a shamanic Prospero might look like, rather than have a version of Thompson's 'magical negro' (see above 153) imposed upon him by a white director.

Becs Andrews's design offered a playful way in to *The Tempest* and produced an overtly contemporary version of Shakespeare that I would nevertheless suggest was historically sympathetic in its conscious theatricality. I began this chapter by suggesting that the Leeds Playhouse programme's figuration of the play as an infinitely open and interpretable text failed to account for the artistic and pragmatic environment of the theatre: theatre companies inevitably make interpretive decisions that open up certain possibilities and close down others. Nevertheless, Becs Andrews's design for Improbable's *Tempest*, in conjunction with director Phelim McDermott's passionate call for productions of Shakespeare to allow performers and audiences to dream (McDermott 2013), makes the case for design that can both offer a particular, detailed and intelligible reading of a 400-year-old play and allow an audience room for interpretive manoeuver. This seems particularly important in a play so fraught with tensions of race and power. Improbable's *Tempest* offered both a culturally diverse group of actors telling a story with a pile of clothes, in which actors of colour are cast in some of the most substantial roles—but also, fleeting moments when that story could be read through the history of African shamanism, or of scavengers on landfill sites.

Conclusions

This chapter has examined costume's contribution to stagings of colonialism in *The Tempest* and explored how costume reintroduces, explores or reiterates issues of race in non-traditionally cast productions. I have discussed costume's role in staging a colonial relationship between white and black bodies in this play, its role in essentialising or foregrounding the construction of whiteness, and its contribution to productions in which actors of colour have been given Prospero's agency and power. Costume design can produce meanings that shift across the experience of watching a play, inviting the spectator, in one moment, to erase race from the mind's eye and consider personal and political interactions between characters and in the next moment to reflect upon their own assumptions and expectations about who can play, or wear, what. This begs questions, following Ayanna Thompson, of how far British theatre and culture has travelled in terms of cultural representation and non-traditional casting. Should we have passed the point in theatre history where casting and costume for *The Tempest* so often bind a black performer up in the histories of colonialism, or do these histories need continual re-telling? Is it more important for costume designers and the actors who wear their clothes to ask audiences to think about histories of race and power through this play, or to enliven them to the potential of diverse casting and performance practice, whereby an actor can get to be Ariel or Caliban, Prospero, Miranda or Third Mariner no matter what their colour or cultural heritage? I suggest that Thompson is correct when she argues that 'we as a society have not been able to pinpoint a stable signification for race' (Thompson 2006a, 8) but that the theatre, a place of unstable significations, can offer audiences worlds in which both black and white people take on, dress up in, and play with the signifiers of power, as well as worlds in which histories of black oppression are critiqued. I conclude that theatre costume has not merely illustrated directors' and designers' concepts of *The Tempest* as a reflection on colonialism and racial power, but has played a significant role in the production and development of these concepts, and has been key to creating theatrical alternatives to them.

PRODUCTIONS DISCUSSED ALL PRODUCTIONS ARE OF *THE TEMPEST*

Cheek by Jowl. 1988. *The Tempest*, Declan Donnellan (director), Nick Omerod (designer), Villa Communale, Taormina, Italy, then touring. https://www.cheekbyjowl.com/productions/the-tempest-1988-1989/.

Donmar Warehouse. 2016. Phyllida Lloyd (director), Chloe Lamford and Bunny Christie (designers), *The Shakespeare Trilogy: The Tempest*, Donmar Kings Cross, London.

Everyman Theatre. 1974. Glen Walford (director), Sue Mayes (designer), *The Tempest*, Everyman Theatre, Liverpool.

Improbable Theatre. 2015. Phelim McDermott (director), Becs Andrews (designer), *The Tempest*, Northern Stage, Newcastle and Oxford Playhouse, Oxford. https://www.improbable.co.uk/portfolios/the-tempest/; http://www.becsandrews.com/stage-design/the-tempest/.

Leeds Playhouse. 1974. John Harrison (director), John Cavanagh (designer), *The Tempest*, Leeds Playhouse, Leeds.

Mermaid Theatre. 1970. Jonathan Miller (director) Rosemary Vercoe (costume designer), John Collins (designer), *The Tempest*, Mermaid Theatre, London.

National Theatre. 1988. Peter Hall (director), Alison Chitty (designer), *The Tempest*, Cottesloe Theatre, National Theatre, London.

Old Vic. 1988. Jonathan Miller (director), Richard Hudson (designer), *The Tempest*, Old Vic, London.

Piccolo Teatro, Milan. 1978. Giorgio Strehler (director), Luciano Damiani (designer), *The Tempest*, Piccolo Teatro, Milan.

Royal Shakespeare Company. 1963. Peter Brook (director), Farrah (designer), *The Tempest*, Royal Shakespeare Theatre, Stratford upon Avon.

———. 1970. Jon Barton (director), Ann Curtis (designer), *The Tempest*, Royal Shakespeare Theatre, Stratford upon Avon.

———. 1982. Ron Daniels (director), Maria Björnson (designer), *The Tempest*, Royal Shakespeare Theatre, Stratford upon Avon. https://www.rsc.org.uk/the-tempest/past-productions/ron-daniels-1982-production.

——— (1988), Michael Boyd (director), Tom Piper (designer), *The Tempest*, Royal Shakespeare Theatre, Stratford upon Avon; The Roundhouse, London. https://www.tompiperdesign.co.uk/gallery/tempestrsc-2001/.

———. 2016. Greg Doran (director), Stephen Brimsom Lewis (designer), Imaginarium Studios (digital character creation), *The Tempest*, Royal Shakespeare Theatre, Stratford upon Avon, Barbican Theatre London. https://www.rsc.org.uk/the-tempest/gregory-doran-2016-production.

Theatre des Bouffes du Nord. 1990. Peter Brook (director), Chloe Obolensky (designer), Theatre des Bouffes du Nord, Avignon Festival.

Theatre Royal Haymarket. 2011. Trevor Nunn (director), Stephen Brimson Lewis (designer), *The Tempest*, Theatre Royal Haymarket.

Works Cited

All references to *The Tempest* and other plays by Shakespeare are from the *RSC Shakespeare: Complete Works* (2007). Ed. Jonathan Bate. Houndsmills, Basingstoke: Palgrave Macmillan.

Akhimie, Patricia. 2018. *Shakespeare and the Cultivation of Difference: Race and Conduct in the Early Modern World*. London: Routledge.

Alexander, B. Interview with Bill Alexander by T. Howard, Black British and Asian Shakespeare Database, University of Warwick.

Annamma, Subini Ancy. 2017. Conceptualizing Color-Evasiveness: Using Dis/ability Critical Race Theory to Expand a Color-Blind Racial Ideology in Education and Society. *Race Ethnicity and Education* 20 (2): 147–162.

Barbieri, Donatella, and with Melissa Trimingham. 2017. *Costume in Performance: Materiality, Culture and the Body*. London: Bloomsbury.

Barton, Anne (nee Righter). 1968. Introduction. In William Shakespeare, *The Tempest*. Harmondsworth: Penguin.

Bassett, Kate. 2012. *In Two Minds: A Biography of Jonathan Miller*. London: Oberon Books.

Berry, Ralph. 1977. *On Directing Shakespeare: Interviews with Contemporary Directors*. London: Croom Helm.

Bevington, David, and Peter Holbrook. 1998. *The Politics of the Stuart Court Masque*. Cambridge: Cambridge University Press.

Billington, Michael. 1970. "Review of The Tempest" (Mermaid Theatre). *Plays and Players*, 17 August.

———. 2002. 'Review of The Tempest' (Royal Shakespeare Company). *The Guardian*, 8 October. https://www.theguardian.com/stage/2002/may/08/theatre.artsfeatures1.

Blake Edwards [dir]. 1979. 10, Orion Pictures [film].

Bloechl, Olivia A. 2004. Protestant Imperialism and the Representation of Native American Son. *The Musical Quarterly* 87 (1): 44–86.

Borsuk, A. 2020. *Pretty Radical Shakespeare*. PhD thesis, Queen Mary University of London.

Brathwaite, Kamau. 1973. *The Arrivants: A New World Trilogy*. Oxford: Oxford University Press.

———. 1993. *Middle Passages*. New York: New Directions.

Brewer, Mary F. 2005. *Staging Whiteness*. Hanover, NH: Wesleyan University Press.

Butler, Martin. 2016. *The Tempest and the Literature of Wonder*. British Library, https://www.bl.uk/shakespeare/articles/the-tempest-and-the-literature-of-wonder.

Cawdry, Robert, and Robert Anthony Peters. 1966. Scholars' Facsimiles & Reprints. In *A Table Alphabeticall of Hard Usual English Words (1604); The First English Dictionary*. Gainesville, FL.

Césaire, Aimé. 1969. *Une Tempête*. Paris: Éditions du Seuil.
———. 2000. *Discourse on Colonialism*. New York: Monthly Review Press.
Coleridge, Samuel Taylor, and N.I. Coleridge. 1836. *The Literary Remains of Samuel Taylor Coleridge*. London: William Pickering.
Curran, Kevin. 2009. *Marriage, Performance, and Politics in the Jacobean court*. Farnham: Ashgate.
de Bry, Johann Theodor, and Philipp Ziegler. 1617. *America [An abridgment of Parts I–IX. of T. de Bry's America and Some Other Voyages]*. Frankfurt: N. Hoffman.
Dowden, Edward. 1877. *Shakespeare: A Critical Study of his Mind and Art*. London: s.n.
Drew, William. 2017. Review: The Tempest at the Barbican. *Exeunt Magazine*, 11 June. http://exeuntmagazine.com/reviews/review-tempest-barbican/.
Dymkowski, Christine. 2000. Introduction. In *William Shakespeare The Tempest: Shakespeare In Production*, 1–94. Cambridge: Cambridge University Press.
Egan, Gabriel. 1997. Ariel's Costume in the Original Staging of The Tempest. *Theatre Notebook* 51: 62–72.
Fanon, F. 2008. *Black Skin, White Masks*. London: Pluto.
Frankenberg, Ruth. 1997. *Displacing Whiteness: Essays in Social and Cultural Criticism*. Durham, NC; London: Duke University Press.
Fuchs, Barbara. 1997. Conquering Islands: Contextualizing The Tempest. *Shakespeare Quarterly* 48 (1): 45–62.
Fulton, Robert C., III. 1978. "The Tempest" and the Bermuda Pamphlets: Source and Thematic Intention. *Interpretation* 10 (1): 1–10.
Goldberg, J. 2002. *The Generation of Caliban*. Vancouver: Ronsdale Press.
Griffiths, Trevor R. 1983. "This Island's Mine": Caliban and Colonialism. *The Year of English Studies* 13: 159–180.
Gurr, Andrew. 1996. Industrious Ariel and Idle Caliban. In *Travel and Drama in Shakespeare's Time*, ed. Jean-Pierre Maquerlot and Michèle Willems. Cambridge: Cambridge University Press.
Hall, Kim F. 1995. *Things of Darkness: Economies of Race and Gender in Early Modern England*. Ithaca; London: Cornell University Press.
Hariot, Thomas. 2007. *A Brief and True Report of the New Found Land of Virginia (1590). Illustrated by Theodor de Bry*. Charlottesville: University of Virginia Press.
Honour, Hugh. 1976. *The New Golden Land: European Images of America from the Discoveries to the Present Time*. London: Allen Lane.
Hope-Wallace, Philip. 1970. Review of *The Tempest*. *The Guardian*, 16 June.
Hyam, Ronald. 2002. *Britain's Imperial Century, 1815–1914: A Study of Empire and Expansion*. 3rd ed. Houndsmills, Basingstoke: Palgrave Macmillan.
Improbable (Theatre Company). Improbable: We Are Improbable. https://www.improbable.co.uk/.

Jarrett-Macauley, Delia, ed. 2017. *Shakespeare, Race and Performance: The Diverse Bard*. Abingdon, Oxon: Routledge.

Jays, David. 2013. Obituary: Rosemary Vercoe. *The Guardian*, 14 August. https://www.theguardian.com/stage/2013/aug/14/rosemary-vercoe.

Jonson, Ben. 2001. *The Masque of Blackness*. In *Ben Jonson's Plays and Masques*, ed. Richard Harp. New York; London: W.W. Norton.

Key, Philip. 1984a. Secrets in an Isle of Magic (Review of *The Tempest*). *Daily Post* [Liverpool], 16 January.

———. 1984b. Big Top Tempest Blows Out the Bard (Review of *The Tempest*). *Daily Post* [Liverpool], 27 January.

Kleber, Pia. 1993. Theatrical Continuities in Giorgio Strehler's The Tempest. In *Foreign Shakespeare: Contemporary Performance*, ed. Dennis Kennedy, 140–157. Cambridge: Cambridge University Press.

Kott, Jan. 1965. *Shakespeare our Contemporary*. London: Methuen.

———. 2002. Interviewed by Alan J. Kuharski 'Raised and Written in Contradictions: The Final Interview'. *New Theatre Quarterly* 18 (2): 103–120.

Kujawinska-Courtney, Krystyna, and R.S. White. 2007. *Shakespeare's Local Habitations*. Łódź: Łódź University Press.

Lamming, George. 1960. *The Pleasures of Exile*. London: Michael Joseph.

———. 1971. *Water with Berries*. London: Longman.

Lamming, George, and Anthony Bogues, eds. 2011. *The George Lamming Reader: The Aesthetics of Decolonisation*. Kingston; Miami: Ian Randle Publishers.

Lindley, David. 2013. Introduction. In William Shakespeare, *The Tempest*, 1–101. Cambridge: Cambridge University Press.

Little, Arthur L., Jr. 2016. Rehistoricizing Race, White Melancholia, and the Shakespearean Property. *Shakespeare Quarterly* 67 (1): 84–103.

London Corporation. *Records of the London Corporation*, London Metropolitan Archives. Repertory xxix.

Malone, Edmond. 1808. *An Account of the Incidents, from which the Title, and Part of the Story of Shakespeare's Tempest were Derived, and its True Date Ascertained*. London: C and R Baldwin.

Mannoni, Octave Jacques Dominique. 1990. *Prospero and Caliban, The Psychology of Colonization* (trans. Pamela Powesland). Ann Arbor: Ann Arbor Paperbacks.

Maquerlot, Jean-Pierre, and Michèle Willems, eds. 1996. *Travel and Drama in Shakespeare's Time*. Cambridge: Cambridge University Press.

McDermott, P. 2013. Phelim McDermott. *The Contemporary Ensemble: Interviews with Theatre Makers*. D. Radosavljević. Abingdon, Oxon, Routledge.

McDermott, Phelim Interviewed by Duska Radosavljević. 2013. Phelim McDermott. In *The Contemporary Ensemble: Interviews with Theatre Makers*, ed. Duska Radosavljević. Abingdon, Oxon: Routledge.

McMillan, Michael. 2017. The Black Body and Shakespeare: Conversations with Black Actors. In *Shakespeare, Race and Performance: the Diverse Bard in Contemporary Britain*, ed. Delia Jarrett-Macauley, 122–134. Abingdon, Oxon: Routledge.

Morgan, Terry. 1984. Review of *The Tempest. Merseymart* [Liverpool], 7 April.

Munday, Anthony. 1610. *London's Love, to the Royal Prince Henrie, Meeting Him on the River of Thames, at His Returne from Richmonde, with a Worthie Fleete of Her Citizens, on Thursday the Last of May, 1610. With a Briefe Reporte of the Water Fight, and Fireworkes.* London: E. Allde for N. Fosbrooke.

Nixon, Rob. 1987. Caribbean and African Appropriations of The Tempest. *Critical Inquiry* 13 (3): 557–578.

Nosworthy, J.M. 1948. The Narrative Sources of *The Tempest. The Review of English Studies* 24: 281–294.

Orgel, Stephen. 1975. *The Illusion of Power.* Berkeley: University of California Press.

———, ed. 1998. *Introduction to William Shakespeare The Tempest.* Oxford: Oxford University Press.

Prison Reform Trust. 2017. Black and Mixed Ethnicity Women More than Twice as Likely to Face Arrest. http://www.prisonreformtrust.org.uk/PressPolicy/News/vw/1/ItemID/465.

Punch. 1970. Review of The Tempest. *Punch,* 24 July.

Radosavljević, Duska, ed. 2013. *The Contemporary Ensemble: Interviews with Theatre-Makers.* Abingdon, Oxon: Routledge.

Saengar, Michael Baird. 1995. The Costumes of Caliban and Ariel Qua Sea-Nymph. *Notes and Queries* 42 (3): 334–336.

Shulman, Milton. 1970. Review of *The Tempest Evening Standard.*

Smith, Ian. 2016. The Textile Black Body: Race and 'Shadow'd Livery. In *The Merchant of Venice, The Oxford Handbook of Shakespeare and Embodiment, Gender, Sexuality, and Race,* ed. Valerie Traub, 170–185. Oxford: Oxford University Press.

Sontag, Susan. 1975. Fascinating Fascism (Review of *The Last of the Nuba* by Leni Riefenstahl). *The New York Review of Books,* 6 February.

Spencer, Charles. 2002. Whipping up a Storm in Spectacular Style. *Daily Telegraph,* 9 May. https://www.telegraph.co.uk/culture/theatre/drama/3577111/Whipping-up-a-storm-in-spectacular-style.html.

Strehler, Georgio, and Thomas Simpson. 2002. Notes on The Tempest. *PAJ: A Journal of Performance and Art* 25 (3): 1–17.

Stritmatter, A., and Lynne Kositsky. 1958. *On the Date, Sources and Design of Shakespeare's The Tempest.* Jefferson, NC: Mc Farland and Company.

Taylor, Paul. 1988. Review of *The Tempest* dir. Jonathan Miller held by V&A Theatre and Performance Collections.

———. 2002. Review of *The Tempest,* Roundhouse, London. *The Independent,* 13 May. https://www.independent.co.uk/arts-entertainment/theatre-dance/reviews/the-tempest-roundhouse-london-9242696.html.

Thompson, Ayanna. 2006a. Practicing a Theory/Theorizing a Practice: An Introduction to Shakespearean Colorblind Casting. In *Colorblind Shakespeare:*

New Perspectives on Race and Performance, ed. Ayanna Thompson. New York: Routledge.

————, ed. 2006b. *Colorblind Shakespeare: New Perspectives on Race and Performance*. London; New York: Routledge.

————. 2011. *Passing Strange: Shakespeare, Race, and Contemporary America*. New York; Oxford: Oxford University Press.

Traub, Valerie, ed. 2016. *The Oxford Handbook of Shakespeare and Embodiment, Gender, Sexuality, and Race*. Oxford: Oxford University Press.

Uhrig, Noah. 2016. *Black, Asian and Minority Disproportionality in the Criminal Justice System in England and Wales*. London: Ministry of Justice Analytical Services, Ministry of Justice UK. https://assets.publishing.service.gov.uk/government/uploads/system/uploads/attachment_data/file/639261/bame-disproportionality-in-the-cjs.pdf.

Vaughan, Alden T., and Virginia Mason. 1991. *Shakespeare's Caliban: A Cultural History*. Cambridge: Cambridge University Press.

Vaughn, Alden T. 2008. William Strachey's "True Report" and Shakespeare: A Closer Look at the Evidence. *Shakespeare Quarterly* 59 (3): 245–273.

Walter, Harriet. 2016. *Brutus and Other Heroines: Playing Shakespeare's Roles for Women*. London: Nick Hern Books.

Zabus, Chantal. 2002. *Tempests after Shakespeare*. Houndsmills, Basingstoke: Palgrave Macmillan.

CHAPTER 5

Conclusion: Practitioner Interviews

This book concludes with interviews of two theatre practitioners who design both set and costumes for the British theatre and internationally. One is Tom Piper, who is particularly well known for his Shakespeare design. The other is Chloe Lamford, who self-identifies primarily as a designer for contemporary work; her interview sits in this book as a challenge to the dominance of the Shakespeare industry in British theatrical culture. A number of the works in the *Shakespeare in Practice* series conclude with practitioner interviews. Here the interviews make a particularly fitting conclusion, because this book has been about how the work of the costume designer—who in current British theatre practice is so often set designer too—makes meaning in Shakespeare production. It has not been the aim to demonstrate what costume design tells us about plays but how the plays and their meanings are produced by clothing on stage. In Chap. 1, on London histories of costuming *Hamlet*, we have seen how costume not only produces different Hamlets but different kinds of dramatic subjectivity. In Chap. 2, on the Royal Shakespeare Company's *Much Ado About Nothing* productions, the focus has been costume design's potential to create and challenge cultural nostalgia. Chapter 3 has seen costume collaborating with and troubling post-colonial constructions of race. To end with the voices of two designers is hopefully to privilege those voices and to foreground the conditions of production that make meaning from Shakespeare today.

B. Escolme, *Shakespeare and Costume in Practice*, Shakespeare in Practice, https://doi.org/10.1007/978-3-030-57149-8_5

The two designers I have had the pleasure to interview have had rather different careers. Piper is well known for his work at the RSC and has produced a huge number of period costume designs. Lamford self-defines as a designer of contemporary work, has largely eschewed historical costume and is concerned with Shakespeare's dominance of the British theatre scene. Thus the two designers reflect a dual concern of this book, and a tension inherent to performing the theatrical past. On the one hand, I have attempted to convey my continuing excitement with the processes of designing for historical theatre. Shakespeare's simultaneous familiarity and strangeness, brilliantly designed for by the practitioners featured in this book, allows his current audiences ways in and out of conversations with the past and present. Costume design for Shakespeare can offer both a past that reflects and teaches the present and a past that is radically different from our contemporary moment. The work of a designer like Piper foregrounds the labour we undertake as audiences to relate to the artworks of the past. His Jacobean *Tempest* set on a structure that recalled the Twin Towers disaster, or his *As You Like It* that starts in an Elizabethan court and ends in modern dress, ask that we watch ourselves making sense of the past. Lamden, on the other hand, works entirely outside of the main producing houses for Shakespeare. She designed *Ophelias Zimmer*, a piece about Ophelia that directly takes Shakespeare to task for his treatment of this construction of femininity; the *Tempest* I discuss with her is the Shakespeare Trilogy production directed by Phyllida Lloyd, discussed in Chap. 4, which eschews a period aesthetic entirely and appears to refuse period drama's nostalgic temptations. I hope that ending this book with the thoughts of these two designers about their own work honours the creative processes I have both praised and critiqued above, and reminds the reader that Shakespeare's multiplicity of meanings are produced in the theatre, visually as well as textually, and in the contemporary moment of the practitioners who do the work of staging the plays.

Practitioner Interviews

Tom Piper

Internationally celebrated designer Tom Piper has been working in theatre design since he was a student in the mid 1980s and has designed both set and costume for a wide range of historical plays, particularly Shakespeare.

He was Associate Designer at the Royal Shakespeare Company from 2004 to 2014. Amongst an extensive range of awards for his work is an Olivier award for best costume design for The Histories at the RSC in 2009. He was awarded an MBE for his services to theatre design and his work on the World War I commemoration installation 'Blood Swept Lands and Seas of Red' in 2014. At the time of writing, he has been a leader in the campaign which has wrapped theatres in bright pink barrier tape marked 'Missing Live Theatre', in support of UK theatres closed due to the Covid19 pandemic. In what follows, the author discusses Piper's design process with him, particularly as it relates to costume for two productions of *The Tempest*.

How did you start out as a designer?

I started by designing shows and posters for student performances at University—I was doing a degree in Biology, then changed to History of Art. Then I started a post-graduate course in Theatre Design at the Slade but left for my first big break, working with Peter Brook's company, on his 1990 *Tempest* at the Bouffes du Nord, Paris. His celebrated statement in *The Empty Space* has always been an inspiration—'I can take any empty space and call it a bare stage. A man walks across this empty space whilst someone else is watching him, and this is all that is needed for an act of theatre to be engaged' (Brook 9). When that person walks across that space, one of the most immediate things you notice is what they are wearing. Even if they're naked, or just wearing tattoos, of course that's a choice! For me, what that person is wearing is the beginning of the designer's journey, it's how you begin to tell the story, to create the world of the play.

Can you describe anything that's common to each creative process when you design?

I've designed a lot of Shakespeare, and the first thing I consider is period—my choices tend to be the period Shakespeare wrote for, Shakespeare's own period, or modern dress. In the RSC's History Cycle [dir. Michael Boyd, 2006–7], we used all three, so in this case period developed through the cycle—the *Henry VI* plays were costumed medieval, *Richard II* Elizabethan, *Richard III* in modern dress. And with Shakespeare I start with the text—I'm fairly traditional that way. So I think about the writer's world and how they've encoded social commentary and critique into their work, what the play offers you in terms of location, who the characters are and their backstory. And although I've done a lot of work for the RSC, my approach is also influenced by the Globe and that dynamic relationship between the actor and the audience. I was part of the team re-designing the Royal Shakespeare Theatre at Stratford. The theatre we re-designed was a proscenium arch theatre, with audience at the back of the upper circle 30 metres away from the stage. The newly designed theatre had audience 270 degrees around the playing space, and the furthest anyone is from the stage is 11 metres. So at the Globe and now at the RST, you're designing costume in the round, if you like, thinking about all of the angles from which it will be seen.

Do you always design both set and costumes?

I sometimes do just design set, sometimes just costumes—but I feel that when you do the two together you're in control of the dramaturgy of the whole piece, you're inevitably a bit more invested in the story telling, its whole arch. If you just do the costumes there's a danger that you just become a stylist who goes 'oh well this is the period we're doing it in and he'd look good in that and she'd look good in that ' and you stop paying attention to what's going on in the story you try to tell.

Particularly with Shakespeare, I find it frustrating not to do both set and costumes because you do need to have control of the story telling. Especially in a space that doesn't really change, that's how you keep the flow of colour and the change of mood and atmosphere as you go through a play. So, for example, my costume design for *As You Like It* with Michael Boyd (2009) went from being constrained Elizabethan, a kind of heightened, puritanical black and white, in the winter, through to contemporary slightly hipster summer style by the end. You can do that with *As You Like It*, you can make a change of period subtle; there are enough scenes where people leave and come back, so that if someone's changed their leather shoes to a pair of Converse you don't quite notice it, until till it all adds up and by the end of the show.

Do you work closely with actors on their costumes?

Yes, of course it's important that people are happy to wear their costume, and the actor's the one who really knows their role so they're a crucial part of the collaborative process. Although too much choice can be impractical; sometimes you're in a position where you're offering an actor something of an illusion of choice—so you might provide a rail of different possibilities at a fitting, choice within relative narrow limits.

Then sometimes a costume that you imagine working on a particular character just doesn't work when they're cast. For *Twelfth Night* with Michael Boyd (RSC 2005), we had Kananu [Kirimi] as Viola, who played Ariel in *The Tempest*, and Gurpreet Singh as Sebastian. But then we had the problem that Kananu pulled out of the production after a run in Stratford and when we went to Newcastle we had to have the understudy play Viola. She was a white actor, almost porcelain-doll-like. The costume Viola had evolved out of what suited Kananu and she'd been using a little bomber jacket in rehearsal and we made her a little almost bolero jacket, a little suit which worked for her—it had flares and cowboy boots. It worked on her and it just about worked on the actor playing Sebastian her brother. But somehow it just didn't work at all on this other woman, so we had to completely change how we were going to say to the audience that these people are twins—and you have to find a costume convention to do it. In the end we ended up going down quite a heavy mask method of doing it. We almost 'whited up' the twins, the Asian 'brother' and white English 'sister' in a Japanese doll-like way; we gave them very stylised make up, really brightly coloured clothes. This all happened in Newcastle, and I was running round the shops in Newcastle buying a velvet jacket and this and that—we completely changed the look because it had to respond to the actors.

How was working with Brook's designer Chloe Obolenski? Was it different to the ways you have worked before or since?

I'd seen the *Mahabarata* and met Chloe and she'd invited me to come and work with the company. Peter Brook's theatre was really like a giant fringe theatre and I did a lot of making. We worked with a model of the Bouffes du Nord. That theatre is a wonderful giant fake, in that it was 'distressed' when Peter Brook first found it, but Chloe enhanced that for the *Mahabarata* and made it redder, used a more Indian palate of colours. Then for *The Tempest*, she spent a month with the painters sanding it back and repainting to get a palate that was much more whites and greens. I designed various pieces for *The Tempest* that are still there now. Chloe got her scenic artist to work with her on the model, which isn't what we normally do in this country, you usually give that work to someone else. She sat there guiding them all for about a month, it really was like making a giant piece of abstract art.

Peter started rehearsing in the space, on a bare concrete floor. The initial models had a bare earth landscape in them; they had contours, they looked like a proper landscape made from earth. We made this by building up a polystyrene base and shipping in loads of earth, with local guys bringing it in wheelbarrows, and Jean-Guy [Jean-Guy Lecat, Brook's technical director and set/space designer] complaining a lot and asking why we were doing this! A lot of Peter Brook's approach came from the casting, and who he wanted to work with. Sotigui [Kouyata] was playing Prospero, he's African, a really tall, elegant man—then the 'funnies', Stephano and Triculo, were Bruce Myers and Alain Maratrat; they were white actors, who played them quite middle class; then Ariel was a black performer, and one of my favourite stories from the production was around how Ariel looked. The huge challenge with *The Tempest* is how you do the first scene because you're launched straight into this storm—how do you get the narrative across and understand who these people are? You should believe that they're genuinely going to die but you should still be able to hear what they say. Peter spent a lot of time trying to rehearse this and they ended up with giant bamboo poles that they waved—and Ariel came out with a rain-stick on his head, so you had the swishing noise of the rain from that, which set up Ariel as the controller of the storm. One of the loveliest bits of 'poor theatre' was when Yoshi Oida, the Japanese actor who played the old Lord Gonzalo, treated the spirits holding up the bamboo stick as if they represented the water level rising. Then for his next entrance, Ariel ran on with this boat on his head—it's in the poster—a boat with little red sails, which I made. This began as an orange crate in the rehearsal room and we thought that in the beginning we might have a little model boat swaying in the space. In true Peter Brook fashion, I was instructed to make a model boat, brought it to the rehearsal room, then the actor picked it up and put it on his head and started playing with it. So then I had to refine it and weight it—but it was still fundamentally the rough boat that I'd made and that became a way of story-telling.

That was always the way with Peter Brook—ideas started big, then were reduced and reduced; we had loads of logs to start with, then that was reduced to three logs that the spirits just rotated really fast between them. And that earth landscape…we ended up taking it all out again, much to Jean-Guy's annoyance! We tried things, like people popping up through these holes in the ground, and I was instructed to make three giant puppets at one point; you're always running behind their process, and that's the hardest thing—you're trying to make something, and they've moved on in rehearsals. So I'd make a puppet, and then they didn't need that any more. There were lots of examples like that. We ended up putting a carpet down on the earth, then that carpet became sand, and there were a couple of rocks on this sand carpet…I spent a lot of time in Paris in the summer trying to dye sand the right colour! And at one point I got the watering of the earth wrong…the substance around the edges of the set was still red earth and you had to dampen down the sand each day to stop it producing huge clouds of dust—but if you got it too wet, the actors' costumes would start soaking up the water and the red pigment in the earth, so for that performance the actors had red colouring all over them.

Did the international cast for this production, the range of national and ethnic heritage, effect or influence costume design?

As a designer, you have to find what unifies the piece. I do feel that in one sense that *The Tempest* was a sort of epilogue to the *Mahabarata*, it felt as though it was slightly hampered, visually, by the huge weight of that. So there was a lot of discussion like 'well, if we change the space to green and white, it won't feel like the *Mahabarata*'—but a lot of the actors were the same, a lot of Chloe's references and styles felt the same—there was earth; no fire this time, as there was in the *Mahabarata*, but there was water...it felt like they were still using the language of the *Mahabarata*. When Chloe designed the costumes, one of the interesting things about it as that she worked with each actor very individually, on their own physique and style. Actually I think this works well with *The Tempest*. Prospero had a very distinct look, then we had two different Mirandas, because they were very young; one was of Indian heritage, Shantala Shivalingappa, one French, Romane Bhoringer. With Yoshi Oida [Gonzalo], Chloe dressed him as if he was in the Nambam Japanese paintings, so he had these ridiculously large britches, which was a bit of an ironic twist, given it was actually the Japanese who drew the Europeans like that, not the Japanese who looked like that. Chloe followed a whole series of different references for different actors—sometimes following their ethnicity, sometimes other aspects, which meant as a whole, it didn't really have that feel of a coherently designed show. It had a good strong sense of style, though, and she used a cutter from England called Barbara Higgins, who came over, and Chloe worked by finding fabrics and references and not doing any drawings, but working with Bar to create shapes and trying them on actors; with some of them, there'd be a costume created in the space with Peter.

You designed one of the *Tempest* productions discussed here in this book, in 2002: the RSC's *Tempest*, which played Stratford and the Roundhouse, London—the company's first production of the play after their move from their permanent home in London at the Barbican. How did the creative process work there?

The big influence on that production was the twin towers, and in this case, some of the ideas for the costumes emerged pragmatically, from this idea for the set, but the aesthetic for the set was pulled together by the costumes. Michael thought that the ship of state that goes down at the beginning was like a tower, like one of the twin towers. This gave us the chance to create a storm which is abstract and made a huge impact. At the Roundhouse, we had a hydraulic mechanism that could tip the stage backwards and forwards and then ladders that would come off it; as the tower broke up, the ladders would sway into different sections. Then we worked with some aerial artists and we decided that the mariners would morph into spirits somehow, so in the storm, they would roll down on ropes and you'd see them floating through the water, like the Bosch paintings of angels, floating off in the water. As the mariners became spirits, they became under Ariel's control, he could use them to be the island spirits. We had to create a look for the mariners that somehow worked for their rope work; they had to have relatively tight-fitting tops and things that didn't roll up, so they had a sort of Jacobean version of an arielist's outfit: Jacobean britches but with a rather tighter shirt. Then the mariner-spirits became everything in the island, even the logs that Caliban had to move around. Their basic spirit costumes were leotards, with little tu-tu dresses over them for the women. It was tricky working in the roundhouse, getting the mechanics of the staging to work—and I remember the tutus arriving all in that same colour scheme and then suddenly the design really came together because the costumes became little male and female versions of these mariner-spirit figures. By stripping back and unifying things, we achieved a choral effect, so that it all felt like one theatrical world, where these figures were just transmogrifying into one thing or another but were ultimately always the spirit-mariners—which up to the point where we saw the costumes hadn't quite worked.

What was your concept for the 'human' costumes for this *Tempest*?

The style was broadly Jacobean throughout. We had a very bold, 'now' set made of steel, and Jacobean costumes in contrast. At the opening we had Alonso, the usurper duke, hanging in the space like a Francis Bacon screaming Pope, stuck as this figurehead of power within this hanging structure, like a Queen Bee that can't get out of the hive.

One discovery I made was that the masque for Miranda and Ferdinand's wedding seemed to us to be Shakespeare laughing at Inigo Jones and court masques—saying 'Well if you want me to do this, I'll do it, I'll write you this ridiculous florid language'. So we actually did it in the style of Stanley Baxter—and it was the Captain and the first mate who came back as Juno and Ceres. They were like dames in a panto, with huge Inigo-Jones-inspired costumes, loads of layers; then when nymphs and shepherds started arriving, those were the mariner-spirits, still recognisable from their costumes. We made up the tu-tu-like skirts for the women. At one point, one girl and one boy started swinging in the space, and it got to the point where it was almost coital when they met in the middle—at which point Prospero goes—'enough'! Because it's getting too rude, too much. So it was a mix of passionate Liz Rankin movement work and also circus, aerialist work.

I should also tell you about the harpy. The concept for this costume emerged from Michael Boyd's principle that everything on stage has to have a consequence, and come out of something else. So the magic feast appeared from a trap in the floor and the centre piece of it was a swan, like at an Elizabethan feast, and some water melons. And one actor stabbed into the watermelons so you had the red and the liquid from the juice, and then the nobles started attacking this swan and ripped its head off. It emerges that the swan was the actress playing Ariel crouched over; she then erupted into the swan, at which point the other spirits arrived with whirling fires —so for me, you saw how it developed as an idea, that your food had become this terrifying thing—rather than, say, a man on a bicycle with some giant wings, floating in. For me that's the power of designing both set and costume—you have control over the story-telling so nothing's a gimmick, a mere piece of spectacle.

Chloe Lamford

Chloe Lamford is an internationally renowned stage designer, working in theatre, opera, music and installation. She trained in Theatre Design at Wimbledon School of Art. She received the Arts Foundation Fellowship for Design for Performance 2013. She is Associate Designer at the Royal Court Theatre, London, and a resident of Somerset House Studios. Here the author discusses Lamford's career and creative process, her discomfort with the conventions of period drama, and finally her approach to working on Shakespeare and Shakespeare-inspired dramas.

How did you start out as a designer?

My parents were both contemporary dancers, so I grew up in theatres—in smelly rehearsal rooms, in the backs of theatres, in the dark, having taken all my toys with me for the day; I've been camping out in theatres my whole life. When I got to my teens, I was doing lots of dancing and was also obsessed with set design—so I knew from the age of 16 that theatre was what I wanted to do. I really loved miniature things—I'd be setting things up, making nice displays! So if you look at my life, there's a complete inevitability that this is what I'd end up doing.

I started out doing a lot of theatre in education and helped out with a youth theatre…I thought I wanted to be a director and then I started designing the shows at Watford Palace Theatre. I worked for free, ended up designing lots of shows for them, then got given a main house show. I met director Vicky Featherstone when I was about 23 and helped her out with a theatre writing workshop she gave, and after that I worked with people connected with her in various ways. I always designed new plays and really discovered what that was like five or six years after I left college—I'd somehow feed the writer and the writer would feed me. I'd be working with the director, too, of course—but in 2009, I worked with Lucy Kirkwood and made a big installation for her play *It Felt Empty*, and that felt like 'that's what I do—I work with living writers'. I've rarely designed a play that was written more than 30 years ago. Working on new plays, I think you're more complicit in the conversation around what you're making and I find that really exciting; I think my best ideas come out of conversation. Always with directors—but also, now, writers know I work with new writing. It's happened very naturally.

Have you usually designed costumes alongside set or have you ever worked with a separate costume designer?

I'm starting to work with separate costume designers a little now. I always designed both until I started working in mainland Europe and there, you can't—the system of making is so different within a theatre building there, you are much more responsible for the delivery of a design than you would be in the UK. Here, the structures are set up to hold everything together—and we make theatre much more cheaply in this country! And much more swiftly too, so we need somebody who does both. It's a practical thing. I really like designing both, because I think my designs are about people, and they hold people. I imagine the people into them and see the total picture. You're creating a little world on stage and there are inhabitants in that world, so you naturally think about them.

Do you ever start the design process by thinking about costume? Or do you always start from the broader scenographic concept?

That also depends on the show. It partly depends on whether you're making things or finding clothes for a character. And if I'm finding clothes for a character in a new play then I definitely work very closely with the actor. They have to inhabit it in such a certain way and you have to hold that conversation quite carefully as it goes through the rehearsal process—and be inside and outside of it at the same time. When working with a new play, you wait for the actor and really listen to them—because it's new, no-one's done it before—you can't come in and announce 'this is a design for your costume'—because we've not ever made this before. And so in those cases, I would discover costume at a later point in the process. I think I can design a costume for an actor that feels quite truthful if I build it with them. I'm fascinated by what makes a costume feel real and what doesn't.

I've never had an argument with an actor about costume; I facilitate, I would never have an ego about putting my take on something in a new play—because we're all discovering it for the first time. Of course, I've got a taste and that taste will appear on stage, because I like certain things, or a rail will appear for an actor in an edited way…but you really do have to listen I think. On the other hand, when you're making costumes, there's a sort of wildness in dreaming them up, particularly if it's something fantastical, like a weird kids' opera or *Amadeus*. I was really obsessed with fashion from a young age. I read *Vogue* from the age of twelve and loved big things, big dresses, so that all comes quite naturally—because I love clothes, I love all clothes!

With something like *Amadeus*, a period piece, or a musical, something that already exists, you want to begin to have your conversation with the piece as you go in, so thinking about costume may well come much earlier. I'm working on something at the moment where I'm definitely thinking about the people a lot as I go into the space. I guess if you think that you're in a world where you can make lots of costumes—which you can't do that often in contemporary theatre—then I would definitely be dreaming them up early on. Doing *Amadeus*, I knew I didn't want it all period; I was asking what my conversation would be with an old play. I'm quite uncomfortable in a period costume world.

What makes it uncomfortable?

It's because I don't think theatre's a museum. And so I always want to play with it. I feel as though if I just did 'period' straight it wouldn't feel connected to why I'm doing the project or why an audience is watching it. So I really fight it. I didn't always, this has just been in the last few years. I'm always asking, why? Why do we have to do it 'properly'? There was a big conversation with *Amadeus* around a modern orchestra who were integrated into the show. And it's set in the late 1700s, so I had a tussle around how to make that. I suppose 'it's not a museum' is my biggest statement when dealing with period drama.

Do you think, then, that the cultural baggage of Shakespeare and his legacy is a problem for British theatre?

Yes, I think it's enormous—that baggage. It's really interesting doing the piece *Shakespeare's Last Play* in Germany at the moment because I'm so annoyed with Shakespeare—he's taken up so much of our theatre space! He's made up so much of our language, his world has dictated how we do everything, what our theatre is—and I think this is part of the reason why my head doesn't conceptually fit in British theatre. It's why I've gone off and worked in Europe and then brought back—I think, I hope—another approach. Because I'm not a word person, I'm a visual person, I think in visual metaphor and I don't think Shakespeare's work does that for me. It's in there—but everyone here is so beholden to the idea we have to do Shakespeare properly, or tidily, or show that we understand the text somehow…

Could you say a bit more about different theatrical cultures? What does working in other European countries enable you to do, and what have you been able to bring back?

I think the key to it is the audience. Culturally, outside the UK, many audiences read idea as well as narrative. I feel like here, they read the story, and *then* the idea, whereas a German, say, or a Belgian audience can hold the concept much more clearly because the cultural education of the audience is different. On the other hand, here we made theatre for a wide range of people—which I think is amazing. The audiences I've had in mainland Europe have been quite elite ones, they read intellectually and conceptually as well. So you can really be bold, because your concept will be understood: it won't be negatively received as 'someone writing an essay about what the play should be'; there's more freedom and more responsibility to try things that come from a conceptual place. It's fascinating to me, how people receive the ideas. Audience is important. Doing Shakespeare in this country, a lot of the stories are known and *owned* by the audience as well—and so when you're making your *Macbeth*, many people come to it with expectations, they already hold the story somewhat and they're like 'oh, you've done *that* like *that*'.

I was fascinated by the severe neutrality of the clothes in *Ophelias Zimmer*. It certainly didn't create the cliché of a young girl's bedroom, or teenage self-expression! What was the process and what led to those decisions?

That aesthetic was a reaction to the Millais painting of Ophelia, as she floats in the river with her long pretty hair and her pretty dress, and the sort of beauty of that victimhood. Why are the young women playing Ophelia often so prettified—the cult of that really interests me and our aim as a group was to deconstruct that image. I don't think we often have very strong conversations about some of Shakespeare's young women. I have strong instincts about how we look at women that I always listen to. I don't want women to be sexualized in theatre unnecessarily. I also did a version of *The Tempest*, an opera, with Katie Mitchell, where Miranda's grown up and stages her own funeral in order to get back at her dad, which we did in Paris last year. But I didn't do the costumes for that but it was a funeral so again the aesthetic was very austere.

For *Ophelias Zimmer*, we began to think—what really happens when you drown? You get bloated. We ended up in a big conversation about how Ophelia could grow bloated over the course of the play—and we knew that we were going to drown her. Although in this play, she doesn't drown, she commits suicide then falls in the water, water seeps into the room. She puts on item after item until she's enormously fat at the end of the play. We tried it with different kinds of dresses, different kinds of clothes—and it kept not feeling precise enough. So the neutrality came in the building of it—once we'd made everything black, that seemed to tell the story more clearly. Often in those conversations with Katie we'd try and think about how you can deliver an idea with the most commitment: let's really take that picture apart, she throws the flowers in the bin every single day, she sees water coming into the room—so we built that image and that's how the clothes became so austere. Alice Birch [playwright] said something brilliant about how in *Hamlet*, Ophelia's so quiet until she goes mad. Hamlet's so loud and rumbustious and shouty, whereas she's very pushed down and quiet—so we didn't want loads of colours or freedom of expression, because we felt she was so suppressed by the play. The piece was as much a conversation with the play as with the character of Ophelia. We worked with this amazing actor Jenny Konig who is so brave, so tough and so rigorous in her conceptual thinking. She played Ophelia and Gertrude in Thomas Ostermeier's production [of *Hamlet*], so she knew everything about *Hamlet*, and there was something about the strength of her playing that role that was amazing—both outside and inside. She almost can't get up at the end of that play because she's soaking wet—it's an enormous effort for her to keep moving around.

For the Donmar Warehouse *Tempest*, how did you work with designer Bunny Christie and the company's prison framework for the trilogy?

Because *The Tempest* was the third in the trilogy, there was already a very clear aesthetic that Bunny and the director had made together. And the piece had a very clear conceit, that each actor had a 'prison character' and a 'play character', so the prison character had to have the conversation about how they were playing the person in the play. The prison characters already existed and we built on top of those—a lot had happened already, already existed—so it was about negotiating those and then finding the magical elements for *The Tempest*.

There's something really interesting about coming to something where there's already really strong parameters—because then your playfulness is already contained in a particular way and I think that's really fun. Out of the three plays of the trilogy, this was the one with lots of magic and strangeness—but there was a strong space that had been created already, and the main area to play with was costume. When you take that concept of the women prisoners as far as it will go, you're thinking—what have you even got available to make things out of? Phyllida Lloyd took me to a prison and I was so struck by how little everyone has and how much decorative work is made with these tiny numbers of things and I found that really beautiful. Lots of those masks and costume elements were very much in conversation with that—though in reality, I'm not sure prisoners would even have been able to get hold of the net curtains and tampons for the wedding costumes, there was some poetic license. Phyllida works with Shakespeare almost like a new play. She really finds what her conversation is with it and responds as she goes, she works very creatively all the way through—and so it was good and interesting to have those parameters, because it meant we could be more cohesive in conversation with the play.

I've written here about the cultural identity and ethnicities of the actors and prison characters in this piece. Was that part of your conversation?

It was discussed in the room, it was part of the process. I think it's good you read the young black characters as being full of energy and hope, that's definitely important. I wasn't so much part of the building of the cast, but I loved that cast for those things, there was such an amazing energy to the performers—that hope you see in the young characters was amazing, it really landed.

Did it make you think you'd like to do some more Shakespeare soon? Or are you happy to leave him behind?

It's interesting because I've now done three interrogations of *The Tempest* in a year, after not having touched any Shakespeare. The Donmar *Tempest* was the first time I'd looked at a Shakespeare play as a grown-up designer! I hadn't designed a Shakespeare play 'straight' like that since I was 22. And what with the Miranda project, *Ophelias Zimmer*, *Shakespeare's Last Play*, I don't imagine Shakespeare's going away. But I always bring a deconstructive head to the work, that's always completely built in, I need a hook or a conversation with it.

Index[1]

[1] Note: Page numbers followed by 'n' refer to notes.

© The Author(s), under exclusive license to Springer Nature   205
Switzerland AG 2020
B. Escolme, *Shakespeare and Costume in Practice*, Shakespeare in
Practice, https://doi.org/10.1007/978-3-030-57149-8

Printed by Printforce, the Netherlands